The
THINKING
Body

A Study of the Balancing Forces
of Dynamic Man

by
Mable Elsworth Todd
NEW YORK, N.Y.

FOREWORD BY
E.G. BRACKETT, M.D.
BOSTON, MASS.

WITH 91 ILLUSTRATIONS

A Publication of The Gestalt Journal Press

This is an unabridged republication of the original edition first published in 1937 by Paul B. Hoeber, Inc.

Copyright 1937 by Paul B. Hoeber, Inc..

Copyright © 2008 by The Gestalt Journal Press

Published by:

The Gestalt Journal Press, Inc.
A Division of:
The Center for Gestalt Development, Inc.
P. O. Box 278
Gouldsboro ME 04607-0278
U.S.A.

ISBN 978-0-939266-54-8

THE THINKING BODY

FROM "FISH TO MAN," BY DR. WILLIAM K. GREGORY

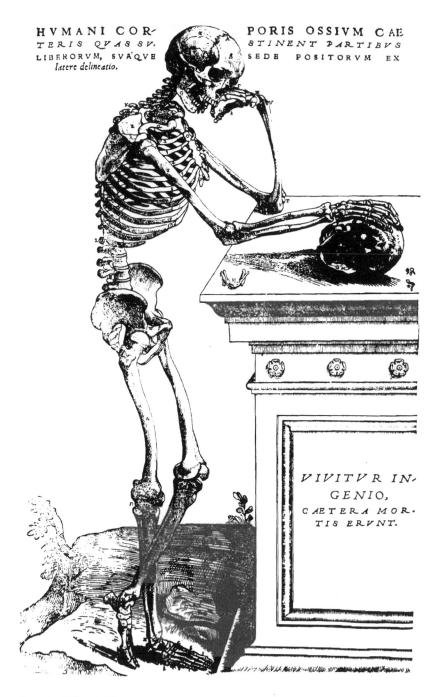

HVMANI COR-
TERIS QVAS SV-
LIBERORVM, SVÁQVE
latere delineatio.

PORIS OSSIVM CAE-
STINENT PARTIBVS
SEDE POSITORVM EX

VIVITVR IN-
GENIO,
CÆTERA MOR-
TIS ERVNT.

FIG. 1. "The Soliloquy." From Vesalius' "De fabrica humani corporis."
Vesalius' drawings were made by Jan Kalkar, a pupil of Titian, which accounts
for their superiority over more modern anatomical illustrations.

Dedicated to the memory of
the late
COLONEL GEORGE FABYAN
of the Riverside Laboratories
of Geneva, Illinois

In grateful appreciation of
his vision of the importance
to life of the subject matter
of this book and of the many
aids extended in furtherance
of its science.

THE THINKING BODY

God guard me from the thoughts men think
In the mind alone.
He that sings a lasting song
Thinks in a marrow bone.

William Butler Yeats:
"The King of the Great Clock Tower."

PREFACE

A PORTION of this text was prepared originally as a syllabus for my students at Teachers College, Columbia University, published in 1929, under the title, "The Balancing of Forces in the Human Being." Since then, the original syllabus has been expanded, particularly in those phases which indicate an approach to "Structural Hygiene," as discussed in the text.

The ideas expressed in this book have been derived from more than thirty years' experience in teaching bodily economy. They are based upon the concurrent study of physics, mechanics, anatomy and physiology.

These theories, essentially empirical, became increasingly reinforced as the observations of such scientists as Sherrington, Cannon and Crile became available, with their emphasis upon the principles of the balance of forces in bodily economy and the determination of form by function, as a law of organic development.

Delay in setting down the material thus accumulated was deliberate; first, to avoid a formulation of ideas before these should have been validated, not alone by my own experience, but by that of others taught by me; and second, to prevent the premature appearance of a "school" or "system," which so often spells the end of creative processes.

A sufficient number of teachers are now applying the ideas daily, in direct instruction of pupils in private studios or incidental to college courses in physical education and hygiene, to demonstrate the fact that these principles work. This is shown by results, both in energy saving in daily living and in their application to special skills.

In the 1929 syllabus, emphasis was laid on the psycho-physical mechanisms involved in the organic reaction to the problem of resisting gravity in the upright position.

Mechanical balance is provided for in the organism, else it

could not have survived its primary encounter with gravity, momentum and inertia, as they were met upon emergence from the water.

The mechanisms for breathing, locomotion and mechanical balance are deeply tied in all bodily tissues and structural adaptations for these functions are closely interrelated. Such a fundamental consideration as chemical balance is not dwelt upon, although it is obvious that the very quality of the bodily substances which makes them capable of support and motion is conditioned finally by their chemical and physical properties. Details of the nervous involvements are presented but briefly, except to describe the proprioceptive mechanism as a prime factor in establishing coordinated movements.

Relaxation is the crying need of our age, but what it is and how to attain it are still unanswered questions. One must learn to recognize it and to deal with it in the stride of life and this book explains ways of thinking about it which will introduce new methods in dealing with it. This text presents the fact that bodily balance in accord with the principles of mechanics is a poignant means for conservation of nervous energy.

MABEL ELSWORTH TODD.

New York, N. Y.
August, 1937.

ACKNOWLEDGMENTS

IN DEDICATING this book to the memory of Colonel George Fabyan, I record my lasting sense of obligation to him for his help during a friendship of many years. The tangible quality of his aid is indicated by the fact that he established a room in his laboratory equipped especially for the use of myself and my assistant teachers, in the study of the facts of physics, physiology and anatomy, as applied to our problems of bodily balance; and by his generosity in furnishing professional instruction and laboratory materials for our use; and by his interest in providing appliances to be used in correction and reeducation of physical maladjustments, including electrical appliances for experimentation in muscle action. All these and many other aids were extended to me because of the vision of a truly great humanitarian.

To my medical friends for their reading of the text and for their most helpful suggestions, I wish to express thanks: Dr. E. G. Brackett, Dr. Robert Osgood, Dr. David Riesman, Dr. Jesse Feiring Williams.

I am very appreciative of the generous consideration shown me by Dr. William K. Gregory, Curator of Comparative Anatomy of the Museum of Natural History, New York, for his helpful analysis and suggestions concerning those parts of the text pertaining to palaeontological and morphological references, and for the use of illustrations.

To Dr. Marshall Fabyan, of Boston, I wish also to express gratitude for his generous and helpful expenditure of time and thought in the years of preparation of this work. And Dr. John Dane and Dr. Adolph Elwyn I wish also to thank for the many favors received from them.

To those who have aided in various ways in the compilation of this text, I wish to express my sincere appreciation: Dr. Louise S. Bryant for her invaluable help in arrangement and documentation of much of the material; Dr. Dimitri von Mohr-enschildt for his help in reading the manuscript; Elizabeth and John Andrews and Kate Pierce Thayer for their kind and careful help in proof-reading and in arrangement of refer-ences. To the latter, Mrs. Thayer, who is the illustrator of this book, I owe the deepest gratitude for her patience in typing material and looking over manuscript, beside her own not in-considerable task of making the many drawings found in the text. I wish also to thank the publisher, Mr. Paul B. Hoeber, and his assistant, Miss Florence Fuller, for their enthusiastic encouragement and continuous helpful suggestions during the preparation of this work for the press.

To all these friends I wish to record my warm appreciation and gratitude.

MABEL ELSWORTH TODD.

FOREWORD

THE author of this book is particularly well fitted by many years of study and practical experience to present her subject. She has had, from the beginning of her career, definite theories of developmental exercise which she has put into practical use and has proved the soundness of her methods by success following their application. This book is not a treatise dealing purely with the subject of Physiotherapy, but presents a study of the fundamental facts underlying the principles of body dynamics as designated in the title which she has chosen.

Some of her opinions of the influences attributable to psychology bring into the picture forces which are not usually accepted, but, in these days, when the psychological processes are recognized to have an important influence on the functions of the body, we can accept all information on this phase of the subject with the open mind of an investigator. Psychological influences so strongly control the character of unconscious activity that they certainly should be used to guide the conscious and voluntary actions. The important part played by psychical activity in the development of the body is so evident that the results of constant muscle action through the unconscious and reflex control need no further proof.

There is a definite plan to that which is offered in this book. The basic principles on which the theories are built are discussed at length and these are used to illustrate the final action and control of the body activity, and the influence of unconscious sensations on body control and body action is stressed.

The author has gone a good way in this present work and has made a radical departure from beaten paths in traditions which govern to a large extent opinions and practices of physiotherapy. The reader will find much to digest, even if he does not accept all of her conclusions. She has brought the result of years of study and investigation to uphold the soundness of that which she has to offer, and this has been a wise provision, for many of her theories, not in accord with much of the teaching and practice in vogue at the present time, may provoke discussion.

In the first part of the book the author has made a careful and complete study and explanation of the mechanism of the body functions in relation to their action. It is preliminary to the conception of corrective exercise as developed in a therapy for the working body. The author describes in detail the component parts of the skeleton, the structures which are formed by their union, and their significance in relation to this function in the body mechanism. The co-relation of their formation with body functions is discussed.

Thus, much more attention is given to the bones, both separately and in their relations to each other, than usually appears in treatises on this subject. They are shown to have important functions other than to form the supporting framework for anatomical structures. The anatomy and the use of the muscles and their action in maintaining body balance and control, especially the muscles of the pelvic girdle, are discussed as a preliminary to a consideration of the development of the conscious muscle control, which is emphasized later in the book.

This first portion of the book will be studied carefully by those who are in need of fundamental instruction in these basic facts, but it can also be perused to advantage by those who are already familiar with this most important knowledge, which is so essential to the intelligent appreciation of the higher conceptions of physiology. In the second part all readers will take a keen interest, for it deals with the practical problems and the application of the principles which have been presented. In this portion of the work, the author has presented her own theories, and her practices of them, and has shown many of the fallacies of so many of the systems which are dealing with the problem of balance and posture.

The importance of conscious and intelligent control of the co-ordinated physical function of the body is emphasized throughout that part of the work which deals with the therapy of physical exercise and its definite direction in all exercise training. The employment of physical exercise in corrective therapy is put on a particularly high plane.

Several functions of the body are given special emphasis. The chapter on Walking analyzes the part played by the different muscles and joints. The imperfection of certain gaits and directions for their correction are clarified. The subject of Breathing is given a particularly complete discussion. The structures involved are considered, with their complex mechanisms, the principles discussed and suggestions made for training and proper use of the breathing function. In dealing with this subject, the author has introduced a particularly intelligent discussion of pain, strains, fatigue, etc., explaining the relation of these conditions to the function of breathing.

The originality of the presentation is attractive even if some readers are not in complete accord with the author's views. New views, even though correct, find their place in the community but slowly; the author of this book, however, has a large amount of material to substantiate her claims for her methods, and she has given this to the public only after long and practical experience, the results of which demonstrate the soundness of her views.

E. G. BRACKETT

CONTENTS

Preface to this Edition ix

Preface xiii

Acknowledgments xv

Foreword xvii

List of Illustrations xxv

CHAPTER I

FUNCTION AND FORM IN HUMAN DYNAMICS 1
BODILY ATTITUDES, 1. HABITS, 4. BONE VERSUS STEEL,
5. BALANCING FORCES, 7. FORM FOLLOWS FUNCTION,
8. POSTURAL PATTERNS, 21. THE PSYCHOPHYSICAL
BASIS OF POSTURE, 23.

CHAPTER II

REACTING MECHANISMS 25
MECHANICS, 25. NERVES, 25. SELF AWARENESS, 26.
NERVOUS REFLEXES, 29. MUSCLE TONE, 30. KINES-
THETIC CONSCIOUSNESS, 31. CHANGING PATTERNS OF
POSTURE, 33. POSTURAL REFLEXES, 34. CONDITIONED
REFLEXES IN POSTURE, 34. PSYCHOLOGICAL REACTIONS
AND POSTURE, 36. WHY STANDING STILL IS HARD
WORK, 37. MUSCLES, MOTION AND REST, 38. BODY
MECHANICS AND STRUCTURAL HYGIENE, 41.

CHAPTER III

MECHANICAL FORCES, FUNCTIONAL ADAPTATION AND
STRUCTURAL CHANGE 45
BIPED PATTERN, 45. STRUCTURE AND FORCE, 46. THE
FIVE MECHANICAL STRESSES, 47. AXIAL AND OTHER
STRESSES, 48. MECHANICAL STRAINS, 49. STRAINS IN

THE BODY, 50. REFERRED PAIN, 53. COMPRESSION AND TENSILE MEMBERS, 54. GRAVITY, MOMENTUM AND INERTIA, 55. BALANCE IN THE BODY, 56. STEEL AND BONE AS BUILDING MATERIAL, 59. SUPPORT OF MOVING WEIGHTS, 61. RESULTS OF LACK OF BALANCE, 62. MUSCLE TIRE, 62. MUSCLE SAVING DEVICES, 63. FASCIA AND MUSCLE ACTION, 65. QUADRUPED INTO BIPED, 66. HANDICAPS IN THE BIPED, 70. BIPED COMPENSATIONS, 70. COMPARATIVE RESULTS, 75.

CHAPTER IV

THE WORKING SKELETON 78
THE VERTEBRATE BODY PATTERN, 78. THE SPINAL COLUMN, 82. THE VERTEBRAE, 85. SPINAL MECHANICS, 87. THE SPINAL CURVES, 91. DEVELOPMENT OF BALANCED CURVES, 93. OTHER ELEMENTS OF SPINAL STRENGTH, 97. THE HEAD AND SPINAL BALANCE, 103. THE RIBS AND STERNUM, 107. THE PELVIS, 113. BRACING THE PELVIC ARCH, 116.

CHAPTER V

DYNAMIC MECHANISMS 118
PELVIC AND FEMORAL MUSCLES, 118. BALANCING ACTION OF PELVIC MUSCLES, 122. PELVIC LIGAMENTS, 123. THE FASCIA OF THE PELVIS, 127. THE PELVIS AS A SHOCK ABSORBER, 131. THE LEGS AND FEET, 134. THE THIGH, 137. THE LOWER LEG, 138. THE ANKLE AND FOOT, 140. BALANCE AND STRENGTH OF LEGS AND FEET, 142. THE SHOULDER GIRDLE AND ARMS, 142. WHEEL-LIKE DISTRIBUTION OF SHOULDER AND ARM MUSCLES, 148. SHOULDER MECHANICS, 155.

CHAPTER VI

BALANCING FORCES TO STAND ERECT 158
STANCE, 158. WEIGHT BEARING AND DISTRIBUTION IN

THE UPRIGHT POSITION, 159. VERTICAL SUPPORTS FOR THE HORIZONTAL BODY, 161. VERTICAL SUPPORTS FOR THE UPRIGHT BODY, 162. STRAINED "HIGH CHESTS," 163. THE DESIRABLE HIGH CHEST, 166. THE SHOULDER LOAD, 170. THE HOOP-SKIRT PATTERN, 171. BALANC- ING THE CHEST AND PELVIC LOADS, 172. ATTENTION STRAINS, 173. "DOWN THE BACK AND UP THE FRONT," 173. NEW POSITIONS AND NEW FEELINGS, 175. BODY BALANCE AND BREATHING, 179. THE PELVIC ARCH, 182. THE FEET AND WEIGHT-CONTROL, 183. THE "FEEL" OF BALANCE, 184. A LONG SPINAL AXIS, 185. PELVIC EQUILIBRIUM AND THE TRUNK AXES, 190. THORAX SHOULDERS AND HEAD, 191.

CHAPTER VII

BALANCED FORCES IN WALKING 194
"THE PHYSIOLOGY OF WALKING," 194. EASY WALK- ING, 199. GRAVITY AND WALKING, 200. TIMING AND THE TAKE-OFF, 204. THE THIGH-JOINTS, 207. KNEES, 208. LOWER LEGS AND ANKLES, 209. THE GAME OF WALKING, 211. RÔLE OF THE EYES IN WALKING, 215

CHAPTER VIII

BREATHING 217
RHYTHMS, 217. CHANGES IN BREATHING, 218. RHYTH- MIC COORDINATION, 219. THE DIAPHRAGM, 221. REST ALTERNATING WORK, 222. TRUNK EXTENSORS AND TRUNK FLEXORS, 225. ANATOMY OF THE DIAPHRAGM, 226. FUNCTION OF DIAPHRAGM, 231. ACTION OF DIA- PHRAGM, 232. INTERRELATED STRUCTURES, 232. DEEP CONTROL OF BODY MOVEMENT, 238. CHEMICAL BAL- ANCE, 240. BALANCED SUPPORT OF THORAX, 241. DIA- PHRAGM AND SPINAL CURVES, 242. INTERDEPENDENT RHYTHMS, 243. TESTING BODILY RHYTHMS, 244.

CHAPTER IX

THE PROPRIOCEPTIVE SYSTEM 247
THE UNLEARNED PATTERN, 247. OLD ANIMAL MECH-
ANISMS, 248. MOBILIZATION FOR MOVEMENT, 248.
THE IMPORTANCE OF EXPIRATION, 250. DIAPHRAGM
INNERVATION, 252. BALANCED FORCES IN EMERGEN-
CIES, 253. SECOND WIND, 256. POSTURE AND SPEECH,
257. ELEMENTS OF SPEECH, 257. CONDITIONED RE-
FLEXES IN BREATHING, 258. ANATOMY OF SPEECH OR-
GANS, 259.

CHAPTER X

PHYSIOLOGICAL BALANCES AND UNBALANCES 262
MAN'S STABILITY, 262. FATIGUE, 263. CHRONIC
FATIGUE, 265. CONFUSION STRAINS, 265. MENTAL
FOCUS, 268. NEURONE STRAINS, 270. OUR NERVOUS
MECHANISMS, 272. EMOTIONAL FACTORS AND CON-
TROLS, 275. CEREBROSPINAL BALANCE, 278. NATURAL
VERSUS UNNATURAL RESTRAINT OF MOVEMENT, 280.
HABIT BUILDING, 282. ACQUAINTANCE WITH DIA-
PHRAGM, 283. TESTING KINESTHESIA WHILE SITTING,
285. BALANCED SITTING, 286. PICTURES TO AID, 288.
EMOTIONAL VERSUS MECHANICAL STRAINS, 288. EF-
FECTS OF HISSING, 290. RELAXATION, 293.

BIBLIOGRAPHY 296

INDEX 299

LIST OF ILLUSTRATIONS

FIGURE | PAGE

1. "The soliloquy" .... *Frontispiece*
2. The diaphragm 11
3. Comparison of bones and joints of horse and man.. 15
4. Inside of upper chest 19
5. Diagram of semi-circular canals in skull of pigeon .. 28
6. Osseous labyrinth of left human ear 28
7. Antagonizers 39
8. Vertebral column as a spring 49
9. Torsion—animate and inanimate 51
10. Small muscles of spine for differential movement of spine and rib joinings 57
11. Use of crouch muscles 64
12. Curves showing fatigue in muscles 66
13. Balanced four-legged position 68
14. Balance in movement 71
15. Pelvic arch showing its depth and depth of thigh-joints 73
16. Action of muscles on vertebrae 77
17. Relationship of bones and lines of hypothetical cylinder 79
18. Three aspects of spine 83
19. Lumbar vertebrae 86
20. How the vertebrae are adjusted for individual spinal action 88
21. Vertebrae with ligaments, front and back views, suggesting mechanics of bridge construction 89
22. Median section through occipital bone, atlas and axis 90
23. Diagrams showing alterable sections and unalterable masses 92
24. Redirection of curves and subtended angles 96

FIGURE   PAGE
25. Cross-section of torso through third lumbar vertebra   98
26. Balance of head on cervical vertebrae   100
27. Skull, side and base, showing pivotal point at con-
    dyles   101
28. Atlas and axis   102
29. Muscles of neck from right side   104
30. Deep back muscles in natural form   105
31. Axes of movement in ribs   109
32. Transversalis and rectus abdominis muscles   110
33. Top aspect of thorax and shoulder girdle   112
34. Section through femur and ilia, showing ligamentous
    bindings   114
35. "Sit on the ischia"   115
36. The bridge that walks and the bridge that we walk
    over   117
37. Lumbar muscles from front   119
38. Deep muscles of pelvis; deep posterior support of
    rotary joint   120
39. Internal obturator muscle   121
40. Deep muscles of pelvis, from within, balancing ro-
    tary joint posteriorly   123
41. Ligaments of pelvis, showing anterior bindings of
    sacroiliac joint   125
42. Right hip joint from front with ligaments   126
43. Ligaments of right half of pelvis, from back   127
44. Fascia and muscles about the ilium   129
45. Radius of revolution of femur and of humerus.....   130
46. Pelvis, top and side views   132
47. Trunk, from side   135
48. Fibula, bronze, seventh century B.C.   139
49. Lower leg and interosseous membrane   139
50. Diagram suggesting action of forces at ankle joint..   140
51. Tibialis posterior muscle   142
52. Shoulder girdle from above   145
53. Executive muscles of back   149

FIGURE   PAGE

54. Deep muscles of back, showing several deep shoulder and pelvic muscles 151

55. Front chest muscles 154

56. Shoulder girdle, rib cage removed 157

57. Four-legged position, using crouch and leg muscles for pulling body backwards, reversing crawl 162

58. Deep muscles of neck from front 167

59. Side view of ligamentum nuchae and stilohyoideus, side support of top ribs 169

60. Relation of shoulder blades to dorsal angles of ribs, quiet and in motion 171

61. Active sitting position 174

62. Arm circling, large to small radius 177

63. Weight of thigh and arm dropping back into sockets, with foot flexion and extension 178

64. Sway back 179

65. Power balancing power through opposed muscle centers 186

66. Cross section passing through body at middle of manubrium 188

67. Lines of force: tensile, gravity, compression 191

68-72. Drawings by F. O. C. Darley for Oliver Wendell Holmes' "Physiology of Walking" 195-197

73. Balance of axial stresses; tension in front, compression in back 202

74. Knee joints 208

75. Hanging in Japanese parasol 212

76. Diaphragm in natural position and form, seen from thoracic cavity 223

77. Trunk extensors of back 229

78. Diaphragm, showing close association of psoas and quadratus lumborum muscles with crura 230

79. Diaphragm 235

80. "Winding up" for power and aim 239

81. Return of sacral curve to front to balance compression and tensile forces at thigh-joint 250

FIGURE   PAGE

82. Ligaments and muscles of respiration and voice in
    larynx 260
83. Suspensory muscles of neck 266
84. Position on side for hip and rib balance 269
85. Diagram of transverse section of spinal cord and neu-
    rone chains 271
86. Spinal nerve 273
87. A good central axis 287
88. Jack-knife sitting 289
89. Relieving spine from strain of leg weights and favor-
    ing a return of blood to heart 290
90. Right posterior wall of thorax 291
91. Anterior wall of thorax, diaphragm removed from
    right side 292

THE THINKING BODY

Chapter I

FUNCTION AND FORM IN HUMAN DYNAMICS

BODILY ATTITUDES

W E SIT AND WALK AS WE THINK. WATCH ANY MAN AS HE WALKS DOWN THE AVENUE, AND YOU CAN DETER-mine his status in life. With practice, a finer discernment will have him placed socially and economically, and with a fair idea of his outlook on life. We judge our fellow man much more by the arrangement and movement of his skeletal parts than is evident at once.

Living, the whole body carries its meaning and tells its own story, standing, sitting, walking, awake or asleep. It pulls all the life up into the face of the philosopher, and sends it all down into the legs of the dancer. A casual world over-emphasizes the face. Memory likes to recall the whole body. It is not our parents' faces that come back to us, but their bodies, in the ac-customed chairs, eating, sewing, smoking, doing all the familiar things. We remember each as a body in action. The individual mental picture gallery knows how Bobby Jones swings, how Nurmi runs, how Helen Wills Moody serves.

Behavior is rarely rational; it is habitually emotional. We may speak wise words as the result of reasoning, but the entire being reacts to feeling. For every thought supported by feeling, there is a muscle change. Primary muscle patterns being the biological heritage of man, man's whole body records his emo-tional thinking.

The explorer and the pioneer stand up; the prisoner and the slave crouch; the saint leans forward, the overseer and the mag-

1

nate lean back. The marshal rides, Hamlet walks, Shylock extends the hands, Carmen requires the weight on one foot, hands on hips, eyes over the shoulder. The postures of dramatic tradition crystallize the theory of the actors, and through their body designs, the young study the portrayal of epic qualities in movement. Guilt, craft, vision, meanness, ecstasy, and lure appear in certain arrangements of arms, hands, shoulders, neck, head, and legs. Thus the stuff of the ages goes into man's thinking, is interpreted and comes out in movement and posture again. Personality goes into structure—by denial or affirmation into person again. It is an aspect of life in evolution.

In self-expression are the mental and emotional equipment, temperament, personal experiences and prejudices, influencing and controlling the relation of the bodily parts to the whole. This equipment includes the working unit for motion—the nerve-muscle action on bones. Muscles act automatically. When acting, they move bones. Man's bones play a large part in his sense of control and position in his world. How he centers them, determines his degree of self-possession; they are continually centered and *ex-centered* in his rhythms of movement. Mechanically, physiologically and psychologically, the human body is compelled to struggle for a state of equilibrium.

The physiological approach to the study of body dynamics is based upon the fact that the neuromuscular system is the unit which determines organized movement. Mechanically, separate units of weight (bones) are moving through space in definite time arrangement. The neuromuscular unit is the motive power. Physiologically, various stimuli prepare the muscles for their responses. These stimuli, being both internal and external, must be correlated. This involves psychological factors affecting the response. Response must be adequate to meet the situation.

The value of the receiving-correlating-responding mechanism in adequate action was very well expressed in my presence by Dr. Jesse Feiring Williams, in these terms, "The intelligence of an individual may be determined by the speed with which he orients himself to a new situation."

For every stimulus there is a motor response. The number of

parts involved in this response is conditioned by the person's social reactions and behavior, as well as by his physical status. The individual is a totality and cannot be segregated as to intellect, motor and social factors. They are all interrelated.

The correlation of visceral, psychic and peripheral stimuli, underlying muscular response, involves the whole of a man. It is the very perception of nerves, viscera and organic life. The whole body, enlivened as it is by muscular memory, becomes a sensitive instrument responding with a wisdom far outrunning that of man's reasoning or conscious control. The neuromusculatures of skeleton and viscera interact, always conditioned by what has been received, as well as by what is being received; and this because of emotional and mental evaluations.

We now realize that in the physical economy of the individual the many systems should be working in balance and unison and that thinking is a very part of their activity. We realize that function preceded structure, thinking preceded mind, the verb preceded the noun, doing was experienced before the thing done. Everything moves, and in the pattern of movement, Life is objectified.

Science has increased our knowledge to the better understanding of these values. Finer adjustments have been attained by balancing the endocrines; by study of the chemical constituents of bodily cells, of chemical contents and balance of needed foods; by the effects of temperature and pressure; by the studies of dress, housing, rest and activity, and a more perfect mechanical balance of the human skeleton. All of this has developed a finer appreciation of the interaction of all these systems in rhythm and harmony.

Parallel with the new knowledge of facts is the new knowledge of the unconscious. The unconscious is treasure-house and charnel-house of the creative and one of the keys to physiology. The "backbone" to which we must join new physiological investigations is the study of the unconscious.

We are told that even in the best human machine, only 15 per cent of the total energy is available for conscious purposes; 85 per cent is used in vegetative processes—heart action and so on.

This leaves us only 15 per cent with which to do the work of the world. Any impairment of the vegetative or unconscious processes will require new energy, and the only source to draw upon is the 15 per cent, which should be conserved for the use of the conscious or distinctively human activities—those activities not shared with other animals. In times of stress, however, the 15 per cent may draw upon the reservoir of the 85 per cent unconscious energy, as pointed out by William James in his essay on the reserves of human energy.

HABITS

Habits being biological, racial and individual, the design of the human mechanism has undergone considerable and important changes during its long process of development. While its general features are determined, its many individual variations are capable of still further modifications by habit and training. Faulty arrangement of parts in the design, through artificial habits, may be corrected. What may originally have been good arrangements may be rendered faulty by furthering wrong habits.

The human body, in addition to other requirements of living, meets the same structural problems of interacting forces as the inanimate mechanism. Bones offer not only protection for our organism, but a suitable framework for support of body weights. Through organized leverage, they give direction and purpose to movement.

Our bodies, we know, have a history outrunning by hundreds of millions of years that of the human mind and that fact is now influencing our attitude toward man in many ways. Even if this scientific discovery be denied, one must admit that in his own case, his baby body was well under way before he woke up and began to think, talk and give evidences of human intelligence. But when, in young children, reasoning powers gradually develop, their attention is directed, not so much to their bodies as to the artfully designed clothes with which they find themselves covered.

Many of us still feel a squeamish distaste when bone and

muscle are mentioned. Confidently ignorant as to what goes on under our skin, we go about our daily doings absolutely dependent upon what lies within but with no more interest in it than the dog has in his anatomy.

Our bodies are brought to our attention usually under disagreeable circumstances—when we are sick or injured, and the clothes have to come off to reveal a wound, burn or fracture. We seem messy inside, for when our skin is punctured or torn, out runs a scarlet fluid which makes a horrid stain and is offensive. When it was rumored that a distinguished Harvard physiologist had had his salary raised, a Cambridge lady in excellent standing was reported to have said that she hoped that the doctor could now afford to do something nicer than to fuss with people's disgusting insides.

Unlike dogs, human beings form habits of managing their bodies badly, through false notions about "holding" individual parts. It may never occur to them that mechanically, action and reaction are as persistent in the living mechanism as in that of any inanimate structure.

BONE VERSUS STEEL

Nature has chosen wisely in supplying us with bone. Bone has the qualities of hardness, stiffness and elasticity which made steel the engineer's chosen medium.

The intelligent person realizes the skeleton alive and whole, inside his entire body, with its living engines, the attached muscles, ready to respond.

In this sense, the daring anatomist was modern four hundred years ago. Vesalius, who died in the year Shakespeare was born, showed a skeleton which might be a Hamlet. Standing by a library table, weight on one leg, left elbow on the table, the figure leans forward a little, hand on cheek. The rock, shrubs and leaves at the feet suggest the unfolding of nature's science; the student's pose and the table look toward the invisible universe of philosophy. The skeleton lives, stands. In a moment it will turn, walk, move body and head in the soliloquy. Impossible not to feel that this skeleton is person!

Beating heart and spurting blood mean life. But behind this redness and liquid stream that stand for vitality is bone. Bone makes blood. It is antecedent to blood. The total number of red blood cells in an adult is computed in billions. The length of life of a single cell is about ten days. Renewal and replacement of cells goes on in the marrow of the bones. Bones live. We must *sense* them alive if we are to understand their interdependence with their adjoined soft tissues. We can then appreciate the importance of their function for the whole body. They aid all other tissues by their protection of cavities, support of weight and manufacture of blood cells. In common with all body tissues, bone has the recuperative quality which is the unique property of all living protoplasm.

Bone, while furnishing protection and support, also furnishes points of leverage for the engines of movement; the muscles. Bones move in response to the neuromuscular unit. Man consciously controls bones. He does not consciously control the neuromuscular unit.

When we command movement of arm or leg, we establish all the conditions to effect the movement of several bony levers in organized action. The wisdom lies not in man's "command," but in the various systems cooperating with the neuromuscular mechanism to establish right conditions.

When a man aims a gun, a whole chain of reflexes is in process of synchronization. These reflexes are preparing as he decides what he is going to shoot, gets his stance, adjusts his shoulder and spine to the weight of the gun, and aims, projecting his eyes. Added to these are internal responses, such as a deep, physical quiet and changed breathing rhythms. He pulls the trigger. Instantly these conditioned reflexes act in accord with principles of mechanics and of organic functioning. He must keep his eye distance correct, his head balanced to insure his stance, and his arm steady. He must absorb the recoil from the gun in his backbone and legs. All these responses are automatic. His duck-shooting skill depends upon the synchronizing of chemical, mechanical and organic conditions. Even the time of the decision to pull the trigger is determined partly by his kinesthetic sense, which he would call his "feeling that all is ready." His freedom of response is also influenced by his optimism. If his body is well conditioned and unhampered by doubts and fears, the duck drops—to his great satisfaction.

With given conditions established, "it happens," exactly as "it snows, it rains" and for similar reasons; conditions are right. Movement is the result of conditions established according to fundamental principles, governing a dynamic living mechanism. Understanding the underlying principles is fundamental to understanding the movements.

None of these responses would be possible were it not for the varying shape and length of bony levers through which the organism effects direction of movement.

The skeleton is made in a way to do certain things, and it is difficult to separate the doing and the making, growth, development and function being so interlaced.

Bone has four functions: the organic, manufacturing blood cells—bone is alive; the protective, it houses the brain, spinal cord and heart, the lungs and viscera—bone is an enclosing casement; the supporting, it bears the weights of the body and supports the organs of motion, the muscles—bone is form. In evolution the needs of function resolve into form—into structure.

The skeleton is nature's mechanical triumph. Lines of force go through its bones and the feeling of motion is in them. The living machine walks.

BALANCING FORCES

The human being is a composite of balanced forces. To maintain his structural support with the least strain on the several parts is a problem of bodily adjustment to external forces, primarily mechanical.

Through balance man conserves nervous energy and thus directly benefits all his activities, mental as well as physical.

At that stage of the evolutionary process when man assumed the upright posture, he secured freedom of motion and a larger command over his environment than is possessed by any other creature. There are, however, mechanical disadvantages and points of weakness in his structural provision that threaten the stability of his support and the protection of his vital processes. To offset this weakness, it is imperative to recognize and properly utilize the principles of mechanics as applied to the main structural units in the vertical position. How does the pull of gravity act upon the spinal curves and upon the flat body walls, which balance at front and back, upon this curved, supporting upright? How do these function to meet the pull of gravity and to keep the skeletal structure supporting its mass of weight? What are the lines of force operating continuously upon the skeleton? These questions and more we must ask ourselves if we wish to solve the mechanical problem of posture and movement of man in the upright position.

FORM FOLLOWS FUNCTION

The principle that function makes form determines the myriad shapes of life, from the earliest single-celled organism to the latest and most complicated plant or animal. The meaning of any structure is to be found by inquiring what the forces are to which the creature possessing it is reacting so that it can maintain its own existence. Force must be met by force, and the structure evolves as the forces are balancing.

Life in the water and life on land are the two great ways of living from which stem two important patterns of structure in the vertebrates. The fish does not have to contend with gravity; rather it seems to work for him, because of the way in which water presses equally from all sides, and up as well as down. The fish, to be sure, has his own problems of gravity in position and direction of movement, and has met them with various fascinating devices. So long as he displaces more than his own weight of water, he does not sink. The land animal displaces less than his own weight in air, so that he must depend on the surface of the ground to hold him up against gravity, which would otherwise bear him swiftly into the earth. As the animal leaves the water for the land, two adjustments must be made simultaneously: to meet gravity through a hard instead of a liquid medium and to take oxygen from a gas instead of from a fluid. As gravity acts perpendicularly upon the body, vertical appendages must develop if the body-weight is to be moved about speedily and freely; and some means must be devised for carrying air into the body, where oxygen may be taken from it for the use of the cells as they live in their own fluid media. Limbs develop to meet the first need, and lungs to meet the second.

Respiration, that is, the exchange of the gases oxygen and carbon dioxide, has two phases in both man and fish instead of one as in the single-celled organism. In the unicellular forms the exchange takes place directly by diffusion at the surface of the cell; in the multicellular forms, certain cells bring the oxygen to the others and remove their gaseous waste products. The entire process takes place in two stages: (1) external respiration, an interchange of gases between the external medium, whether this be water or air, and the circulating fluid of the body; and (2) internal respiration, an interchange between the tissue cells and the circulating fluid by simple diffusion, as in the single-celled organism. Lavoisier, who discovered oxygen and its rôle in the body, called the external phase primary, and the internal, secondary breathing.

Fish and man differ in their organs of external respiration. The gills of the fish present a large surface, well supplied with blood, over which water continually passes, while the blood takes the oxygen gas from the water and gives out the carbon dioxide from the tissue cells. Lungs contain numerous air sacs, in which the renewal of air is effected by respiratory movements, while the blood circulates rapidly just beneath the surface of the sacs, through which it takes oxygen from the air and yields the carbon dioxide it has taken up in internal respiration.

The shift from water to land was not made at once, but by gradual stages, represented today by various amphibians which, as their name implies, live both in water and on land. Some live in mud and are able to breathe either water or air as need arises, by means of gills, or by rudimentary lungs, or by special adaptations of their skin. Others, like the toad and the frog, have an early tadpole life in the water, quite like fishes, and upon emerging as adults, lose gills and tails and acquire lungs and legs.

In a real sense the living organism never loses its dependence upon water for its essential vital processes, and however far from the water the animal or plant may get, it carries about within it, its old watery environment in the form of tissue fluids, without which the individual cells cannot live. About 70 per cent of the human body is water, and any departure from this proportion produces serious consequences.

The apparatus for locomotion and for breathing, which appeared simultaneously in the racial pattern as vertebrates came onto the land, continue to be closely associated in the growth of individual organisms and in their functions. They are intimately related through mechanical and nervous tie-ups between appendicular and respiratory structures, also between both these and the cardiovascular system by which blood is conveyed from heart to lungs for aerating and back to the heart with its load of oxygen. And in man, the particular parts of the skeleton and musculature which operate to maintain the spinal curves and to keep the trunk erect are most closely associated with the bony and muscular parts involved in breathing.

The land creatures had not only to learn to breathe air instead of water, but they had to support their weight above ground. This meant adjusting to reduced pressures from above and from the sides, and meeting the downward force of gravity through their own tissues, which had also to withstand the upward push from the ground. This required the development of limbs and a different sort of a skeleton or hard supporting structure. The limbs of land vertebrates developed from special fleshy fins grown by fishes which learned to come up onto the shore and to get about in the mud. These fishes were called "lobe-fins" and were contemporary with the "lung fish" that acquired the earliest type of air-breathing lung, from which the later forms are supposed to have developed.

Out of water, the skeleton had to be both light enough to move about and bulky enough to afford attachments for the

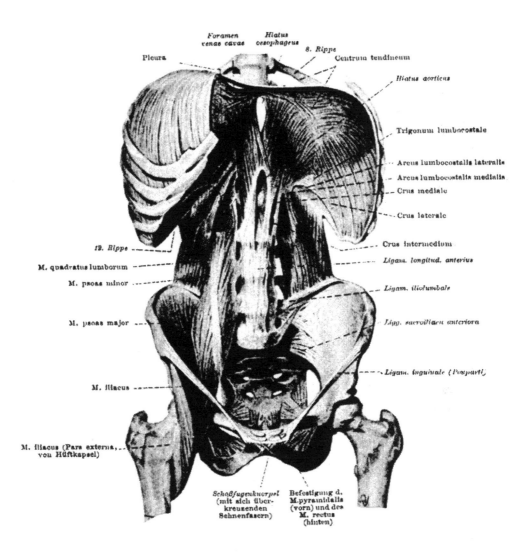

Foramen
venae cavae

Hiatus
oesophageus

Pleura

8. Rippe

Centrum tendineum

Hiatus aorticus

Trigonum lumbocostale

Arcus lumbocostalis lateralis

Arcus lumbocostalis medialis

Crus mediale

Crus laterale

Crus intermedium

12. Rippe

M. quadratus lumborum

M. psoas minor

M. psoas major

Ligam. longitud. anterius

Ligam. iliolumbale

Ligg. sacroiliaca anteriora

Ligam. inguinale (Pouparti)

M. iliacus

M. iliacus (Pars externa, von Hüftkapsel)

Schoßfugenknorpel
(mit sich über-
kreuzenden
Sehnenfasern)

Befestigung d.
M.pyramidalis
(vorn) und des
M. rectus
(hinten)

FIG. 2. The diaphragm. Back abdominal wall and diaphragm. Natural position of bones and natural shapes of muscles. At right, a part of diaphragm is cut away above lumbocostalis, to show upper origins of psoas and quadratus lumborum. (From Braus.)

[11]

strong muscles that were needed to move it. Thus it appears that the type of spine and the shape and manner of attachment of the limbs differ in the various types of veretebrates according to the kind of locomotion adopted. The snake gets on without arms or legs because its spine is so very flexible that tiny movements from side to side, communicated through the ribs, serve to pull the body along. The actual motion in the snake depends upon friction between the ground and the transverse oblong scales which cover the under-body wall. In all the reptiles the skin tends to be either very tough or quite hard, as in the turtle, and since the legs do not raise the body much, an exoskeleton is needed for protection against ground shocks.

Bird and mammal both derived from the reptile but followed divergent patterns in their supporting and moving mechanisms. The bird, in taking to the air, exchanged a flexible spine for a rigid one, selected light, hard, and relatively hollow bones, and specialized in powerful forearms, with a highly developed clavicle and a large sternum, giving an attachment and a fulcrum for the strong wing muscles, while ignoring the legs except as accessories.

The mammal lifted himself up from the ground on all fours, and at first used both arms and legs fairly equally in locomotion. When the ancestor of the primates (monkeys, apes and men) got off the ground and began to live in the trees, a change in the type of locomotion became necessary, with a differentiated use of arms and legs. In the trees the arms and hands were used to pull the body up from one level to another, and as progression had to be vertical a great part of the time, the lower limbs bore the bulk of the weight both in climbing and in resting.

The four-legged animal on the ground had to do many things with his head that the tree animal learned to do with his forepaws. Grasping and climbing developed the hand and its power of manipulation. This ultimately freed the head and enabled it to serve increasingly the needs of the special senses of seeing, hearing, smelling and tasting without having to undertake such acquisitive movements as seizing and holding. The animal could rest and pick up food or some other object and bring it to his mouth, or hold it to smell it or to look at it, without having to move the head toward it. Consequently, more kinds of impressions could be obtained simultaneously, and the need for the correlation and coordination of a multiplicity of impressions coming at once through sensory channels brought increased need for relay and storage centers in the neuromuscular system. This gradually resulted in higher and rounded brain shapes, and since the bones accommodated themselves to the brain growth, skulls became higher and rounder, culminating at length in the relatively huge, dome-shaped head characteristic of the human being. The growth of the skull to match the brain is characteristic of the way in which, in the body, hard tissues are altered by soft tissues.

While the primate lived in the trees, the arm and hand were developed for long-range action as compared with their simpler use in quadrupedal locomotion. This developed the characteristic shoulder girdle of the primate, especially the clavicle, or collarbone. The scapula, or shoulder blade, had already been developed as a supporting structure for the forelimb and a protective roof for the shoulder-joint, distributing the muscles and attachments of the arm in such a way as to shield the upper thorax from their action. The extension of the clavicle laterally in a plane nearly at right angles to the breastbone, or sternum, strengthened the protective function of the shoulder girdle as the increasing variety and vigor of the arm movements brought greater hazard to the heart and to the respiratory mechanisms of the chest.

Returning to the ground, however, the ape did not develop upright posture in the human sense. For a long time locomotion continued to be largely on all-fours, and when the animal rested it was in a sitting, or rather squatting, position; only in emergencies and for brief periods did it stand on its hind-legs. Walking on two legs became a regular procedure only with the development of the frontal brain and consciousness of self in man. Dr. Gregory, in his "Bridge-that-Walks,"* gives a fas-

* The Bridge-that-Walks, an essay by William K. Gregory.

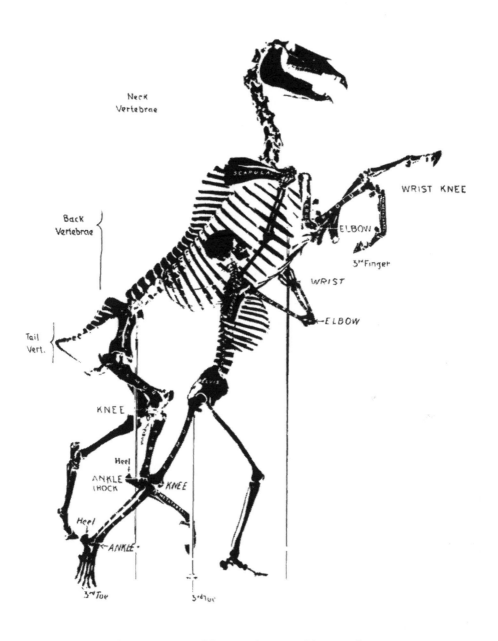

FIG. 3. Comparison of bones and joints of horse and man.
(From Gregory)

[15]

cinating picture of the gradual development of the human locomotor mechanism.

The course of development involved in the erect carriage is reflected in the history of the individual. In the embryo both the arms and legs develop rather late, with the lower limbs relatively inconspicuous, even for some time after birth, while the arms and hands are comparatively strong in the newborn. The legs and pelvis do not begin to get their later proportions until they are needed for walking. They are prepared for this use in the creeping stage of the baby's activities.

The spine remains the fundamental basis of support and movement for all of the various vertebrate structures. The strength of arms and legs depends upon their closeness of association with the strongest parts of the spine. Thus the great muscles binding the pelvis and legs to the spine extend deep into the trunk, and some reach high up into the thorax, where they are attached at a level opposite the lower end of the sternum.

These are the important muscles for support and movement in walking, so that we walk with the help of our lower chest structures as well as by the more obvious muscles of thigh, calf and foot. Shoulders and rib-cage are likewise connected with the lower spine and with the pelvis through the strong muscles of the back and sides. Strength of movement of the arms, in throwing or grasping, or in lifting outside weights, is dependent upon the underlying support and strength of loins and thighs. The essential structures for the support of body-weight and for the control of movement are thus to be looked for in the lower spine, where the oldest and best-established patterns of neuromuscular activity are found, as well as in the legs.

Activity, when following the primary patterns of the animal, reveals the intimate association of the vital processes of the body, as well as the structural interrelationships and coordination. As soon as the body must function actively as a unit, as in walking or running, or dealing in any direct way with the environment, the structural lines of connection are drawn tighter and the bony and muscular parts are moved toward center, so that there may be as much economy of effort as possible. Witness the crouch of the animal or the preparation for a race or a pole vault.

In the neuromuscular mechanism the oldest and therefore the strongest associations between one part and another, center along the vertical axis of the spine. Here lie the central tubular structures of the circulatory, respiratory and digestive systems, constituting the "service supply" for the whole. Along this axis also, safely protected by the spine, lies the "service of communication," the nervous system. The spine is the power center, the protective center and the coordinating center for both structural and organic rhythms.

When the animal is resting quietly, as after eating, and the rhythm of organic function may be perceived, there appears only a passive relationship between the various parts of the body; there is the look of an all-pervasive comfort and well-being and of little effort in the living processes—the cow comfortably chewing her cud. All the organic activity is along the central axis, in the central tube-like structures of the circulatory, respiratory and digestive mechanisms. The service of supply is preparing for future expenditures.

As the animal begins to move about or to react in some positive way to his environment, the functional interrelation of bodily parts becomes evident. Breathing is deepened and speeded up, as required by the increased need of the active muscles for oxygen. This means deepened action of the diaphragm. Its great sheet and stem alternately contract and relax, to make the chest cavity larger and smaller, until not only diaphragm and intercostal muscles are moving but additional groups of muscles in abdomen and pelvis are engaged, actively and obviously, in working the pump. Finally the muscles extending between the chest-wall and shoulder girdle become engaged; in fact, all skeletal muscles may be called upon to take part under the stress of extreme exertion.

The heart muscle, too, responds to hasten the blood on its way to the lungs, and then to carry oxygen to the clamoring

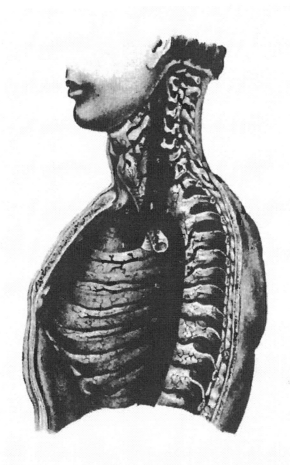

FIG. 4. Inside of upper chest, showing depth of spine and relation of main arterial trunk to spine. (From Goddard.)

muscle cells. The digestive apparatus is affected, not so much in its immediate chemical activities, which are abated by violent exercise, as in the gross movements of its muscular walls. These movements propel the columns of food onward and speed the absorption of the prepared food by the lymphatic vessels, which then hasten to pour it into the blood stream, so that the blood sugar used in muscular activity may be restored.

Maintaining a balanced relationship of spinal parts to the long axis is an important aid to the primary rhythms of breathing. The vertical action of the diaphragm to its greatest depth along this axis is necessary if full dimension of the oxygen tank is to be established. A short spinal axis reverses this picture. It widens the curves and interferes with ligamentous and muscular functioning at the segments.

As the diaphragm deepens its action through the lumbar region of the spine, the muscles of the lower spine which extend from deep within the pelvis take a stronger hold and a basic lower trunk support is established. As the breathing deepens, the whole body comes alive, ready for action. Or, as is the case in sleep, the potential energy which hangs in the balance, ready for use, drops nearer and nearer to the perfect balance leading toward rest. Thus in sleep as in waking hours the centers for locomotion and for breathing are coordinating and the body acts as a unit in making the two adaptations necessitated by its land environment, that is, supporting its upright weight on a narrow base, and breathing air.

To understand these processes and the bodily adaptations, we must begin with an outline of the structural provisions for bodily reactions and know something about the mechanism of nervous and muscular coordination by which its reactions are effected.

POSTURAL PATTERNS

In applying the principles of mechanics to the human body, considering it both as an entity in the midst of universal forces and as a unit made up of a large number of parts, each definitely related to every other, the words "postural patterns" offer a convenient terminology. Should the term seem to convey a fixed outline or shape, recall that the body, like all other known objects on earth, is continuously subject to the pull of gravity and to inertia and must incessantly meet them. As it is being drawn toward the earth's center, it maintains itself by virtue of constant movement of the various parts; and it must as persistently withstand a tendency to continue moving in the same direction, or to remain at rest. The shape, or pattern, of the body is therefore a moving one, dynamic, not static.

The laws of gravitation and of motion were derived through the observation of falling bodies. Without a working knowledge of these laws the high steel skyscrapers and great bridges of today would be impossible. Through experience man has learned that unless he combines his materials, whether wood, brick or steel, in certain ways his structures will fail to meet the stresses thrown upon them by the interacting forces exerted by weights which push or pull upon them, by air pressure, or by jars and shocks in the ground. Through much testing of materials in divers types of construction and terrain, he has learned how forces act upon materials and how these must be arranged to meet the constant impact from such forces. The pattern will vary with the substance, and with the use for which it is destined.

In the human body it is the same: the postural pattern is that of many small parts moving definite distances in space, in a scheme perfectly timed, and with the exact amount of effort necessary to support the individual weights and to cover the time-space-movement. These delicate, accurate and intricate regulations are made in the substrata, below the "threshold of consciousness." Through such adjustment, man preserves his unity and copes with his world.

If we keep to the concept of ceaseless motion from a great play and flux of forces, and the resulting action and reaction between all objects, we can better understand the mutual resistance in balance that gives the physical universe its solid, secure look. So with the human body. Even the individual cells of the body are organized by balancing forces. The great authority on the cell, Edmund B. Wilson, tells us that cell*

* The Cell in Development and Heredity, by Edmund B. Wilson.

bodies do not necessarily have confining walls, but that in some cases forces acting within them hold them to their individual shapes, while they remain "masses of naked protoplasm." Again, within the cell there is a configuration of particles varying with the cell's activities, and in constant motion. This may be seen in the micro-movies of living cells and growing tissues of plants and animals.

To attain conscious control of the structural balance of the human body, we must know its component parts, their relationships, and the forces acting upon and within them. We must understand its materials and their functions and behavior. Understanding the mechanical principles of weight support which apply alike to animate and inanimate structures must be a part of this knowledge.

The bones are the weight-bearing parts, and gravity the primary force to which they are subjected. The balance of bones at their contacting surfaces, the joints, as well as their movement by the muscles, must be considered if economical adjustment of materials of the body is to be attained.

This adjustment involves psychophysical reactions as well as the purely physical reactions to the forces of gravity and inertia which operate alike on organic and inorganic mechanisms.

THE PSYCHOPHYSICAL BASIS OF POSTURE

In the building of artificial structures, the engineer's prime concern is with the character of the materials available for his use. He must know their inherent qualities and their behavior under stress of external forces before he makes a choice: for certain structures, stone or wood; for others, steel. So too, the intelligent use of our bodily mechanism depends upon our understanding of the nature of its materials and their behavior.

Without attempting to enumerate the components of the human body, we note that the important characteristic common to all is a capacity for responsive action. This capacity is inherent in the protoplasm, which constitutes the living material of all organisms, plant or animal. As more is learned of the complexity and variability of protoplasm, the more difficult it is to define. Thomas Huxley called it *the physical basis of life*; this is as near to a satisfactory definition as we are likely to come. For there appears to be no single substance which can be called protoplasm; there are rather an indefinite number of protoplasms, varying not only from cell to cell in chemical make-up, but even within a single cell.

This primordial moulding matter is neither solid nor fluid; it is both. It is just sufficiently solid to keep a form it assumes, and just sufficiently fluid to change to some other form at need. Any protoplasm is a mixture of extremely complex chemical compounds arranged in a minute cell structure, which is usually differentiated into a nucleus and surrounding substance called cytoplasm. The structure is found in its greatest complexity in man. All the myriad cells of the body have characteristics in common, but each lives a somewhat independent life of its own in a fluid medium. Each breathes, assimilates and displays irritability, and in varying degrees all can repair and reproduce themselves. In addition to these common cell functions, which are shared by all organisms from the single cell to the most elaborate multicellular plant or animal, each individual cell has a special rôle to play in the functioning of the whole structure.

The cells for the various functions combine into groups known as systems, such as muscular, bony, nervous, epithelial, vascular or glandular, which severally react to a variety of external and internal stimuli. Glands react primarily in emotional changes and muscles execute movements, both responding to stimuli transmitted through the nervous system. The reactions of all parts are so coordinated and integrated by several different factors, chemical, physical and nervous, that we perceive the individual as a whole rather than as a collection of parts.

Chapter II

REACTING MECHANISMS

MECHANICS

IN THE MECHANICS OF THE HUMAN ORGANISM, ITS TOTAL REACTION TO THE FORCES OF GRAVITY AND INERTIA ARE important, as it supports itself and moves about in an erect position. Particularly important are the structural and functional interrelations of the parts of the bony framework with the muscles through which movements are executed and upon which all sensations and motions depend.

In the nerves and muscles, we have a receiving and responding mechanism developed to a capacity to perform patterns of movement, ranging from the delicate repairing of a tiny watch to the highly intricate and inspired movements of the ballet.

NERVES

The nervous system is an organization of millions of highly specialized cells, which together perform for the whole body the functions which keep a single-celled creature a responding unit. An ameba, as Jesse Feiring Williams points out, shows, among others, the essential qualities of excitability, conductivity and integration. Thus, "if a needle pricks the amoeba, it is excited, the stimulus is conducted throughout the cell, and the protoplasm shows an integrated action by withdrawing from the offending needle."*

In the higher forms each of these processes is effected by means of special nerve cells, and in place of the "all-over" excitability there are "receiving cells" so differentiated as to respond selectively to stimuli through the various sense end-organs, as those in the nose, the eye, the skin, and so on.

* Atlas of Human Anatomy, by Jesse Feiring Williams.

Conduction is by means of elongated nerve fibers; and integration is accomplished in nerve centers, or ganglia, the highest referring center being the brain. Here excitations from several areas and of different kinds can be sorted and redirected in the form of coordinated impulses to muscles and glands for their characteristic responses. These three phases of the nervous process are carried out by means of highly intricate structures, of which the integrating centers in brain and spinal cord are the most elaborate.

With its infinite branches forming a network throughout the body, the nervous system is constantly acting on all structures and organs, conveying impulses to and from the centers in brain and spinal cord. Ceaselessly stimuli are producing reactions. All are recorded somewhere in the nerve centers; some we become aware of at once; others do not rise immediately into the field of consciousness.

There can be no such thing as fixity in such a fluctuating mass. Every sensation from the outside world, every activity and thought within, causes a change somewhere in the organism, which nevertheless has a marvelous capacity for running smoothly and accurately. Its balanced adjustment may, however, be disturbed by imposed jarring forces, whether they be physical or chemical, and the balance can be impaired seriously by the deliberate imposition of a fixed idea or an "emotional set." Hypertension in the human being is like rust in metal machinery.

SELF-AWARENESS

Awareness of our own motion, weight and position is obtained from within the body itself rather than from the outside world. It is accomplished by means of sensations arising in certain nerve end-organs, which are as definitely specialized to record them as are the sense-organs in communication with the outer world for seeing, hearing, smelling, feeling and so forth. Otherwise we should be unable to stand or move about with any certainty without guidance from some outside source through the senses of touch, sight or smell. But the body possesses the power of reacting to gravity, inertia and momentum, the primary forces of the physical world, by means of that part of the nervous system known as *proprioceptive*, or "perceiving of self," as distinguished from the *exteroceptive* mechanisms by which the outer world is perceived.

The proprioceptive sensations, also called "organic," are grouped, according to their origins in various parts of the organism, into three general types: the "feeling of movement," in all skeletal and muscular structures, called kinesthesia; the feeling of position in space, derived from organs in the inner ear and known as labyrinthine; and miscellaneous impressions from various internal organs, as of digestion and excretion, called visceral.

Altogether, the proprioceptive system, acting in conjunction with all the outer senses, serves to guide our total reaction to the outside world in terms of motion toward or away from particular objects, and to give us our ideas of space and time. More than any other factor the proprioceptive system is responsible for the appearance of the individual as an organized unit when he is moving about.

Kinesthetic sensations from extremely numerous and scattered end-organs in muscles, tendons, joints, ligaments, bones, cartilage and other tissues of the supporting framework, make us aware of movement, whether passive or active, resistance to movement, weight pressure and the relative positions of the parts of the body.

Awareness of our orientation in space is derived from sensations arising in special end-organs of the inner ear, which are closely associated with, but not part of, the acoustic sense. These organs are located in a bony chamber called the labyrinth, or vestibule, and the sensations from them are therefore termed labyrinthine, or vestibular.

The labyrinthine sensations record two kinds of impressions: the position of the head and thus of the body, in relation to the earth, and the direction of movement in space. Two distinct organs are involved, the otoliths and the semicircular canals.

The precise way in which labyrinthine sensations are transmitted is not known, but it is agreed that knowledge of the position of the head in relation to the horizontal plane is derived from movements of the otoliths, little particles of lime

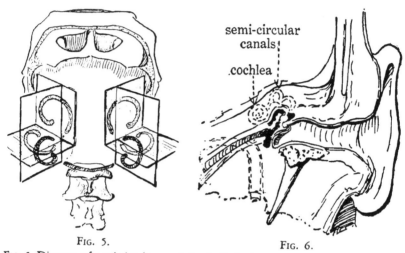

FIG. 5.   FIG. 6.

FIG. 5. Diagram of semi-circular canals in skull of pigeon. (Redrawn after Ewald.)
FIG. 6. Osseous labyrinth of left human ear, containing fluid and membranes which serve the sense of balance. (Redrawn after Morris.)

imbedded in tiny hairs in the vestibule of the ear; whereas the direction of movement of the head, particularly its rotations in any given dimension of space, is perceived by means of fluid moving in the semicircular canals. The semicircular canals, of which there are three in each ear, together represent the three dimensions of space, as shown in Figures 5 and 6.

However the result is accomplished, the fact is well established that the otoliths and semicircular canals are the seat of impressions of position and direction of motion in space; and that they are combined in the brain with the kinesthetic sensations of movement, weight pressure, and relative position, coming from other parts of the body, to give us our minute-to-minute information as to the movements of our limbs, neck and trunk, where we are at any given moment, and how we can get somewhere else.

Besides the kinesthetic and labyrinthine, there are sensations coming from the viscera and the vascular system which are communicated to the central nervous system and utilized in various ways. The particular manner of communication is not clearly understood. There are no definite impressions associated with them in consciousness, so that we do not at once refer the visceral sensations to their origin. They are not related directly to the motor apparatus save in certain areas, as in the control of the two ends of the alimentary canal. A feeling of fatigue, for instance, may mean a culmination or sum-total of unrecognized stimuli from fatigued stomach, liver, other viscera or muscles.

NERVOUS REFLEXES

Reflex is the term applied to the threefold nervous process of the receipt of a sensation, the transmission of it to a center, and the acting upon it by means of a motor impulse conveyed from the center to a muscle or viscus. Reflexes may be relatively simple, with only one kind of sensation and one type of movement, or they may involve multiple sensations and a corresponding number of movements. However complicated the structures may be that are involved in a reflex, the three phases are always present, and the sequence is normally continuous and complete. Incoming sensation, followed by registration and outgoing motor impulse, constitutes the "reflex arc."

Organic impressions are dealt with by means of complicated reflexes, resulting in appropriate movements. They are constantly set up by the activities of the body and its many parts, in muscles, bones and joints, in the viscera and in the head. They are combined in various ways with impressions from the other senses, particularly those of the eyes and the skin. The basal ganglia for the coordination of all these related impressions are in the cerebellum, in the vernacular the "little brain." Most of the operations involved in the guidance and control of our bodily movements are entirely unconscious. The original sensations and the chain of reflexes are not necessarily brought so far as the seat of consciousness in the upper brain, or cerebrum. The multitude of fine adaptations and adjustments of the body, and of its several parts, which enable it to keep a balanced relation with the forces of gravity and inertia, constitute primary patterns of behavior millions of years old, and all are dependent upon nervous reflexes.

The proprioceptive system is responsible not only for the special organic sensations, but for regulatory functions as well. It serves as a governing mechanism to regulate the extent of each motor discharge. It prevents overaction of the muscles in reaction to external stimuli and may evoke compensatory reflexes in the opposite direction.

It is this function of regulating and limiting muscular activity that is disturbed when damage is done to the labyrinthine apparatus, or to the cerebellum. Starling describes the effect as being similar to that of destroying the governor of an engine.* The movements of muscles in response to stimulation from the peripheral nerves become excessive and conflicting. These movements can and often do occur without disorder of the cerebellum, from disturbances in peripheral nerves or spinal pathways, as for example the disturbed muscular coordination in the disorder known as ataxia. Power of motion continues, but the movements are clumsy, disorganized, usually excessive, and badly directed. The other senses, as sight and touch, can take over the direction of movements to a certain extent, but this is both difficult and time-consuming.

MUSCLE TONE

Another closely related proprioceptive function is the production and maintenance of tone in muscles, and also in ligaments and fascia. This steady slight contraction observable in most skeletal muscles is quite independent of surface sensibility and depends entirely on the proprioceptive end-organs in the muscles and their accessory structures.

Tissue tone is of great importance in posture and support, and the tone of our muscles moreover largely conditions our bodily endurance, since muscles do not fatigue so readily when their

* Principles of Human Physiology, by Ernest H. Starling, 1912.

tone is properly maintained. The explanation seems to be that the constant slight contraction is not due to a shortening of all the fibers at once in any given part, but rather that the muscle fibers work in relays. For this reason, muscle is not being fatigued by its inherent tone. Normally, tonus to some degree is always present.

Unbalance of this special tone function is often the accompaniment of neurotic disturbances called, if exaggerated, muscle hypertension, or if diminished, muscle hypotension, or flabbiness, which physical exercise alone does not serve to correct.

In order to comprehend posture, it is necessary to have some understanding of the proprioceptive mechanisms and the nature of muscular activity.

KINESTHETIC CONSCIOUSNESS

We are unconscious of most of the small movements involved in posture and locomotion. Usually we are not aware of the initial sensation that starts the reflex or of the movement that completes it. This is true both of movements resulting from exteroceptive sensations and from the proprioceptive sensations. A vast number of these are habitual, that is automatic, though they may have been evident to consciousness at some period, as when learning to walk, to use a special tool or acquire a motor skill. However, it is possible to bring the organic impressions and resulting movements into consciousness and thus to control the adjustments. This fact underlies the learning process in purposive movement and conditions any improvement.

The nature of the kinesthetic process may be seen by an analysis of the way in which we become aware of the distance of objects. We are able to say that a table is four feet away or a piano ten feet, not, as one might suppose, because of any special quality of vision or a specific reaction to light, but chiefly by means of the muscular sense. The ability to differentiate distances is built up from a multitude of impressions conveyed from the eye muscles used in focusing the visual image upon the retina. The degree of muscular adjustment that is necessary varies with the distance and size of the object, and also with its shape. Impressions of the work done by the eye muscles as they move are reported to the brain, where they are interpreted as indicating a certain distance in space. This interpretation in turn is effected through an association of ideas or memories of various cumulative experiences, muscular and tactile, and of visual impressions of color and size. This is due to memories of former experiences—movements of the eye, movements of the body in going toward objects and reaching them, together with tactile impressions of their shapes, extent and textures derived from handling them. This spatial perception built up from past experience of the body muscles is remembered in conjunction with the impressions from adjusting the eye muscles. If this were not so, we could not distinguish between a large table ten feet away and a smaller one five feet away, since the visual image and the amount of muscular adjustment by the eyes might be identical.

Similar associations of ideas, also aided by the labyrinthine sensations reporting the position of our heads in relation to the earth, enable us to perceive an object in its actual position, right side up, although the retina receives an image that is upside down as projected through the anterior refracting surfaces and media of the eye.

Through our developed kinesthesia we are able, by nicety of adjustment of muscles and the recognition of slight movements in coordination, to estimate the power, distance and span of movements required by such acts as lifting weights, climbing stairs, throwing balls or jumping rope. The muscular reactions are automatic. We do not measure the number of pounds that we are about to lift or the number of stairs we are about to climb before we change our coordinated movements to lift our bodies or to adjust them to a level plane after climbing; nor do we measure the distance of the rope from the floor before we jump over it, nor apply a yardstick to the field before we throw the ball.

All these skills arrange themselves simultaneously in patterns of movement in response to impulses set up in the nervous system. These impulses activate muscles, and muscles move bony levers in orderly fashion according to the mechanical laws of leverage. Our object should be to know more of the fundamental principles upon which these operations are based, so that we may facilitate freedom and economy of effort and motion—think straighter and throw a straighter ball.

CHANGING PATTERNS OF POSTURE

The ability to improve a pattern of support and movement for the reduction of mechanical stresses comes, not through the development of bulk and power in individual muscles, but from the study and appreciation of the human body as a weight-bearing and weight-moving structure. Kinesthesia, the feeling of movement and of weight, is the important source of our information. Through it we are able to bring about a better balancing of parts, and thus coordination of the whole. Our real interest then is a knowledge of mechanics, aiming to establish mechanical freedom and organic unity.

By securing balance at all weight-bearing and weight-transferring points in the structure, we equalize the pull on the antagonizing muscles under passive conditions, and thus release a greater amount of energy for their use in action. Why hold the bony parts of our body when we can let them hang or sit? In movement, they must alternately depart from center and return, if coordination is to take place.

When "doing exercises" under instruction we are apt to think that we move or direct the moving of muscles. What actually happens is that we get a picture from the teacher's words or his movements, and the appropriate action takes place within our own bodies to reproduce this picture. The result is successful in proportion to our power of interpretation and amount of experience, but most of all perhaps to the *desire to do*. In any case, the final response is automatic and not the result of any consciously directed movement of particular muscles. It is the result of a combination of reflexes, no one of which can be selected as in itself "causing" the movement, or pattern of movement. As Starling has pointed out:

"We have no objective phenomenal experience of our muscles. All that we are aware of and can judge of by our other senses is the movement as a whole, and our sensation of movement is therefore referred to the whole movement and not to the individual muscles."*

POSTURAL REFLEXES

Underlying all activity of the whole body, as in locomotion or in the various athletic skills, are the postural reflexes, by which man gets his bearings and keeps them. These are the reflexes that attend constantly to the important task of adjusting his weights along the upright of the spine, and maintain the spine itself in its supporting curves. Even the eyes are secondary in this process. They are constantly adjusting themselves as the messages come in from the labyrinth registering the positions of the head in relation to the earth.

The dog or the cat can balance itself with far greater ease than man, because at any given time three of his four feet can be on the ground at once and thus establish a plane. Even man finds that on steep or uneven ground he can progress better by using a stick for a third leg, to get a plane for balance. The tripod, because of its third leg, can be set down anywhere, on the most uneven surface, and thus makes surveying possible in the roughest territory.

CONDITIONED REFLEXES IN POSTURE

Posture attitudes of an animal are unconscious, while man's are largely determined by preconceived notions as to how he ought to look. The automatic character of response to a notion of what is desirable in posture is evidenced by the behavior of the average adult upon hearing the words: "Stand up straight." The chest is thrust out, the head and chin drawn stiffly back and up, in the effort to look "tall and straight." Actually the spine may become more curved than before, though in another direction. The height may thus be shortened, while the whole structure is handicapped both for general support and for move-

* Principles of Human Physiology, by Ernest H. Starling, 1912.

ment, as the spinal curves are thrown out of relation to the vertical axis.

This familiar response is determined by our conditioned reflexes. That is, the sensory-motor chain of reactions in our nerves and muscles has been gradually modified through association of ideas derived, not from mechanical or physical considerations of what balance means or how a really straight back looks, but from moral, that is, social concepts.

The words "straighten up" imply traits of integrity and self-reliance. We try therefore to look like someone brave and strong, and the soldier on parade, preferably the leader, is usually taken as the pattern, reinforced by suggestions from picture, story and song. For long years, the only "official" bearing was that of the soldier. The conventional command for it was descriptive: "Shoulders back, chests up, chins in, toes out!" Now these, and especially the requirement of pointing the toes outward, are no longer stressed even in military circles and are not found in gymnasium directions, but the average adult still responds through his conditioned reflexes to these old social and group suggestions. To most persons a word is all that is necessary to produce a characteristic pose: the symbol of a strong supporting character is a "stiff backbone"; the person who can take punishment without whining "takes it on the chin." The old adage, "Don't carry your wishbone where your backbone ought to be," reflects the moral suasion of a past age—good morals, perhaps, but bad anatomy.

Conditioning the reflexes, thus establishing fixed muscular patterns follows the imposition of these mechanically false ideas. But the system would react with equal ease to the right mechanical idea, and it is a fortunate circumstance that the structure adjusts itself to varying inner as well as outer stimuli, because we can alter the position by altering the stimulus. That is, we can substitute for the artificial or morally perfect position, the mechanically perfect, or naturally balanced position. To do this we must make use of the kinesthetic sensations coming to the central nervous system from every bone and joint, every ligament and muscle, just as surely as and more constantly than the peripheral sensations of touch, sight or sound.

PSYCHOLOGICAL REACTIONS AND POSTURE

The organic, or proprioceptive sensations, usually unconscious, are most significant in all movements involved in reflex action, and therefore in the process of learning or of habituation in practically all skills.

Postural reflexes have more widespread significance than is generally realized, since they enter into and modify other physical processes, such as breathing and the circulation, and may even affect mental activity. William James, in his "Principles of Psychology," pointed out that bodily postures definitely influence the emotions.* Certainly the reverse is also true, and the peculiarities of posture associated with mental diseases and abnormalities of various types have long been observed.

Laboratory experiments have shown distinct differences in the ability to make sensory discriminations according to bodily position. For example, pitch is best determined in the vertical posture, which is also favorable for testing the strength of grip and the accuracy of tapping; while the tactile sense and the visual and auditory memory appear to be best in the horizontal position. Many scholars have reported that they were able to do their best intellectual work while lying down.

These facts may explain the instinctive choice of the standing position for certain activities, even where the conditions of space do not demand it, as in the case of a musician, who must constantly adapt to the pitch of others, like the tap-drummer or castanet player, in an orchestra; or where delicacy and precision as well as strength are required as in fine surgery, mechanical drafting or machine-tending. Lying down, however, may best serve the person sizing up a situation in mental review, or planning for some future activity, where passive receptivity to ideas is needed rather than alert preparedness for immediate response to an outside stimulus.

William H. Burnham, the noted educator, remarked that

* The Principles of Psychology, by William James.

"conditioned reflexes of the utmost significance to physical and mental health may be developed in connection with posture."*

WHY STANDING STILL IS HARD WORK

The reflexes induced by the effort to stand still have been compared to the activities in a signal and switching station of a great railway, where half a hundred possible wrecks must be averted simultaneously. In our bodies there is a continuous tendency for gravity and inertia to unbalance the various units of weight and a continuous counter-effort to keep them balanced. The signaling between the various parts of the body and the cerebellar switching station is like that in the dispatching office, only far more complicated. Save in the artificial surroundings of the old-fashioned classroom or the Army, we have actually little occasion to stand still more than momentarily. But consider what happens when we "stop, look and listen" at cross-streets and the speedy dispatching that must be done through our various nerve centers to prepare arms, legs, spine and head to act together in a sudden backward jump that may be necessary to meet a threatening situation. When the wild creature stands still it is generally in some similarly critical situation, in which the impending choice for flight or attack leaves no time for deliberation; all must be "set to go" in any direction. This means a fine balance, as close to unbalance as can be, so that the slightest impetus will release the appropriate chain of motions.

Walking, as we all know, is easier and less fatiguing than standing, since the process of losing our balance and quickly recovering it causes less strain than the effort to keep our very flexible, delicately poised mechanism in one position. In standing there are actually many more small movements of more small parts cooperating. We must, moreover, impose our wills upon our bodies, since the attempt to stand still is not "natural" and must be directed consciously. This is more fatiguing than any movement that follows an unlearned pattern. Muscles

* Posture as a Condition of Efficient Brain Activity, an essay by William H. Burnham, American Posture League.

can be held in one position or continuously contracted only for short periods without fatigue; and the pattern of muscle action is that of alternate contraction and relaxation, which may be exhibited either by the whole group of muscle fibers making up what we call "a muscle" or by separate bundles responding within it.

Motion allows for rhythmic alternation and variation in the use of muscle fibers, and gives time for the individual bundles to rest, that is, to resume their simplest state of elementary tone. However, when standing, if the three bulks of weight—head, chest and pelvis—are held in alignment at their own spinal levels and balanced at their bony joinings, the muscles do not have to work nearly so hard to keep them there as when they are held out of alignment. Gravity itself is harnessed when we keep our weights balanced. By cultivating our sensitivity to kinesthetic impressions we can learn how the various parts feel when they are balanced, and by frequent reference to this consciousness we reduce strains and stresses within the structure.

MUSCLES, MOTION AND REST

The nature of muscle action with its alternate contraction and relaxation may be best exemplified by the heart beat. Cannon states that the heart, during twenty-four hours, works nine hours and rests fifteen; such are the proportionate periods of contraction and relaxation in systole and diastole which enable it to keep going for a lifetime. The alternate rhythm is especially marked in the heart because of the presence of two types of muscle tissue, the striped, which is like that in the skeletal muscles, and the unstriped, like that in the intestinal canal and in the walls of the blood vessels. Unstriped muscle is characterized by a tendency to continuous and rhythmic contraction and relaxation.

Striped muscle tissue also partakes somewhat of this tendency. As muscles work in pairs, actors and antagonizers, when one set contracts the opposing set relaxes, allowing it to be stretched. Through the agency of the proprioceptive mechanism, the tension in this set produces in the muscles a tendency to contract, thus initiating the next movement. That is, in extending the whole leg from the body, all muscles about the thigh joint take part. As those in the front of the leg contract, the ones in the

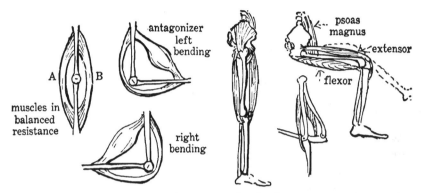

Fig. 7. Antagonizers. As a muscle on one side of a bone contracts, its opposing muscle stretches.

back relax and thus can be stretched; otherwise the leg would not move. There would be instead a tug of war between the two sets of muscles. When the hamstrings contract, the leg bends backward and as this happens, the quadriceps muscles relax and are stretched in turn, with the result of producing in them a tendency to contract, reversing the movement again. And so this alternation continues, in all activities such as walking, riding, running, bicycling or climbing.

The accompanying diagram shows schematically the action of the two sets of muscles about a joint, the bones being represented by two rods, with muscles attached to both sides.

The timing system controlling this alternation in muscular movements lies in the proprioceptive mechanism. The action of the legs is facilitated by the timing of the alternate contraction and relaxation of muscles. This timing is perfected by repetition and practice, until an intricate series of timing reflexes is built up for each type of movement involved in establishing new skills.

The motions of the various parts of the body used in standing or walking involve many pairs of muscles which move the spinal segments, so that the weights of head, trunk and pelvis are balanced upon the jointed column, and these combined weights are transferred through the legs to the ground. Muscles should not be called upon to hold special parts away from center in response to notional concepts. The muscle task is to move the bones, balance them at their spinal contacts along the axis of the spine, and transfer their weights as directly as possible to the base. Holding them in any preconceived position results in strain. The only way to avoid this is by keeping the joints properly aligned and the muscles as free as possible to move the bones and transfer or alter their direction of movement. Such result can be reached only through an understanding of balance and weight-thrust at the joints. A knowledge of mechanics is essential. We need not worry about appearance, because the balanced posture is bound to be beautiful. Indeed, when we analyze our impressions of posture, we find that it is the carriage showing poise and quiet strength which attracts us, while the strained attitude, with local rigidities, communicates to us a sense of discomfort.

On the other hand, a subjective impression of "comfort" in a particular position cannot be safely identified with mechanical balance. From long habit one may become accustomed to a wrong position even though it creates stresses throughout the mechanism. Because of nervous adjustments that have been made in establishing it, it may feel comfortable, especially if we complacently regard it as proper. Any readjustment, even to a balanced position, may produce at first the discomfort attendant upon change. Thus, a person who has been holding his chest high, in response to some notion of duty or brave front, feels when first told to disregard his chest in accordance with better mechanical adjustment, that he is losing some of his moral force by so doing. This is plainly a reflex which will require reconditioning or a process of re-education to change. After the body weights have been shifted from positions where they were held by muscle power to positions where they are balanced at their bony joinings and sit or hang in line with their supports, new reflexes (powerful enough to displace the old ones) must be smoothly established so that the new position is maintained with the least sense of effort. Then effective responses to these new sensations and better coordinated action will bring about new habits, or new patterns of posture, which in time will feel comfortable.

BODY MECHANICS AND STRUCTURAL HYGIENE

Throughout the entire bodily structure run two forces: the one is mechanical, operating on all parts of the body in the same way that it acts on any similar combination of weights, levers and supports; the other is the living force exerted by the neuromuscular mechanism. In our dynamic organism, correlation is accomplished in two interrelated ways: by mechanical changes through direct transmission of pressure or tension, and by organic changes through the excitation of living tissue. The effect of the neuromuscular force is to move bones about, while the effect of the mechanical force is to move them in accordance with the principles of natural balance. In the absence of the neuromuscular connections, the spine would collapse in response to purely mechanical force. This happens in paralysis. However, the adjustment of our bodily mechanism to the forces about it must follow the same principles that govern other structures with the same mechanical problems. There is no valid reason for believing otherwise. To secure conscious control of balance in the bony structure of the human body we must begin with an understanding of its mechanical design and then trust to the long-established automatic machinery of the neuromuscular system to make the necessary space-time adjustments. But this automatic process is interfered with whenever we attempt to force into a new position any particular part without reference to the pattern of the whole.

Exceptional performance in any one activity is not involved, nor emphasis upon a special set of muscles, but rather a cultivation of habits of thinking which secure the balance of the separate units of weight at their points of support. Contemplate the facts, and you will find your body responding with comfort in sitting, lying and standing, and with a new freedom

in activity. Economy of effort is a component of this new freedom. Functional design and the balance of forces in materials
must be studied and applied to establish economy and to form
a basis for structural hygiene.

Structural hygiene, then, may be defined as the application
to the human body of the principle of organic development
that *form follows function*. The prime mechanical function
of the bony skeleton is to resist gravity and to support the
weight of the body above the ground. Its form has developed
for this purpose. The prime function of muscles is to move
bony levers by furnishing power at appropriate points. They
should be used for this purpose, and not to do the work
assigned to the bones. This muscular action, directed by the
nervous system, performs the patterns of time-space-movement.

As the organism becomes more elaborate or meets increasingly elaborate hazards, with new needs at new levels of consciousness and interest, it can make special adaptations of
particular parts only by means of the old neuromuscular mechanism. The superimposed interests do not and cannot be made
to supplant the old basic concern of survival amidst the contending forces of gravity and inertia. New functions do not
replace the old, they are simply added to them.

The function of the skeleton is protective in its primary
sense, even before it is supporting, and the supporting phases
must not be allowed to interfere with the protective phases.
When man lifted his body-weight from the ground in assuming
the erect posture, the added handicaps of support through his
narrow base were met by various devices for management as
well as by structural change. These changes, however, have
proved to be inadequate in themselves to solve the problem of
easy balance under the new conditions. As a consequence, the
functioning of the skeleton as a protective mechanism is often
jeopardized by poor mechanical adjustment. Human intelligence must be applied to this problem.

If muscles are called upon to lift and to hold weights unnecessarily instead of to move bones in balanced relationship,
such action violates their relation with the nervous system, as

the organic sensations then sent to it are not designed to induce the appropriate reflexes. The holding of parts in fixed and strained relations impedes circulation, and the resultant congestion of one part and the defrauding of another can work havoc throughout the system. Quite limited breathing may suffice for the exchange of oxygen and carbon dioxide in the lungs, as may be seen in cases where the lung capacity is greatly reduced by disease and yet life is maintained. But the failure to utilize to the full all the chain of muscles that normally take part in the mechanics of breathing, such as the deep-lying abdominal and pelvic groups, robs the body of one of the natural coordinating mechanisms by which, for example, lymphatic and venous circulation, liver action, and peristalsis are promoted.

"Posture" is incessant. Even in sleep, organic functions such as breathing and digestion are still continuing in their rhythms, and structural parts assume relationships to each other, varying in their freedom and tension according to the strains of the day's activities. Small strains and tensions then assume an importance quite incommensurate with their initial dimensions. The stimuli constantly transmitted to the nervous system from joints and muscles are cumulative in effect, and often persist and hold over in muscular patterns of fatigue, which may not be completely relieved by sleep.

If these fatigue signals continue, as they may when there has been over-long contraction without rest, even when individually imperceptible, their effect piles up until enough is collected to produce a reaction in the nervous system. This reaction may partake of the nature of "shock" and be violent and incalculable in its effect, since the neuromuscular system, in its effort to deal with unassimilable impressions, may engage many more side chains of reflexes than ordinarily would be necessary. The end-result may be extreme inaction or an explosive overflow of nervous energy, according to the nature of the stimulus, and of the reacting organism. In any case, the particular reaction to fatigue depends to a great extent upon the emotional balance of the individual.

The type of postural maladjustments which consume energy and fatigue us most are those connected with our daily activities as we sit at a desk or sewing table, at a typewriter or a microscope—activities employing small movements of the eyes and hands and necessitating many small decisions and judgments, and constant attention. Attention means tension, a readiness to move with no movement taking place, which spells fatigue, for the reasons we have reviewed. This is doubly the case when to attention we add worry as to the outcome of our work, or anxiety for the future. Even when the anxiety is quite apart from the work in question, or when we are not sitting at a small, constraining task, our emotional undercurrent will express itself in some postural pattern. Emotion constantly finds expression in bodily position; if not in the furrowed brow or set mouth, then in limited breathing, in tight-held neck muscles, or in the slumped body of discouragement and listlessness.

These are some of the more important, though elusive strains to which the body may be subjected, through violation of the principles of mechanical adjustment, in the primary function of supporting itself against gravity.

There are ways and means which we may consider of achieving and maintaining primary body balance between these two sets of forces—the living and the mechanical. If sometimes we seem to be insisting on the obvious, let us remember that the ideas which need the most clarifying are often those to which we say, "of course."

Chapter III

MECHANICAL FORCES, FUNCTIONAL ADAPTATION AND STRUCTURAL CHANGE

BIPED PATTERN

STRUCTURAL BALANCE, AS WE KNOW IT, BECAME A PROBLEM WITH THE SLOW EVOLUTION OF A BIPED WHOSE STRUCtural arrangements had been developed over thousands of years of ancestral functioning on all-fours. In the quadruped pattern the separate units of body-weight hang from a horizontal spine like a girder, and the whole load is distributed quite evenly over a broad base resting on four supports. The biped pattern involved shifting the units from their vertical suspensions to positions where they are slung on a curved upright column and their accumulated weight concentrated on a narrow base, whence it is distributed through only two supports to the ground.

That man's organic and structural balance are not yet perfectly adjusted to the upright position is evidenced by the many functional disturbances associated with the support and movement of his body-weights. These functional disturbances arise from various strains expensive to the bodily economy, producing swayback, spinal curvature, visceroptosis, and so forth. The functions of the supported tissues and organs may be disturbed by the effect of the strains that are being communicated to them from the framework. The significance of postural patterns is recognized in certain functional as well as structural difficulties.

In 1927 the Public Health Service of the United States published "A Résumé, with Comments, of the Available Literature Relating to Posture," by Dr. Louis Schwartz.* In this the author enumerates the various bodily changes which have been

* *Public Health Rep.*, 42:1242-1248, 1927.

ascribed to the shift from the horizontal to the erect posture, including advantages with the disadvantages. The number and variety of disabilities, which seem to involve every region and almost every organ, appear incredible until one remembers the intimate interrelationships between the parts. One author, W. C. Mackenzie, is quoted to the effect that "if generalizations were to be made about the causes of human diseases, it would be along the line of failure of accommodation to the erect posture."

Reassurance, however, is brought by the list of notable advantages to human living, which more than compensate for the difficulties, particularly as these difficulties may be counteracted by attention given to the proper mechanical adjustment and use of the bodily parts. Intelligent adaptation depends upon a knowledge of the mechanical problems involved, the nature of stresses and strains, and of nature's provisions for meeting and preventing them, both in inanimate structures and in the human body, and particularly the principles of balance as applied to the weights of the human structure on its bony framework.

STRUCTURE AND FORCE

Structure is an arrangement of material designed to meet the action of forces whether by transmitting or resisting them. The action of forces is continuous throughout the material universe. All matter represents a balance of forces. To carry the subdivision of matter no further than the molecule, the quality and texture of any given substance depend upon the relations of its constituent molecules in their mutual coherence or their mutual repulsion. This inherent quality is displayed by the manner in which the substance meets impinging forces.

The nature of the mechanical problems confronting the human structure may be more readily understood by observing the same problems in inanimate structures where they are relatively simple.

The science of engineering is built, first, upon the mathematical determination of the degree and direction of the forces that are acting, or that will act, upon any projected structure, and second, upon the selection of suitable substances to meet these forces, and their combination and arrangement so that the result will be stability. This will produce the least strain upon the materials of the structure.

In the physical universe, action and reaction are always equal and opposite. There is no such thing as a force acting by itself, or upon an evironment in which there is no reaction. A force moving in one direction is met by an equal force, or combination of forces, which together are equal and opposite to the original force. That this is not always evident is due to the different kinds of structure which materials possess. Air, water and solids such as wood and stone have different ways of reacting, or of offering resistant force to an attacking force. Fluids, gases and solids differ from one another by virtue of the difference in the way their constituent molecules cohere. And within the groups the various substances differ between themselves: gases in their densities; fluids in their thickness or liquidity; while solids are light or heavy, soft or hard, tough or brittle. These differences reflect molecular disposition and determine their reaction to the forces coming from without.

THE FIVE MECHANICAL STRESSES

Under action applied by an outside force, any structure, whether simple or compound, will hold or give way according to its ability to meet the force with a resistance opposing and at least equal to the onslaught.

Thus, pressure downward upon any part must be equalled by an upward thrust in the opposite direction. A force pulling in one direction must be met by an equal pull in the other; a force causing twisting in one direction must be counteracted by an equal twist in the opposite direction; a force that causes sliding of one part upon another must be resisted by a force great enough to keep it from sliding; while a force that causes a tendency in a structure to bend along its axis must be countered by a force sufficient to keep it from bending.

The direction in which any force acts upon an object in relation to its internal axis determines the nature of the stress endured by the object. Any force operating upon an object induces some degree of stress within, since no action can occur without a reaction. Thus pressure will result in compression stress being set up within the object; that is, its molecules will be forced nearer together and will spring back in reaction. Pulling causes tensile stress: the molecules are drawn apart and tend to come together again in reaction.

AXIAL AND OTHER STRESSES

Compression and tensile stresses are called axial, since both operate along the axis without altering it. Three other stresses may be set up which involve the axis in some way or another, if the forces of pushing and pulling are combined, or if they are directed in such a way as to interfere with the axis. They are torsion, shear and bending.

Torsion stress occurs when pressure or pull is so exerted upon a structure as to cause its particles to twist about the axis. Analyzed, torsion is found to involve an alternate compression and tension, or pushing together and pulling apart of the particles, without disturbing the axis, although the structure is weakened for support in the area affected.

Shearing stress, or shear, is caused by a force directed against a structure at an angle to its axis so as to cause one part to slide over the other, disrupting the axis. This may be caused either by a single force directed against one part, with the rest of the structure rigid, or by two equal forces in opposite directions operating on adjacent parts.

Bending is a combination of tension and compression applied in such a way that the axis is curved, so that the structure is weakened for support. This may be caused by an unevenly disposed side load, or a too heavy top load. It is the most serious of the stresses and the hardest to counter.

These stresses may and usually do occur in various combinations and degrees. If the structure is homogeneous the stresses will naturally be different from those induced in structures of combined substances; also, a continuous structure will react differently from a segmented one.

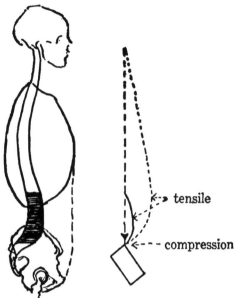

tensile

compression

FIG. 8. Vertebral column as a spring. Balance of axial forces, compression and tension on swinging block. (Redrawn after Braus.)

MECHANICAL STRAINS

Every stress within a structure threatens its integrity by altering the cohesion of its molecules. If the stress continues beyond the ability of the substance to resist, the structure will give way. Substances vary greatly in their ability to resist the various stresses, and their quality is determined by their reaction under stress. Thus, an elastic substance is one which can stand pull or pressure or combined stresses even to the point of actual elongation or shortening, returning to its previous state of molecular cohesion when the force ceases to operate. Some substances when pulled, pounded, bent or twisted do not break, but do not return to their original shape after the force is withdrawn: these are malleable. Substances that are brittle or too soft will break or tear under similar stress.

The point at which the integrity of a substance begins to be interrupted marks the beginning of strain. It is not necessary that a substance show deformation by tearing, breaking, crushing or pulling apart, for it to be under strain. Strain may begin long before it is manifest of itself, and may be cumulative. Such latent strain is even more dangerous than the obvious strain since it conveys no warning.

In order to provide against the hidden existence of strain, which may be coincident with stress, engineers insure endurance in a structure by providing a material, or a combination of materials so arranged that together they can offer resistance to an amount of stress several times as great as is likely to be set up within them. In computing the stresses which a structure like a tall building or a bridge must meet, engineers can predict with fair accuracy not only those imposed by the external forces of gravity, wind, and the pressure and jar from objects moving upon the structure, but also those from the mutual reactions between its several parts. Parts of a structure must balance each other as well as meet the outside forces if the structure is to maintain its equilibrium.

STRAINS IN THE BODY

We cannot as yet predict with mathematical precision what to expect in the way of opposing forces exerted upon a human body, nor the degree of stress likely to be set up within it. For the equilibrium of the body is determined, not alone by the physical principles of statics and dynamics operative in the case of inanimate structures, but also by an inherent capacity for change and adaptation in a living substance, which is lacking in the inanimate.

In the human body the fact that action and reaction are at all times equal and opposite is not always discernible, because the body is able to oppose force with living force and to bring from other parts new supplies of energy to a part in need; so that weight may be balanced by energy, instead of by weight alone. This makes the problem of planning for stresses and strains more complicated without changing its essentials. Years of teaching experience have shown the fundamental principles of engineering to be equally valid in the case of the bridge, the skyscraper and the human mechanism. Observation of engineer-

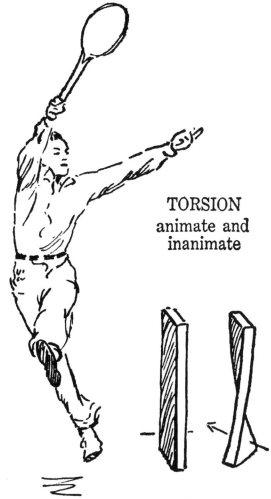

TORSION
animate and
inanimate

FIG. 9. Torsion—animate and inanimate.

ing principles and their application enables us to reduce bodily strains and to economize human energy.

The body is composed of substances of all degrees of fluidity and density, from water to solid bone. This very variety is an element of strength, and is one reason why the body can change and adapt itself so constantly in reaction to the play of universal forces that their action upon it is not noticeable. Furthermore, it is able to repair broken or worn parts and to accumulate energy against a future need. Indeed nature does for the body what the engineer does for the bridge or building by providing for resistance in excess of what is likely to be required.

Under ordinary circumstances we do not realize this, but let an accident occur and the safeguarding principle is readily seen in operation. For example, when a bone breaks, both edges begin to grow new cells toward each other, and the new portions are always larger than the parts replaced. It is due to this fact that the surgeon, in order to prevent a too long, buckled, or humpy leg-bone, must cut away a considerable rim on either side before putting on the connecting plate that bridges the gap until repair is effected. In the same way scar tissue grown over a cut or burned area is usually thicker and stronger than the original tissues.

The principle of excess replacement applies to energy as well. Thus, after a shock as from an operation, or in convalescence from a serious illness, the body acquires new energy in excess of that needed from day to day in a relatively inactive existence. This sometimes gives an illusory sense of strength which leads the patient to overexert, and he may suffer relapse or take longer to recover. Actually, the shock or illness has used up the reserve of energy which it has taken a long time to acquire, and it is to replace this reserve that the new surplus is needed.

In holding up its own weights the body may exert muscular effort far beyond what is really called for; and it can continue to do this because of its reservoir of energy. But in so doing, if the parts are held out of alignment and away from the axis of gravity, peculiar strains are put upon the spinal structure, which may give way, with results of a quite unforeseen and disastrous nature. Sometimes the end-results are remote from the site of strain; and moreover symptoms may be misleading because of the nature of referred and reflected pain.

REFERRED PAIN

The diagnosis of reflected and referred pain presents many difficulties. The literature is an extensive one and several titles are included in the bibliography for those interested.

From "Pain" by Dr. Richard J. Behan I quote:* "Referred pain is the name given to that class of pain in which the irritation occurs along the course of the nerve fibers, and the pain is felt as being produced in the somatic peripheral distribution of the affected nerve or nerves."

Three places where irritation may cause referred pain are:

> The cord.
> Posterior roots and ganglia.
> The nerve trunks or nerves.

As examples of referred pain he mentions:

Pain in the groin caused by a mole on the foot.

Pain in the knee from a corn.

Pain in the left clavicle from volvulus of the small intestine.

Pain in the arm and hand from pressure on the brachial plexus by a supernumerary rib.

Pain in the little finger due to pressure on the ulnar nerve from a growth on the first rib.

Pain in the thigh (anterior and posterior) and in the groin from a psoas abscess.

Pain in outer side of the hand, from irritation of the musculospiral nerve due to fracture of the upper part of the middle third of the humerus.

Of the difference between reflected (or deflected) pain and referred pain Dr. Behan says: ". . . in reflected pain there is a transfer of painful stimuli from one neuronic system to another; while in referred pain there is no transfer but only a misreference of the pain by the sensorium."

When strains manifest themselves in the form of "referred

* Pain: Its Origin, Conduction, Perception and Diagnostic Significance, by Richard J. Behan.

pain," their causes are difficult to trace as they are closely tied
to the vegetative function.

Starling makes note that "When the afferent autonomic
fibers of a nerve are the seat of pain, the primary referred pain
is in the area of the cutaneous somatic fibers of the nerve."

COMPRESSION AND TENSILE MEMBERS

The elements of a structure through which weight is directly
transferred to the ground are called in engineering parlance the
compression members. These are the uprights in any structure.
The tensile members are the suspensory parts which direct
weight to points on the uprights where it may be received and
transferred to the ground advantageously—in the living structure, through bones. The direction of forces in the compression
members is downward, with gravity, while the direction of
forces in the tensile members is opposed to gravity.

In a bridge, the compression members are the uprights which
rest firmly on the ground and, in all but the most primitive or
temporary structures, are sunk well into the solid earth; while
the long cables stretched from the uprights to the cross-pieces,
holding them up, are the tensile members. All the accessory
parts, like the shorter and graduated cables connecting the
long cables with the sections of the cross-pieces, the braces,
trusses, ties and cross-beams, are either compression or tensile
members. That is, they either resist the downward compression
force of gravity by an upward push of their molecules, or they
hold the weight up by virtue of their ability to resist stretching,
their compression or tensile force being at least equal to the
force of the gravity pull on the weight.

Compression members must be hard; and they may be rigid
like wood or stone, or elastic to some degree like steel. Tensile
members may be either rigid like metal or wood; or they may
be pliable like ropes of hemp or cables of drawn steel. If
elastic they must be capable after stretching of immediate return to their original dimensions.

Compression stress may also be met by rigid structures diagonally disposed, as in arches or brackets. The arch may be

reinforced by buttresses, beams and ties, and the bracket by added suspension members. Tensile stress is met in any axis by those substances which can successfully resist stretching. Pliable or soft tensile members operate only in a vertical line if uncombined with rigid structures.

GRAVITY, MOMENTUM AND INERTIA

The engineer's problem resolves itself into finding means for meeting the forces of gravity, inertia and momentum, which affect all objects whether at rest or in motion. This problem becomes complicated when the active forces of air or fluids are interposed, as in the pressure of wind, temperature changes, or the drive of water. Whatever function the structure is to serve, whether for dwelling, roadway, bridge, automobile, or other human use, the materials must be arranged, first and foremost, so as to meet without collapse the inevitable, continuous action of universal forces.

So with the human structure: its first mechanical obligation is to meet satisfactorily the constant pull of gravity toward the center of the earth; also it must meet inertia, which so conditions any object that when it is at rest it tends to remain at rest, and when moving it tends to continue moving in a straight line. Since all parts of the human body are constantly moving, each separate unit is dropping of its own weight; the momentum is determined by the size of the unit, its density, type of support and distance from the ground. These forces, which operate exactly as they do upon weights outside the body, must be met by the body with resistance equal, or more than equal, to counter them in their manifold expressions and combinations.

The body's original material endowment is such that resistance to the several mechanical stresses of compression, tension, bending, shear and torsion is provided for in the tissues and organs themselves. The way in which the structures are actually used, however, can modify profoundly their ability to withstand the stresses they constantly undergo. Hence the importance of understanding the mechanical principles involved in their arrangement. These principles of support, balance, and movement of weight are the foundations of structural well-being, and so are deeply implicated in the rhythmic conduct of all vital processes of the entire organism.

In comparing the body to a building or a bridge, however, we must remember that there is in the body no single compression member nor upright, but that the spine and other supports are made up of a number of parts, alternately compressive and tensile in function. If the frame were rigid or in one piece, movement would be impossible—we should have no take-off, no spring-board; we should be static, not dynamic.

BALANCE IN THE BODY

In maintaining a balanced position amidst contending forces, stresses are set up within a structure, the degree of which varies with the position, the weight, and the resistant properties of the several parts. If strain occurs, its degree is proportional to, and varies with, the degree of the stress.* To have a minimum of stress, and therefore of strain, within the body, not only must the structure as a whole be in balanced relation with the outside forces, but each part must be in balance with every other part within the system. This means that each part must be properly related to every other, remote as well as adjoining, if true mechanical balance is to obtain.

Movement of any one part away from the gravitational axis of the body involves the movement of an opposing part in an opposite direction, or the application of sufficient muscular force to restore the balance of the whole. This was explained by a simple analogy in an earlier article, as follows:

"Place on one side of an evenly balanced rod a fifty-pound weight. If you wish to retain the equilibrium of the rod you must either place the same weight on the opposite side or apply your own energy to the amount of fifty pounds' pressure.

"Move the fifty-pound weight back to the center of the rod and no effort is required to hold it up. It is balanced.

"Mechanical law explains that the nearer to center weight

* Hooke's Law.

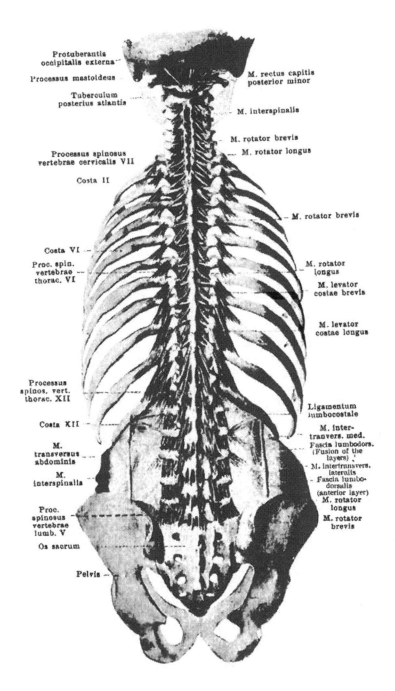

Protuberantia
occipitalis externa

Processus mastoideus

Tuberculum
posterius atlantis

Processus spinosus
vertebrae cervicalis VII

Costa II

Costa VI

Proc. spin.
vertebrae
thorac. VI

Processus
spinos. vert.
thorac. XII

Costa XII

M.
transversus
abdominis

M.
interspinalis

Proc.
spinosus
vertebrae
lumb. V

Os sacrum

Pelvis

M. rectus capitis
posterior minor

M. interspinalis

M. rotator brevis

M. rotator longus

M. rotator brevis

M. rotator
longus

M. levator
costae brevis

M. levator
costae longus

Ligamentum
lumbocostale

M. inter-
tranvers. med.

Fascia lumbodors.
(Fusion of the
layers)

M. intertransvers.
lateralis

Fascia lumbo-
dorsalis
(anterior layer)

M. rotator
longus

M. rotator
brevis

FIG. 10. Small muscles of spine, for differential movement of spine and rib
joinings. Note lumbar fascia for attachments of transversalis. (From Spalteholz.)

[57]

is maintained, the less expenditure of energy is required to keep it in equilibrium. It is evident, therefore, that if we discover the position of the best mechanical advantage, this position must correspond to anatomical fact."*

In the upright body, weights are not arranged horizontally on rods, but one above the other, making the problem of altering and restoring balance somewhat different. Imagine three blocks in perpendicular alignment. If the median line of the structure passes directly through the center of the weight of each block, gravity will exercise an equal pull on all alike, and the structure will stand. But swing one block out of alignment and its relationship to the center of the whole is disturbed: if it is to keep that position, external force must be applied.

In the human structure the three principal units of weight are the skull, the thorax and the pelvis. If these are balanced at center in relation to the axis of gravity there will be no unequal strain upon ligaments or muscles about the joints. But if any one of these three bony blocks is not supported at the center of the structure in its natural alignment, more muscular effort must be exerted to maintain its position in space, which involves an unnecessary strain and waste of energy.

STEEL AND BONE AS BUILDING MATERIAL

An engineer is concerned primarily with the qualities of the materials to be used in any structure and their ability to endure the stresses that it must meet. These will vary with the use. The pillars of a bridge must be able to withstand the effects of moving weights as they pass across it, as well as the weight of the various parts of the structure itself. Steel has been found to be the most valuable material for bridges because of its strength and durability, and especially because of its elasticity, by virtue of which it can successfully resist both the axial stresses, compression and tension.

In these particulars bone resembles steel, with strength for

* Principles of Posture, an essay by Mabel Elsworth Todd.

endurance, substance and stiffness to resist compression, and a degree of yielding to sustain shocks. Bone is a lacy network of living fiber, intimately combined with chemical substances which give it the necessary hardness and firmness to support weight.

An understanding of the physical and chemical properties of bone is important in our consideration of its mechanical function. The animal or organic part, composed of gelatin and blood vessels, makes up about one-third of the weight, and the other two-thirds are mineral, largely lime salts of various kinds, especially calcium phosphate. If the animal portions be burned away the calcined residue retains the form of the original, but is fragile and far more readily crushed. If, on the other hand, the mineral parts are removed by dilute hydrochloric acid, the decalcified bone, though it retains its form exactly, is tough and flexible, and a decalcified rib or ulna may be easily tied into a knot.

The physical properties of the living bone enable it to resist both the axial stresses of compression and tension so that it is neither crushed nor torn easily, while it is still relatively light. Its resistance to pressure is extraordinary. "A five-millimetre cube of compact bone of an ox when calcined will resist pressure up to 298 pounds; when decalcified, up to 136 pounds"; while "under normal conditions, up to 852 pounds, the pressure being applied in the line of the lamellae."*

In its dual resistance to both compression and tensile stress, bone is quite remarkable. Substances generally differ greatly in their power of resistance to crushing and tearing. In this respect Piersol notes that cast iron can withstand a crushing stress five times as easily as it can a tensile stress of the same power; and wrought iron is only half as resistant to crushing as it is to tearing. Bone, on the other hand, has an almost equal resistance to both crushing and tearing, the ratio being as four is to three. If, therefore, we indicate these relative resistances to compression and tensile stress in terms of per cent, the three materials would stand as follows:

* Human Anatomy, by George Arthur Piersol.

	Resistance to	
	Crushing	Tearing
Cast Iron	100	20
Wrought Iron	100	200
Bone	100	75

It is obvious from this that if either cast or wrought iron were to be used alone to resist both stresses together, a large amount of material would be required, which would mean a great increase in weight and bulk. This makes either cast iron or wrought iron unsuitable for building purposes, while steel, having resistance to both stresses, can be used for tall buildings or large bridges, where both stresses must be met. And bone, which is not ordinarily subject to a great deal of tensile stress, can resist a degree of tension three-quarters of that needed to resist compression without tearing or crushing, and this without sacrificing its most important quality of lightness.

SUPPORT OF MOVING WEIGHTS

The chief mechanical function of the bony framework is to bear the weights of the body as they pass downward, accumulating from level to level, from head to trunk to pelvis to legs, thence through the feet to the ground. Such an arrangement as will produce the least stress in fulfilling its supporting function when at rest is obviously the one which will also make for the best mechanical advantage in movement of its parts.

Here again we perceive the similarity between bone and steel. Its inherent qualities allow steel to meet successfully the stresses of weight support in tall buildings where, besides the accumulated weights from floor to floor, the forces of wind, moisture and temperature, at play over large surfaces, make greater and more varied stresses than in the low buildings of the past, for which the less variably resistant stone or wood sufficed. So its elastic bony framework enables the human structure to meet the similar problems of height and the arrangement of weights at various levels along a vertical axis.

But the body must do what no skyscraper, with its supporting shafts sunk deep into the ground, need do. It must carry the weight through a flexible column of jointed and movable segments and transfer it through a rocking base to two jointed supports that rest on the surface of the ground. This involves a balancing of parts, which, as in a bridge, is attained by an equal action between compression members and tensile members. The lines of direction of weight-thrust through the compression members, the bones, indicate the varieties and amounts of pull upon the surrounding and attached tensile members, the muscles, ligaments and other soft tissues.

RESULTS OF LACK OF BALANCE

If the line of thrust is centered through the joints, the resulting pull will be equal upon the tensile members about them. If it is not centered, there will be unequal pull on muscles, ligaments and fascia, with consequent strain.

Muscles are responsible for the movement of bones. They should have the greatest freedom possible for this function and should not be called upon unnecessarily for the support of weights, still less to bear the burden of weights off center. An unbalanced adjustment of weights not only strains the muscles, which must contract against the pull of gravity, but if maintained long enough it may even injure the bone itself, and certainly it must affect unfavorably the circulation of the blood at the joints, in the bone and in adjoining tissues.

MUSCLE TIRE

The effect of unbalanced weights falls most seriously upon the muscles, and this for several reasons. A muscle operates by means of the contraction of multitudes of very small fibers that make up its body. These are held together in bundles, called fasciculi. These little bundles are again united by sheaths of fascia into the larger bundles making up the muscle mass, which acts as a unit through tendons attached to bones. These move the bones like the arms of a lever.

If a bone is securely supported by ligamentous union with another bone at a joint, so that its weight rests evenly on the bone below, a relatively slight contraction by a muscle will serve to move it, just as a small child can move a heavy door that is securely upheld on well-oiled hinges, although he could not begin to lift the weight itself. If, however, the muscle must not only move a given weight, but while contracting for this operation, must also lift the weight through space, it is put under a greater handicap. It is stretched by the weight and must contract against the tension, which affects the entire muscle body. As a result, the muscles must contract more powerfully, and more of the muscle fibers are brought into action simultaneously than would be required simply to swing the bony lever on its fulcrum. This rapidly fatigues the muscles. They cannot rest between contractions either as units or by that relayed action of their several bundles which is nature's saving provision against muscle fatigue.

MUSCLE-SAVING DEVICES

Muscle tire can be largely prevented by the intelligent use of the mechanisms coordinating in bodily activity. Thus vision, hearing, and the sense of touch combine with the proprioceptive sensations to prepare our thinking to accord with the demand for muscle action.

Prepare for the load. If a weight be lifted during a contraction, even a light object will fatigue the muscle speedily. If a muscle is to lift a weight it should contract before the load is taken on. This is a prime rule in the conservation of muscular energy: *prepare for the load.* Try, with fingers relaxed, to lift this book; note how heavy it seems and how it almost slips from your grasp. Now put it down, and with a sense of its weight in mind grasp it and feel how light it seems. This also explains why even a heavy object, if firm, can be lifted more readily than a light one that is floppy. Thus the muscles can adjust to the weight of a board, whereas a soft bundle like a bolster or mattress will fall about and have to be caught at unexpected points by unprepared muscles.

Muscular tone is nature's provision against fatigue. It is a

form of preparation whereby, when a muscle "contracts in response to a stimulus, there is, so to speak, no 'slack' to be
taken up before the muscle begins to pull on its attachments."*

FIG. 11. Use of crouch muscles. Convert a pull into a push.

Ordinarily, when carrying heavy objects, we quickly take
advantage of various mechanical aids. We somehow convert a
pull into a push, a suspension into a support from below, as by
a shoulder or head strap. Or we distribute the load so that
both sides share it, and we frequently stop and rest.

However, we cannot do any of these things advantageously
unless the main units of body-weight are balanced, one above
the other, as the design of their supporting structure, the spine,
allows. Otherwise, a certain number of muscles must be occupied continuously in supporting the units away from their
central axis. This results in unequal pulls upon these muscles,
and in strains, not only upon the particular muscles that are
directly affected, but also upon others at various points along
the whole spinal axis, as one part after another tries to aid in
restoring balance. The very integrity of the spinal mechanism
depends upon balanced action throughout: first, between the
two sides in maintaining the bilateral symmetry which is one
of the strongest features of the spine; second, between the

* Principles of Human Physiology, by Ernest H. Starling, 1912.

various tiny muscles along the spine engaged in balancing the vertebrae one upon another evenly, so as to properly house the spinal cord; and third, to maintain the curves which enable the spine to function adequately as an upright support.

FASCIA AND MUSCLE ACTION

If muscles are either extended or held continuously in contraction, the fascial sheets in and about the muscles are subjected to too long stretching or distortion, and the capacity of the muscles to act effectively is impaired. It is the fascial structure about and between the separate bundles that makes the contracting parts cohere. If they do not cohere, the cumulative effect of the separate contractions is lost, and power is thus dissipated.

Muscle strain, if kept up, can have very serious effects, not only because of the pain and discomfort that it causes, but because the muscles themselves become chemically injured by the piling up of lactic acid within their tissues. This may result in their becoming incapable of responding to nervous impulses; they may become over-tense and unable to relax, or they may lose tone and become flabby. In either case the condition is a serious one, which may take some time to overcome.

An impressive example of what this means is the familiar laboratory experiment of stimulating a muscle, removed from the leg of a frog, by means of an electric current. The contraction of this muscle, which is registered graphically on a moving drum, is sufficient to lift a tiny weight. When the weight begins to drop, if the muscle is at once rested and bathed in salty water, it will "come back" quickly, perhaps requiring five minutes' rest before it can begin to contract upon stimulus, and again lift the weight. If, however, instead of stopping the work when there is a reduction in the power of the contractions, the muscle is kept under stimulus and made to work longer, the registered curve will drop quickly until it disappears; that is, until the muscle stops contracting. Now it will take, not five minutes, but at least twenty-five, or an amount of rest equal to the square of the first period.

Consider what this means when, instead of one muscle, hundreds are involved. The cumulative effect may be imagined. Postural strains thus assume importance in the bodily economy.

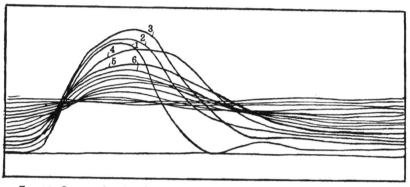

FIG. 12. Curves, showing fatigue in muscles in consequence of repeated stimulation. First six contractions are numbered and show initial increase of first three contractions. (From Brodie.)

Anything that will reduce them will have favorable repercussions throughout the whole organism.

Insurance against such strains comes through organized balance of the units of weight at their bony contacts, the joints. As the body moves, weights shift, and if readjustments are to be made with the least possible strain on the muscles, the various units must be constantly brought back to balance at the joints.

QUADRUPED INTO BIPED

The nature of the mechanical problems presented by the upright position can best be understood by comparing it with the four-footed position, and noting the changes in weight thrust brought about by the shift.

There are three ways in which weights may be supported in any structure—and only three. They may sit, they may hang, or they may be braced. Stiffness must be a quality of the supporting members for sitting or braced weights. The upward thrust against a sitting weight must be vertical, and against the braced weight it must be diagonal. In the arched support, the thrusts must be diagonal and bilateral. A hanging weight must be suspended in a vertical line from its support, but it may hang on either flexible or rigid material.

The skeleton supports weights in all three ways: the head sits upon the spine; the arms hang from the shoulder girdle; and the ilia brace the sacrum. Assumption of the upright position has meant changing the direction of support in several respects from that in the quadruped. Thus the function of the separate parts and their interrelationships are changed, so that some parts sit that formerly hung suspended, and so on. To make the best use of the skeleton for support we must note where the several parts sit, where they hang, and where and how they are braced. Observation of these facts, followed by appropriate adjustments, will reduce mechanical stresses in the human framework, and will save the soft tissues from unnecessary strain.

In the standing quadruped the body-weights hang from the horizontal spinal column, which serves as a girder, distributing the whole load more or less equally between the two ends, whence it is transferred through the shoulder and pelvic girdles to the four supporting legs. At each of the vertebral joints the weight is divided equally, being passed in an approximately vertical line through the articulating surfaces, one facet resting or sitting upon the other.

The contents of the body wall are enclosed in an irregular cylinder, somewhat larger toward the front part, with most of the viscera so disposed that they gain considerable support from the thorax, or rib-cage. The spine, braced by the ribs, forms the upper border of the cylinder, with the lower border made up of the sternum, or breastbone, and the long, strong muscles of the abdomen. Both borders are flexible. The heavy muscles in the shoulder and pelvic regions are directly above the forelegs and hind legs, and their placement is such that the viscera are protected from their action. Finally, the hind legs are so disposed that they form a powerful spring, with the knees so far forward that the femora make an acute angle with the spine, and there is little chance for shock to the spine in the transfer

of the body-weight to the ground. There is also in the quadruped little occasion for strain on the ventral body wall in any
position.

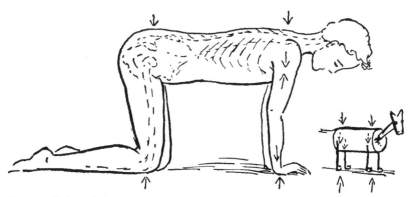

FIG. 13. Balanced four-legged position, with spine as a ridge-pole, lateral and
dorsal planes of body parallel.

To get the feel of this easy support, stand on hands and knees
with back parallel to the floor, as if in preparation to take a
load. Keep the sternum and the pubis as close together as
possible, without arching the back. This makes a compact
cylinder with relatively parallel borders above and below, and
the viscera held neatly within.

Consider what happens when this compact cylindrical structure is brought into the upright position; appreciate the changed
structural and organic problems of support and movement.
Were it not for the strength of the ventral wall by virtue of
the linea alba, the strong central tendinous aponeurosis to which
the several layers of powerful abdominal muscles are attached,
we should be in a sorry plight.

The weights of the body, which have been distributed over
a broad base through a horizontal spine and four legs, are now
transferred through a vertical spine onto a narrow base and
thereafter carried through two legs to the ground. Mechanically, this involves new lines of weight-thrust upon supporting
bones all the way from the occiput to the ground, with adjust-

ments at each point or surface of contact in the joints. As a result, the visceral contents of the body and the soft tissues of the body wall itself must change their functioning to meet the new responsibilities. All parts of the body are affected, and it is important to understand in some detail the way in which the changes are brought about.

In the first position, the weight of the spinal girder and of all the parts hanging upon it passes through the paired posterior facets on the articular processes of the vertebrae and rests upon the tops of four shafts, the two humeri in front and the femora in the back. There is nowhere an accumulation of weight downward through a single axis, but instead, side distribution through many short axes along the spine, with terminal distribution through the shoulder and pelvic girdles at either end. The lumbosacral connections at the posterior facets through which the weight passes from the spine to the pelvis are in alignment with the thigh-joints through which it passes from the pelvis to the femora. The supporting shafts of the femora are in alignment with the superior rami, or upper branches, of the pubis as they curve forward into the ilia.

In the erect position the forward supports are removed so that all weight is supported by the legs, which now have a different angle in relation to the spinal axis. The result is a change in the general direction of the weight-thrust throughout the structure, and in the particular parts of the vertebrae through which the weight passes. The facets, or articular surfaces, between the vertebrae being now in vertical alignment instead of horizontal, weight transfer is no longer directly through them, but the weight passes instead through the bodies of the vertebrae and the intervertebral discs.

Next, we find that the direction of the weight-thrust from the spine to each leg is now oblique, from the lumbosacral joint forward to the heads of the femora. The spring-like design of the legs is also changed, since the femora are now in discontinuous alignment with the spine, and the lower bones of the leg and ankle are much more nearly vertical in their direction.

HANDICAPS IN THE BIPED

Several handicaps to easy support and balance of the body-weight result from the erect posture. Instead of the weight being divided as it is transferred from one vertebra to the next, the load is more concentrated upon a single area at each level. Since the weight must pass through the cartilaginous, and therefore flexible, intervertebral discs as well as through the bony bodies, there is a constant possibility of shearing stress, not present in the quadrupedal mode of transfer. While this hazard is checked somewhat by the vertical articular facets, which now serve to limit sliding motion across the spinal axis, this in turn makes for a certain loss of flexibility.

The ribs, at the new angle, are reduced in their service as buttresses to the vertebral arches in the thorax. The support of all the weight upon the two rotary hip-joints is not nearly so stable as the four-legged form of support. Finally, the spring-like action of the legs is lessened by the more vertical adjustment of the several parts, replacing the shifting diagonals of the hind legs of the quadruped.

The mechanical significance of this change in the relative axes of legs and spine is not fully realized until the movement of the human body is compared with that of the quadruped. The animal, by swinging back on his hind legs gets the necessary leverage for springing, or for starting a vigorous run. The horizontal distance between his leg joints provides the needed space. In the human being, this space is reduced in the knees and in the ankles; and, in the pelvis, to the very small interval between the sacroiliac joints and the heads of the femora.

BIPED COMPENSATIONS

These handicaps, however, are more than compensated for by the fact that it is these very changes in weight transfer, and especially the new routing through the bodies of the vertebrae, which make possible the establishment of the four opposing spinal curves that enable the spine to function in the upright position.

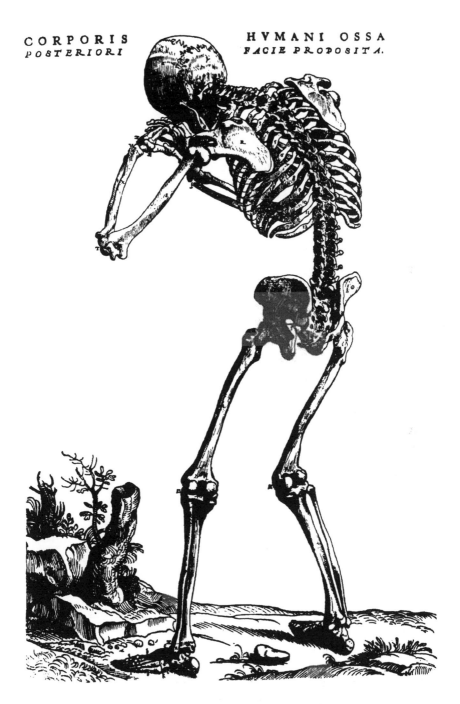

CORPORIS
POSTERIORI

HVMANI OSSA
FACIE PROPOSITA.

FIG. 14. Balance in movement. (From Vesalius.)

[71]

The biped position gives a wider range of movement to the rotary joints of the hips, and thus to the legs, although the support is less stable than in the former arrangement. The free-

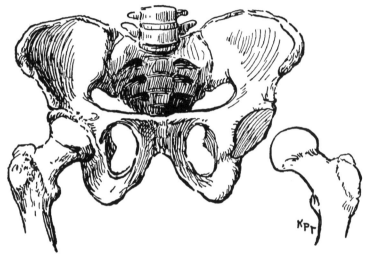

FIG. 15. Pelvic arch, showing its depth and the depth of thigh-joints.

dom of the arms from weight-bearing gives them that significant sweep which they would not otherwise have. No quadruped can move his fore and hind legs so far from center to either side as man, nor can many of them move the limbs much above the back.

Next to the hands, the pelvis and legs have changed most from the quadruped pattern because of the changed nature of the mechanical problem. Instead of forming a cross-piece resting upon two uprights under one end of the spinal girder, the pelvis is now a base for the whole column of weights. For a clue to the way in which weight is at once supported by and transferred through the pelvis to underlying moving supports, we turn again to engineering—this time to bridge-building. The pattern of the human pelvis resembles that of a short cantilever bridge, in which the weight delivered at one end is supported at the other end.

In the upright position, it is the space in the pelvis between the points of weight-thrust on the sacrum and the points of support at the thigh-joints which make the forces act through the pelvis like those of a cantilever bridge. The compression forces act through the flaring bones of the pelvis in such a way as to require balanced action of all tensile members traveling upward from the front of the pelvic arch, and of the ties reinforcing the inner sides of the arch. The equal action of these compression and tensile forces secures balanced adjustments of weights at the sacrum and at the heads of the femora.

The pelvic bridge is connected with its supporting pedestals by rotary joints which allow movement in three planes. These joints are further to the front than is commonly realized, since the centers of the acetabula, into which the heads of the femora are fitted, are only a hand-span apart across the front of the pelvis. This type of joint gives the maximum freedom for the variety of adjustments needed in moving body-weights about and in meeting the constant shocks made by the varying impacts coming up from the ground at each step. The force of these impacts or jolts equals exactly the force with which the body-weight hits the ground, and this varies with the amount of the weight and the distance that it travels and its speed. The fact that action and reaction are equal and opposite is appreciated when we step off a curb that is higher or lower than we expected. The jolt is felt throughout the whole body. The mechanisms which serve us in walking become habituated to the usual height of curbs and the muscles prepare automatically to absorb these shocks. The feeling of the jolt is due to the unpreparedness in the muscles to adjust the mechanisms to the unexpected.

The really important effect of the erect position was to free the arms and hands from responsibility for support and locomotion. This enabled them to develop their own motor and tactile skills, a circumstance which underlies the productive potentialities of the human being, since without these skills art, literature and the sciences would be impossible, at least in the forms in which we know them.

Speculation about the rôle of the upright posture in determining civilization is outside the province of this book, but Dr. Schwartz, in his résumé of the literature, remarks on its profound influences along at least two lines: psychological and physiological. First: "The range of vision and hearing was increased, and these senses were, to a large extent, substituted for smell, leading up to a psychology based on sight and hearing rather than on smell, and thus to the development of art and music."* On the purely physiological side, it is suggested that "the better drainage from the brain may explain the distinction between the intelligence of animals and the intellect of man."†

COMPARATIVE RESULTS

The total result of the change from quadruped to biped is to make balance more easily disturbed. The ever-present possibilities of upset from top-heavy situations and of various strains and stresses become characteristic of the biped. But this very insecurity is a source of power over the environment, since movement in any direction is facilitated, not only for the parts but for the whole.

In the biped position, the gravity pull on the spine is at a different angle in each part, as compared with the quadruped position, and the connecting soft tissues must meet the oblique strains. The shearing stresses in the spine tend to produce visceroptosis and swayback. Resulting symptoms are exaggerated in proportion to the distance between the pubis and the sternum. Were this space bridged by bone, the hazards of the erect position would be greatly reduced, but movement would be seriously hampered. In fact, if we had a ventral as well as a dorsal spine, this book would never have been written! Our activities would be exceedingly limited, and knowledge of mechanical principles and design in the body quite unnecessary.

The simplest way to secure balance of the inward parts is by

* J. Knox Thompson, quoted in: A Résumé with Comments on the Available Literature Relating to Posture.
† Leonard Williams, *ibid.*

keeping the ventral and dorsal walls as nearly parallel as possible, and the rotary joints of the hips as freely movable in all
directions as is compatible with secure support.

Our real problem, then, is to maintain the body compactness
of the quadruped position, and at the same time so to arrange
the joints that the weight passes through them to the ground
with the least strain and loss of balanced action of all the adjoining structures. Careful analysis and intelligent understanding of the lines of force playing through these joints is necessary
if we are to manage them economically.

To understand the mechanics of the body, we must regard it
from the point of view of function, in which movement is implicit; we must study the shape, size and relative position of
the various parts, which are themselves the result of functional
adaptation. When this is done, the principal underlying mechanical bodily adjustments assume a logical sequence in the
imagination. These are referable to the proprioceptive system,
the central system of balancing forces. Arbitrary postures of
static design lose their grip on an imagination informed by a
philosophy of poise in movement.

Considered functionally as a moving and weight-bearing
structure, emphasis is placed first on the balance of weights at
the bony contacts, the joints. A human skeleton, stripped of
muscle, though not of ligament, might be balanced sufficiently
to retain a sitting posture. Bones are firm and able to support
the various weights at their several levels, head on atlas, the
lowest lumbar vertebra upon the sacrum, acetabula upon the
femora, and so on. Ligaments are tough fibers which bind the
bones together, and limit their radius about the joints. In this
limiting action ligaments are also aided by atmospheric pressure,
i.e., suction, but more by the arrangement of muscles in connection with the joints, particularly in large and powerful composite joints like the pelvis, or in such a system as the lumbar
spine. Muscles contract and thus move the bones by means of
their attached tendons, aided by their fascial sheaths and by
the suction that holds them close against the bones. The muscles

are automatic in action, responding to stimuli from the nervous system, which controls and integrates the activities of the whole body, making them coherent and purposive.

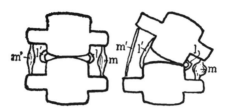

FIG. 16. Action of muscles on vertebrae; also ligaments limiting movement. Contraction of muscle *m* stretches its antagonist *m'*. (Redrawn after Hough and Sedgwick.)

The solution of the human structural problem depends primarily upon the mechanical principles of dynamics and statics, applied in the same way as in any successful building, bridge or skyscraper, modified only by physiological and psychological factors. Bones are the weight-bearers. Both at rest and when operated as levers in movement they transfer and control weights at the joints. In such situations they are the compression members, and should be so used. All the other structures involved in the movement and arrangement of bones, including muscles, ligaments and fascia, are the tensile members, and should be freed so far as may be from the direct support of weight.

Conscious direction of a moving function rather than a holding function should be the emphasis where bones, muscles and ligaments are concerned, since man presents a dynamic problem.

Chapter IV

THE WORKING SKELETON

THE VERTEBRATE BODY PATTERN

THE GENERAL BODY DESIGN IS SIMILAR IN ALL ANIMALS WITH BACKBONES. IN SUCH DIFFERENT CREATURES AS fishes, amphibians, reptiles, birds and mammals, the spine is the essential basis for their framework. It is made up of segments called vertebrae, which give the name to the whole group, the vertebrates. The spine developed to protect the central nervous system in water-living creatures long before arms or legs were needed for support and locomotion, although the head had long been a distinct unit. The spine divides the trunk into two canals, one dorsal and the other ventral. Within these canals the essential life processes are carried on.

The dorsal, or neural canal houses the central nervous system, surrounding it completely by a bony wall made up of arched vertebral processes. The ventral, or visceral canal, in which all the vital organs are lodged, is much larger and walled by the bony and cartilaginous extensions or attachments of the spine for only part of its extent. It depends for cover largely upon the common body-wall of muscles, ligaments, fascia, and integument which surrounds both canals. The general body design is shown in the accompanying diagram. (Fig. 17.) Two parts of the framework are distinguished: the axial skeleton, which develops from the primitive notochord, and the appendicular, which starts within bud-like projections in the body-wall.

The axial skeleton is made up of the spine with its immediate outgrowths, the head, ribs and sternum. Along it are disposed all the essential systems of the body. The central nervous system (the brain and spinal cord) is located at top and back in

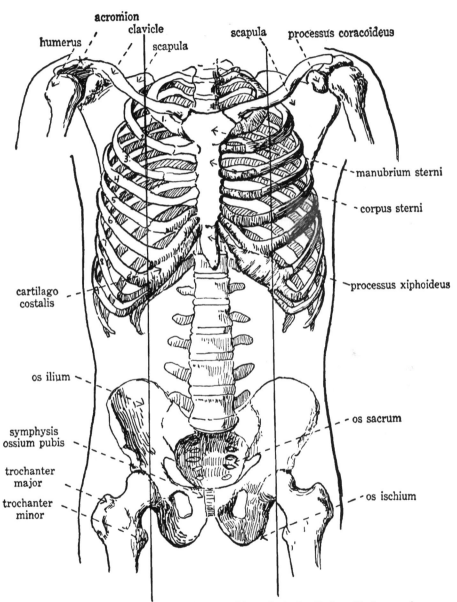

acromion

clavicle

humerus

scapula

scapula

processus coracoideus

manubrium sterni

corpus sterni

processus xiphoideus

cartilago costalis

os ilium

os sacrum

symphysis ossium pubis

trochanter major

os ischium

trochanter minor

FIG. 17. Relationship of bones and lines of hypothetical cylinder. (Redrawn after Eycleshymer and Schoemacher.)

the dorsal canal. To the front in the ventral canal is located the digestive apparatus with its associates and derivatives, the circulatory, respiratory, urinary and reproductive systems.

The main differences between the axial skeleton in man and in the other vertebrates are in the position of its parts, owing to the upright posture, and in the relatively larger size of the head and pelvis.

The vertebrae vary in shape and size according to the nature and contents of the neural and visceral canals in the different areas of the body. The bones making up the skull are not derived from vertebral bodies and processes but compose a complex structure of capsules and walls, for olfactory, optic and otic organs; basis cranii, containing remnants of notochord; roofing and surface bones; visceral elements comprising oral, hyoidean and branchial arches, and surface bones, maxillae, dentaries, etc.

The appendicular skeleton, with a very different origin in the embryo, makes the supporting framework for the limbs. It consists essentially of two girdles, the thoracic, or shoulder girdle, and the pelvic, to each of which is attached a series of bony levers making up the arms and legs. The design of the bony frames for arms and legs is quite similar, in spite of superficial appearance. In each, a long upper bone is attached to two lower bones, which in turn are connected with a series of short bones arranged in a mosaic pattern, and to these again are attached five radiating digits.

The shoulder girdle consists of two clavicles and two scapulae, and lies outside the chest, superimposed upon the axial skeleton. It has no direct bony connection with the spine. In contrast, the pelvic girdle, composed of ilia, ischia and pubes (when fused called the innominates), is attached firmly to the spine and forms part of the wall and base of the abdominal and pelvic cavities.

As a working mechanism, the skeleton cannot be understood if considered only as a bony framework. Since ligaments bind the bones together at the joints, and muscles move them, and the activities of the whole are governed by the nervous system, no one of these elements acts independently.

The physical characteristics of bone, the densest form of connective tissue, described in the preceding chapter, are its high resistance to both compression and tensile stress, its lightness, and its elasticity. These are the principal properties also of steel.

Bones, most of which develop from cartilage, an antecedent tissue, are conveniently grouped by their general shape into long bones, which have a shaft and two extremities, as in the arms and hands and in the legs and feet; flat bones, such as certain skull bones, the ilia, and the scapulae; and irregular bones, such as those making up the spine and the weight-bearing parts of the foot. The long bones are the most interesting in their mechanical features. The shaft is a hollow cylinder of compact bone containing marrow in which the red blood corpuscles are formed. The hollowness of the shaft takes from its weight, and this shape makes for strength since it "conforms to the well-known law that a given quantity of matter is much stronger, both lengthwise and crosswise, when disposed in a hollow cylinder than as a solid one of equal size and length."*

Bones are held together in joints of various degrees of fixity and movability by ligaments, which are a tough though flexible form of connective tissue. Ligaments also support other structures, such as viscera. Sometimes ligament is elastic, but as a rule that about the joints is inelastic. Certain long ligaments in the spine which unite a series of irregular bones and joints are notably elastic. Nearly all joints are surrounded by capsular ligaments, flexible, tube-like structures enclosing the ends of the opposed bones. The actual articulation and movement takes place within the capsule. These capsules vary greatly in their weight and strength. As a rule the articulating surfaces of bones are covered with cartilage, and nearly all are furnished with lubricating structures known as synovial membranes. These membranes secrete a fluid which prevents friction.

Skeletal muscles, some of whose characteristics were described earlier, are sheathed by fascia, another form of connective

* From Human Anatomy, by George Arthur Piersol.

tissue. They are attached to bones or to other muscles, and sometimes to thick, fascial bands, by tendons—very tough, dense fibrous tissues, entirely non-elastic. Tendons are sometimes round and sometimes like straps, and sometimes are in flat sheets.

For a convenient description of their various functional relations, the skeletal muscles are commonly grouped in several ways: into such pairs as actors and antagonizers, characterized by alternating contraction and relaxation on opposite sides of the bone; into adductors and abductors; into flexors and extensors, according to the direction of movement of bony parts which is effected by them.

For our immediate purpose of interpretation of the mechanical functions of the body, we are to distinguish muscles as "centering" and "ex-centering," according to whether they draw parts toward or away from their center of support. Under varying conditions, centering and ex-centering may involve any or all of the activities indicated by the terms of the other types of grouping.

THE SPINAL COLUMN

Viewed from front or back, the backbone is seen.to be a column, broadening quite regularly toward its base, so much so that it can be described as an extended pyramid. Viewed laterally, the effect is somewhat different, as one side, the anterior, is a long S-curve and the other, the posterior, is made up of a series of blades, the outlines of which mark a curve which is so flat as to be nearly straight in some areas. (See Fig. 18.)

The depth and the breadth of the spine, and its three-dimensional character, can be appreciated by looking at the accompanying figures, which show that the spine is as deep as it is wide. At all levels the column is deep set and occupies about one-half the diameter of the body from back to front, as may be seen by the median section of the body in Figure 18.

The central position, bilateral symmetry, and pyramidal shape of the spine are what give it its great strength for the support

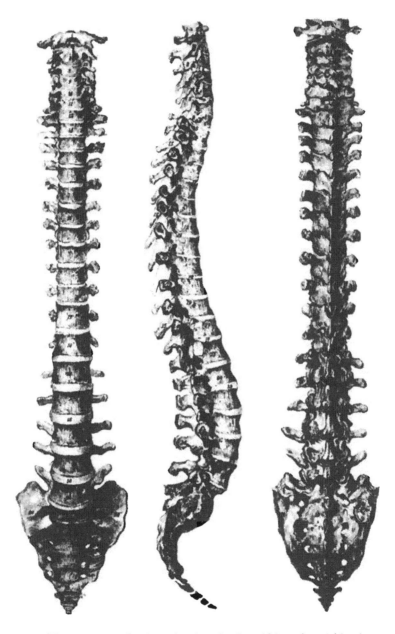

Fig. 18. Three aspects of spine, showing depth, width and variable shapes of vertebrae. (From Quain and Wilson.)

of the whole body. The S-shaped curve gives it power to support weight while upright.

THE VERTEBRAE

The individual vertebrae vary greatly in shape, but are all formed on the general plan of a rounded disc, or body, with an arch extended from it. (Fig. 19.)

In the human spine the body of the vertebra is the principal weight-receiving part. The neural arch extends dorsally from the body, its two sides meeting above and forming a rounded opening through which the spinal cord passes. Lateral and dorsal processes on the roof of the arch complete the structure.

The vertebral bodies enlarge in all dimensions toward the base of the column to support the increasing loads, since not only are the separate parts and attachments larger and heavier, but each level must carry the accumulated weight of those above it. The largest part of the spine, accordingly, is at the level where the entire weight of the head and trunk is being transferred through the pelvic arch to the legs, that is, at the sacrum.

The shape and size of the dorsal and lateral processes also change, as well as the bodies of the thirty-three or thirty-four vertebrae, so that no two are identical, though there is a general resemblance between them. The vertebrae are grouped in sections as follows:

(1) Seven cervical vertebrae compose the neck, hold up the head, and indirectly and partially support the chest, shoulders and arms. It is a curious fact that this number is almost constant in mammals, even the giraffe having only seven vertebrae in its neck.

(2) Twelve thoracic vertebrae, from which the ribs extend, form with them and the sternum, or breast-bone, the protective and supporting wall for the thoracic cage which surrounds the heart and lungs and the upper abdominal viscera.

(3) Five lumbar vertebrae, the largest and deepest of all, complete the flexible portion of the spine.

(4) Five sacral vertebrae, the bodies and processes of

which, in the adult, are fused into a single curved, shield-shaped plate, the sacrum, to which the pelvic girdle is attached. The upper part of the sacrum is

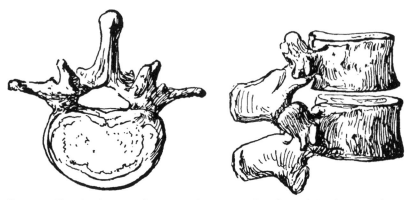

FIG. 19. First lumbar vertebra, top view; second and third lumbar vertebrae, side view.

broader than the lumbar vertebrae, but it is much shallower throughout and tapers in all dimensions toward the coccyx.

(5) Finally, four or five small vertebrae, lightly fused, make up the coccyx, the dwindling remnant of a tail.

Our common impression of the spine as being a shallow structure just below the surface of the back is derived from the only part of it that we can feel, the rounded points that mark the dorsal spinous processes of the vertebrae. These are the individual "spines" of the vertebrae from which the column gets its name. The dorsal spinous processes extend backward from the neural arches which surround the spinal cord and are important protective structures. They furnish attachment for the long spinal muscles and ligaments that not only move the body but also serve to pad the covering wall for the delicate nervous system.

Both these dorsal and the transverse processes of the vertebrae are modified in thickness and length according to the number and kind of muscle fibers needing attachment along their surfaces at the various levels. The dorsal muscles attached to the spine take no direct part in supporting weight except to aid in the control of the posterior portions of the spine in maintaining its curves. Their main function is to extend the trunk and to unite the pelvis, thorax and head.

SPINAL MECHANICS

We are chiefly concerned with the supporting function of the vertical spine, and especially the adjustment along it of the various loads, head, chest and pelvis, at their several levels, and the transmission of this accumulated load to the ground. The adjustment of weight in the upright position is made by means of the same muscles and bones as in the quadruped pattern, but with new angles at which the forces operate, and with a corresponding difference in the attack of stresses within the structure. The old basic neuromuscular coordinations therefore are utilized, with the newer nervous patterns superimposed upon them. The old pattern is retained, not lost, in the process. This may be seen in the creeping baby and in the ability of the adult to support himself, and even to move about after a fashion, in the four-footed position.

A somewhat detailed understanding of the spinal mechanism is important for its proper use, and especially for avoiding its abuse. This includes the way the spine is formed, the way it acts to meet the constant pull of gravity upon itself and its loads; and finally the influence of inertia and momentum under the new conditions of life on land, with the human responsibility for locomotion in the upright position.

The shape and substance of the spine give it great strength and flexibility. Most important for the latter is the alternation of the cancellous bony bodies of the vertebrae with the intervertebral discs of fibrocartilage, the latter forming about one-quarter of the whole length of the column. The discs both separate and bind the bodies together. The binding strength comes from the way in which their outer layers of tough fibers are slanted, first in one direction, then in another, with some of them lying almost horizontal.

In each disc is a central core of yellowish pulp containing fluid that is so strongly compressed as to make a resistant ball within the more yielding fibers. This device, with a construc-

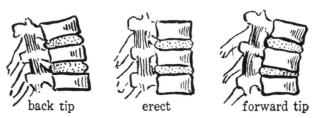

back tip   erect   forward tip

FIG. 20. How the vertebrae are adjusted for individual spinal action. (Redrawn after Mollier.)

tion something like that of a golf ball, keeps the vertebrae from pressing against each other and also limits the degree of deformation that the discs themselves can undergo from the constant weight pressure upon the joints. The close apposition of the vertebrae and their discs and the flexibility of the joints, protects the spinal nerves as they emerge from the cord. The discs are relatively larger in the more flexible portions of the spine, so that they form about 40 per cent of the length in the cervical region, 33 per cent in the lumbar, only about 20 per cent in the thoracic, and are not present at all in the sacrum.

The ligamentous bands interlaced along the spine, connecting the bodies and processes of adjoining vertebrae, resemble the trussings and ties of a bridge, some vertebrae having single, and some double trussings. This arrangement augments the strength of the column to meet compression stress; also it allows for great flexibility, while friction is countered by lubricating sacs at each joint.

Finally, the spine is made a working unit by the universal longitudinal ligaments that extend from one end to the other, connecting all the bodies, discs, laminae, and dorsal spinous processes. The most important ligaments are the anterior and posterior common and the supraspinatous and flava. (See Fig. 21.)

The flava ligament, because of its highly elastic quality, has an especially important mechanical rôle in the integration of the spine. Elastic connective tissue is yellow; hence the name flava. Its broad, flat bands connect the laminae, or top portions

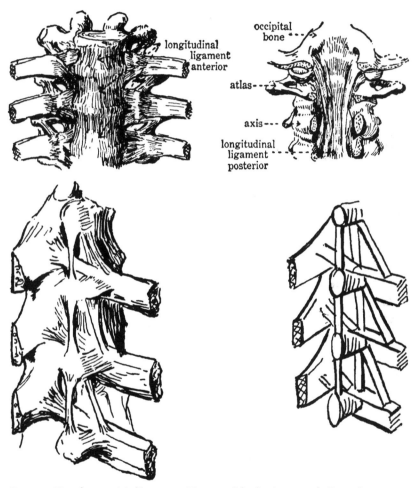

FIG. 21. Vertebrae, with ligaments. Front and back views, and (lower) suggesting mechanics of bridge construction.

of the neural arches, and run throughout the flexible portions of the spine from the axis, or second cervical vertebra, as far as the sacrum. The fibers of the flava are inseparably united with the fibers of the capsular ligaments which surround the joints

between the vertebrae, and by their inherent tension prevent
the formation of folds in these capsules. They also tend to bring
the bones back into position from the innumerable slight dis-

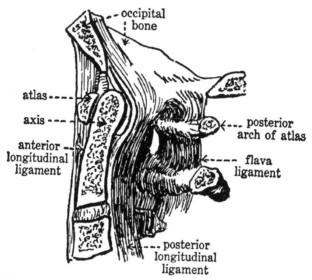

FIG. 22. Median section, through occipital bone, atlas and axis. Note ligaments.
(Redrawn after Spalteholz.)

placements to which they are subject. The flava further interdigitate with the other longitudinal ligaments, so that the
restorative effect is communicated to them. As Piersol points
out: "That this replacement is effected by a purely physical
property of the tissue, instead of by muscular action, implies a
great saving of energy."*

The stable relationship of the vertebrae and discs that makes
them able to bear weight in the upright position is due largely
to the tonus of the ligaments, particularly that of the anterior
common ligament. This in turn is affected by the action of the
muscles which control the spine and the relation of the trunk to
pelvis and legs.

Strains on the spinal ligaments can be prevented or relieved
considerably if one understands the line of direction of the

* Human Anatomy, by George Arthur Piersol.

forces acting upon the joints to which they are attached, as well as the design of the spinal structure, which is essentially one of continuous and opposing curves.

Considered as a mechanism for weight support, the spine is a flexible, segmented structure in dynamic equilibrium, having its axis of movement within. Since the spine must be able to move both itself and its attached weights at various levels, the column is curved.

The spinal curve is a composite one, continuous, and with no interposed angles or straight portions between the concave and convex phases, one phase merging imperceptibly into another as they cross and recross the spinal axis.

The component curves, which are named according to the anatomical region in which they occur (cervical, thoracic, lumbar and pelvic), do not correspond exactly with the phases of convexity and concavity of the spine as a whole. Thus, observing the spine from the front, the cervical convexity culminates between the third and the fourth cervical vertebrae, at a point where the spine starts to curve backward and the long primary concavity commences. This long curve does not end until the fourth lumbar vertebra is reached. The two terminal vertebrae of the main spinal curve, from the point of view of spinal balance, are thus in the middle of the neck and the lower part of the lumbar region. The most nearly horizontal vertebrae are those that bound this curve, the third cervical and the fourth lumbar, and those in the middle of the curve, the sixth, seventh, eighth and ninth thoracic.

This symmetrical bow, which might be called the working curve of the spine, takes up nineteen of the twenty-four movable vertebrae, including four cervicals, twelve thoracics and three lumbars. The remaining areas are not particularly flexible. At the top the first and second cervical vertebrae act as a unit to support the head, and at the lower end, the fifth lumbar is sunk well into the pelvic base, where the pelvic concavity begins.

Each anatomical curve partakes of the character of its adjoined curve at the areas of redirection, and each therefore has a convex and a concave phase. There must be mutual direction

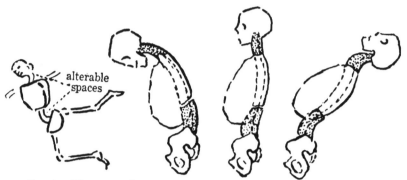

FIG. 23. Diagrams, showing alterable sections and unalterable masses.

and resistance between the individual curves of the spine or power for movement of the whole would be lost.

Taking in turn the main weights of the body (head, thorax and pelvis) we find that the actual transfer of weight comes at the points of contact between the occipital condyles with the atlas, the twelfth thoracic with the first lumbar, and the fifth lumbar with the sacrum, the sacrum with the ilia, and the acetabula with the femora.

The weight-bearing relation, taken in order between these points of contact, is mutual, continuous and cumulative. If there is true mechanical balance at these points, all muscles and ligaments between the balancing structures will be under the least strain possible.

The transition between cervical and thoracic areas begins, as we have seen, with the fourth cervical and continues to the second or third thoracic. Also, the eleventh and twelfth thoracic and the first and second lumbar vertebrae mark the transition between the thoracic and lumbar areas. These vertebrae tend to resemble each other in shape, especially in the angles of the transverse and dorsal processes. The latter are so related to each other as to make the vertebrae act together and to be definitely limited in their range of movement, thus offsetting the mechanical weakness that would result from a change in the curve, where so much weight is being redirected.

DEVELOPMENT OF BALANCED CURVES

In the newborn infant, the spine is straight and very flexible, with all joints movable. The first muscles to attain power are those of the lumbar spine and the pelvis, which the baby uses even before birth, squirming about, moving and straightening the lower back, drawing up the knees, and throwing them out in the "kick" familiar to all mothers. For some time after birth the active muscles are those which are centering, that is, holding the parts back against the spine, which is their center of support. Thus, arms and legs tend to be held close to the body, as before birth. Later, when more expansive movements take place, the excentering muscles, that is, those pulling weights away from centers of support, become active in response to self-determined impulses and desires for movement.

The spinal column must carry and control all its superimposed weights. To attain movement, compensatory curves must be developed. A straight, segmented column is unsuited to carry a lateral load, that is, one off center, like the thorax. Such a load will tend to cause shearing stress and bending stress since the spine will sag at the level of the unbalanced weight. A curved structure, on the other hand, is not best suited to carry an axial or top load, like the head, because it will tend to increase the existing curve. In either case, when the column starts bending, all loads bend it more and more until it gives way. Therefore, to carry either an axial or a lateral load, a flexible supporting column must develop, first, a basic curve in the direction opposite to that in which the load is tending to bend it. With this basic curve established, the auxiliary, compensatory curves will be developed and reinforced throughout the structure.

The two primary curves, the thoracic and the pelvic, are implicit in the spine at birth, because of the design of the bones of the rib-case and pelvis, which are attached to them, and by their positions in the universal curve of the developing embryo. In the lumbar and the cervical regions, where there are no bony appendages, the curves are barely indicated. If the young baby is held without support at the back, the weights of his head and chest will topple the spine over in any direction that offers. The curves necessary to complete the spinal system of curves to support the body-weights are still to be formed, compensatory to those in the thoracic and pelvic regions.

By much vigorous kicking and crying during the first months of its life, the baby develops those muscles which are needed to produce and stabilize the lumbar curve into its convex direction toward the front, to counteract the primary concavity of the thoracic curve. Not until this curve has been established is the baby able to hold its head up, to sit or to stand alone. In the standing or sitting position this load is passing through the thoracic spine into the lumbar region along a short diagonal axis, directed toward the front. It must be met there with a counter-thrust from the opposite direction if the spine is not to collapse at this point. The lumbar curve furnishes the necessary counter-thrust.

The effect of the weight of the skull as the top-load of the spine is to produce another curve in the cervical region. This is slightly convex, to oppose the long concave thoracic curve, and, with the lower lumbar curve, it completes the stabilizing of the spine to bear weights in an upright position.

Gradually the infant develops power in the minute muscles and ligaments about the vertebrae which control the secondary curves, by throwing his arms and legs about, turning his head from side to side and lifting it while prone. Active movements and the resulting deeper breathing bring about the coordinated action of the entire spine. This process is greatly aided by spells of crying and screaming, since the diaphragm and the lower lumbar and pelvic muscles are so closely associated.

In this way, by means of what may appear to be discomfort or distress, an axis of opposing curves is being established in the spinal column for the adequate support and movement of the body-weights. The head cannot be held up until this long axis is established. Power to sit, stand, and walk comes only after this axis has been made secure by the strength of the spinal muscles and ligaments, whose intricate balancing action at the individual vertebrae has produced the opposing curves.

Not only are there four curves, alternately convex and concave, in this arrangement, but the shape, length and degree of each is adapted to the nature of the load and its movement. The cervical curve is the slightest, as the head is balanced centrally on the top vertebra, and its weight, though considerable, is a single unit instead of an assemblage of weights like the other loads.

The thoracic curve is much deeper. Its strength is derived from its length and its symmetry and the way in which it is balanced, not only by the other curves along the spinal axis, but also by the curved surfaces established by the ribs and the equal and opposite curve of the sternum, with the ribs bracing between.

The lumbar curve is relatively short and deep in proportion to its length. Although it includes only five vertebrae, these are massive and with their attached muscles constitute a large proportion of the lower trunk. The action of the lumbar spine is therefore very powerful, and as it is more flexible than the thoracic, it clearly dominates the action of the whole trunk, and of the shoulders and arms, as well as the legs.

The sacral, or pelvic, curve is the sharpest of all. Since the vertebrae are fused in the adult it is in itself entirely stable, which is a necessary condition for the base of a curved column. Even in relation to the lumbar curve above, which gives it whatever adaptability it can have, the sacral spine has a relatively small range of movement. Its curve is continued downward and forward through the coccyx, by joints, ligaments and muscular attachments, to other portions of the pelvis. Together the sum of the angles subtended by these curves is equal to the sum of the curves of the spine in the vertical axis; that is, they equal two right angles, and balance the upper curves. (Fig. 28.)

Furthermore, the actual shape of the pelvis, with the strong, curved arches of the sacrum and the ilia at the lumbosacral and sacroiliac joints, and the division of the weight through the ilia

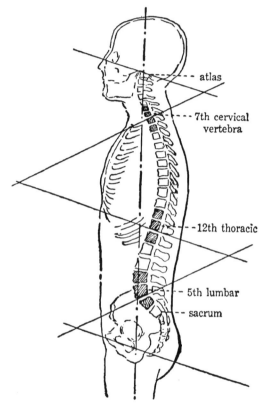

Fig. 24. Redirection of curves and subtended angles.

to the heads of the femora, makes a situation essentially differ- ent from that of the flexible portions of the erect spine above. The base curves extend in three dimensions through solid sup- ports, and in any dimension must be considered as continuing to a point at the front of the pubis.

The way in which the spinal curves balance each other is shown also by the fact that in spite of their difference in length and depth they subtend angles that are equal. Thus, if lines passing through the intervertebral discs at the terminal vertebrae of each curve are extended, they form angles which are equal to each other although at unequal distances from the spine and from the line of gravity. Moreover, if the lines making up the several angles are further extended and joined, they bound parallelograms. This suggests the possibility of a mathematical determination of the stresses and strains of the bodily mechanism in terms of the resultant forces, and thus measurable. On the basis of such measurements might be erected a system for individual betterment, mechanical and physiological, pointing toward a practical structural hygiene.

If the weight and position of the loads of the head, chest and pelvis are in balance with respect to the spinal curves, their bending effects will oppose and thus neutralize each other. If not, the bending forces will tend to disturb the balanced action of the curves about the spinal axis, and outside force must be exerted to reestablish the balance. In the body, balance cannot be effected by opposing weight for weight, as it can in artificial structures by such means as putting an equal weight opposite and at an equal distance from the center, or a smaller weight farther away. The essential supporting mechanism is a compact, flexible column, whose integrity depends upon the closeness of the various compression members to a central axis and to each other. If, therefore, weights are held out of balance, this must be done by throwing extra work on the small muscles and ligaments about the individual vertebrae in order to accent, or even distort, the normal compensatory curves; or by tightening suspension muscles or tensile members, as in the neck, causing them to bear more weight than is their proper task.

OTHER ELEMENTS OF SPINAL STRENGTH

Considered mechanically, the strength of the upright spine to bear loads accumulating toward the base depends in great part on the curves. However, other factors are:

First, the shape of the spine as a whole, particularly its bilateral symmetry, which is extremely important in making

possible the curves from front to back; second, its position in
the trunk and the breadth and depth of the vertebral bodies and
transverse and dorsal processes, which together form a large

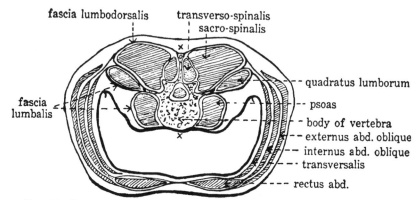

FIG. 25. Cross section of torso, through third lumbar vertebra. Fascia and
tendons half schematic. Note depth of spine between crosses at anterior border
of body of vertebra and end of posterior process. (Redrawn after Braus.)

part of the transverse and antero-posterior diameters of the
axial skeleton at each level; and third, the graduated sizes of
the main units of weight and of the main attachments.

At all levels, the spine is more nearly centered in the body
from front to back than is generally thought. At the top, the
front of the atlas is half way between the front and back of
the head; and in the lumbar region the front of the spine is at
the center of the body. The lumbar spine, with all its heavy
muscles and ligaments, occupies one-half of the entire cubical
area at this level and constitutes more than half of the weight
of the lumbar segment of the trunk since the soft, front parts
are so much lighter in this region. (See Fig. 25.)

The bodies of the vertebrae increase steadily in all dimensions
and vary in relation to the transverse diameter of the axial
skeleton. At the top of the chest the body of the first thoracic
vertebra is nearly a quarter of the width of the rib-cage, and
that of the fifth lumbar is a quarter of the width across the top
of the pelvis. Lines drawn from the top of the first thoracic

vertebra to the broadest part of the sacrum touch the outer tips of the lumbar transverse processes.

The vertebral processes also enlarge. The curves and the direction of the spinous processes enlarge at the same levels and to about the same extent as the transverse processes. Thus one finds enlargement both laterally and antero-posteriorly at the upper thoracic and lower lumbar regions, where large surfaces for attachments are needed by the great muscles. In the cervical region, the dorsal spines of the vertebrae are relatively large in comparison with their bodies to accommodate the large muscles at the sides of the spine and in the neck.

Another element in mechanical balance and strength is the comparative sizes of the main attachments and loads on the spine. The head is seen to be a trifle over a third of the breadth of the shoulders. The pelvis is approximately the width of the shoulders, excluding the arms, and is as wide as the widest part of the rib-cage. The three main spinal loads, head, chest and pelvis, are of nearly the same diameter at their deepest points from front to back. This fact makes possible a flatter body wall, both back and front, than is usually imagined. If flat boards were placed at front and back so as to touch the head, chest and pelvis they could be kept approximately vertical and parallel.

The head makes an axial load on top of the spine. It sits evenly balanced upon the atlas, and thus is the type of load which can be borne most easily by an erect, curved and moving column. The points of connection are two relatively small, shallow projections, the occipital condyles, having convexly curved surfaces. These condyles, situated on the base of the skull, about half-way between the front of the upper jaw and the back of the head, fit smoothly onto the concavely curved surfaces of the atlas, with which they articulate.

This arrangement allows the head to rock backward and forward easily, without displacement. The head sits upon the spine at a point just back of the articulation of the jaw, in line with the entrance to the ear, and not, as one is inclined to imagine, somewhere near the back of the neck. It may thus be seen to rock easily on a little cradle at the center of its base, rather than to swing from a hinge at the back.

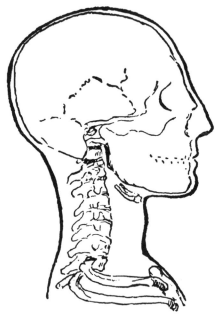

FIG. 26. Balance of head on cervical vertebrae. Note position of hyoid bone and slant of first two ribs.

The center of the head as a whole would be marked by a line crossing the two axes of balance at the condyles. This is not evident upon superficial view, owing to the varying contours of the skull and face.

This centering of the head is necessary, as the organs which report to us the position of the head in relation to the earth and keep us informed as to our place in space at any given time, are located immediately above the condyles. These sense organs are housed in the vestibule of the inner ear, and the ear is in line with the condyles. The slightest change in plane of the head is at once recorded by the vestibular or labyrinthine sense organs and the important information is instantly conveyed via the cerebellar reflexes to the eye muscles, so that the eyeball rolls appropriately to adjust to the new level of vision.

This same messenger system acts upon other muscles of the body to move or prepare them for movement. Such a sensitive mechanism requires that the balanced weight be exactly cen-

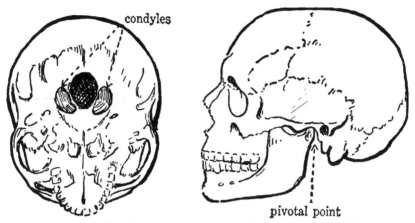

FIG. 27. Skull, side and base, showing pivotal point at condyles.

tered, with the center of gravity of the head directly in line with the center of the articulating surfaces. Otherwise, the head would have to be held by outside muscular force, enormously complicating the proprioceptive problem.

A head which is held habitually in an unbalanced position, on one side or too far back, with the throat sagging, not only fatigues the muscles holding it, but must produce confusion in the proprioceptive mechanism.

The head weighs from 15 to 20 pounds. This weight must be balanced. If, while keeping the chest supported, you let the head hang forward of its own weight, you may realize how heavy it is.

An intricate arrangement of muscles and ligaments connects the head with neck, shoulders and trunk, and the various vertebrae with each other.

The ligaments uniting the head with the atlas and axis, and these with each other, are arranged so as to give maximum strength and flexibility for motion. The whole mechanism is protected by the presence of synovial joints, which provide lubrication.

The condyles are not parallel, but converge toward the front

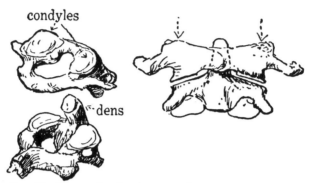

Fig. 28. Atlas and axis. Arrows indicate where head sits.

and are slanted downward from the middle line. They present a wedge-shaped appearance along the border of the great foramen through which the spinal cord emerges from the skull. The position and shape of the condyles limit the range of rocking motion by the head on the atlas and prevent side bending and rotation here. The latter motions are effected by action between the atlas and the underlying cervical vertebrae, especially the second, commonly called the axis. This action involves a complicated arrangement of muscles and ligaments in the entire region of the neck and is quite different in character from the simple mechanical balancing of the head on the atlas at the condyles.

In all the motions of the head, save nodding, the atlas and axis act together. In rotary movements the atlas turns on pivots on the axis about the so-called dens or tooth of the axis.

The atlas is very broad, forming two-thirds of the diameter of the base of the skull between the mastoid processes, so that altogether the atlas-axis mechanism furnishes a strong platform for the double condyloid articulation of the head. Sir Arthur Keith, the great British anatomist, describes the head mechanism most interestingly in his "Engines of the Human Body."

THE HEAD AND SPINAL BALANCE

The head is a good starting place to get a feeling for balance in the axial skeleton. Start the head nodding gently like a toy mandarin. This will bring a sense of the place where the head rests on the spine. While rocking the head as a delicately balanced weight, note how the eyes move automatically against the direction of the head and how their vision is kept focused on the horizon. The eye and neck muscles are being adjusted at the same time by their primary reflexes through the labyrinthine mechanism. When an attempt is made to keep the eyes directed so as to move with the head instead of against it, the primary reflexes have to be interrupted, which at once brings a sense of strain and tension. The strong muscles at the back and sides of the head and neck are brought into action and the nature of the head movements is changed from a mechanical balancing to a forcible pulling back and forth of the weight of the head by the muscles.

The learned pattern is not so economical of energy as the unlearned. The eyes habitually adapt themselves, without consciousness, except for the visual result. When, however, we bring into consciousness the ordinarily unconscious process of contracting the eye muscles, it disturbs the whole mechanism and brings into play many more muscles and motions than are needed. This is exemplified in the use of prisms in exercising maladjusted eyes.

The neck and head muscles are very strong. They must be, to balance and move such a heavy weight as the skull, supported as it is on so small a surface in relation to its size.

This necessitates many guy ropes, which are amply supplied on all sides by tough muscles and tendons running from ribs, sternum, scapulae and clavicles to the head and reinforced by side ties between ribs and cervical vertebrae. The spine affords the head a secure upright support through its opposing curves and its powerful longitudinal muscles and ligaments.

If the occipital condyles rest evenly on the surface of the atlas, a balanced relation between the atlas and other cervical vertebrae will follow, and muscular freedom and ligamentous tone about all their attachments is assured. This in turn favors the adjustment of the rest of the spine to its loads, since in the

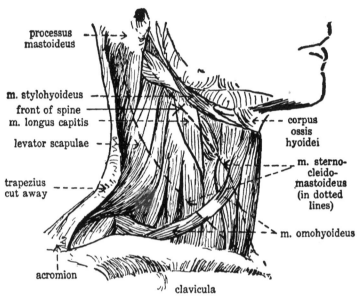

processus
mastoideus

m. stylohyoideus
front of spine
m. longus capitis
levator scapulae

corpus
ossis
hyoidei

trapezius
cut away

m. sterno-
cleido-
mastoideus
(in dotted
lines)

m. omohyoideus

acromion

clavicula

FIG. 29. Muscles of neck from right side. Note stylohyoideus muscle attaching hyoid to skull and omohyoideus attaching to scapula. The latter aids in swallowing. (Redrawn after Spalteholz.)

erect position, the head furnishes the cue for the balance of the whole body.

With the head off center, the upper or cervical curve of the spine will be disturbed. Consequently, it loses its balanced opposition to the underlying spinal curves in the thoracic, lumbar and pelvic regions, and compensatory strains must be set up through the entire length in order to restore the axis of support. These strains are evidenced by pinched areas and stretched areas in various parts of the spine. The head should be centered. Hang by your head from a star, as you walk, and feel the release of bodily strains.

The thorax is a side-load on the spinal column beginning at the base of the cervical region, and receives its main support

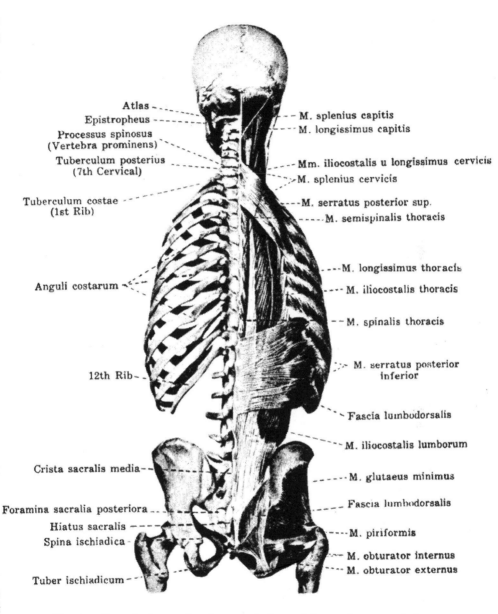

Atlas
Epistropheus
Processus spinosus
(Vertebra prominens)
Tuberculum posterius
(7th Cervical)

Tuberculum costae
(1st Rib)

Anguli costarum

12th Rib

Crista sacralis media

Foramina sacralia posteriora
Hiatus sacralis
Spina ischiadica

Tuber ischiadicum

M. splenius capitis
M. longissimus capitis

Mm. iliocostalis u longissimus cervicis
M. splenius cervicis

M. serratus posterior sup.
M. semispinalis thoracis

M. longissimus thoracis
M. iliocostalis thoracis

M. spinalis thoracis

M. serratus posterior
inferior

Fascia lumbodorsalis

M. iliocostalis lumborum

M. glutaeus minimus

Fascia lumbodorsalis

M. piriformis

M. obturator internus
M. obturator externus

FIG. 30. Deep back muscles, in natural form. Splenius is removed, hence space between serratus posterior superior and erector trunci. Two bands of lumbodorsal fascia are retained on right and serve both serrati as aponeuroses of origin. Other fascia removed. Note egg-shaped chest and width of chest at ninth rib. (From Braus.)

[105]

from the thoracic spine, which is curved concavely, opposing the cervical and lumbar convexities. The thorax is primarily a protective mechanism for the heart and lungs, also for the upper portions of the alimentary canal with its accessory organs. It aids in the specific functioning of all these viscera.

The supporting function of the thorax is distinct and important. It consists in the provision in ribs and sternum of strong, widespread attachments for the tensile members of the trunk, which make up the great muscular and tendinous wall for the front of the body. This wall extends between the thorax and the pelvic girdle, and is suspended from the head, neck and upper thoracic spine, by way of the thorax. The sum total of the action of these tensile members produces a force equal to that provided by the compression members of the back.

The general shape of the thorax and the intricate arrangement and kind of movement of its many parts subserve the protective function. It is a strong, egg-shaped cage with movable walls capable of expansion in all dimensions, formed by twelve pairs of ribs which are securely articulated with the spine in the back and, save for the last two pairs, the so-called "floating ribs," are united with the sternum in front by cartilaginous extensions. The upper rim of the cage is formed by the first ribs, uniting the first thoracic vertebra and the top bone of the sternum, known as the manubrium. Separating the cavities of the chest and the abdomen is the great expansive muscle of breathing, the diaphragm, forming the floor of the cage and with roots extending well down the spine.

The chest is far narrower at the top than we ordinarily realize. The upper rim, formed by the first pair of ribs, is only about one-third the diameter of the shoulders. The broadest part of the chest is in the plane of the ninth rib in front and the first lumbar vertebra in the back.

THE RIBS AND STERNUM

The peculiar shape and slant of each pair of ribs determine the characteristic contour of the thorax. This enables it to function as a strong protective cage and as a moving part of the breathing apparatus, and at the same time to act as a support for body-wall structures. The support and motion of the ribs favor the maintenance of a symmetrical cavity for the heart and lungs, with relatively slight changes in the shape of any one part at the expense of another, during the various respiratory phases. The relation of breathing to general body balance is significant, as the mechanics of breathing and locomotion developed simultaneously. The supporting framework of the thorax is so constructed that its weight and movements are balanced in relation to those of the upper and lower portions of the body.

The ribs look quite unlike the other bones of the body, and no two pairs are alike in shape, size or direction. They are flat, curved bars of light bone with well-defined heads and necks at the spinal ends, while at the anterior ends are open cup-like concavities for the cartilaginous attachments of the sternum.

The ribs hang from the spine, being articulated with the vertebrae by two series of joints, the heads in each case joining with the bodies and intervertebral discs, and the necks with the transverse processes of the vertebrae. These double contacts make for strength and flexibility. They also limit the range of movement of any single rib, or pair. The joints are slanted somewhat acutely in relation to the spinal axis, and the ribs continue to slant downward as they swing outward and backward until they reach a level with the dorsal spinous processes of the vertebrae. Here at what is called the dorsal angle of the ribs they turn toward the front. Thereafter, they continue to curve and to slant outward and downward so that the front end of each rib is considerably below the level of its spinal attachment, some being as much as 6 inches lower.

As they approach the front of the body, the direction of the ribs changes in varying degrees. The five upper ribs, as they pass the middle side line, tend to become horizontal, and the first three pairs are quite horizontal as they approach the sternum.

The last two pairs of ribs, the floating ribs, which have no cartilaginous connection with the sternum in front, hang free and do not extend beyond the mid-lateral line. They function mainly as attachments for the rim of the diaphragm in the back and also for some fibers of the quadratus lumborum

a vertebrosternal rib   a vertebrochondral rib

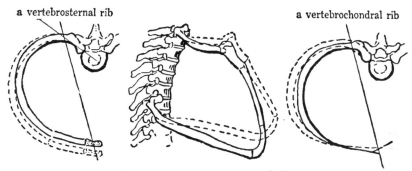

FIG. 31. Axes of movement of ribs.

muscle, which connects the thorax with the pelvis, and of the transversalis abdominis muscle. These muscles, the quadratus and transversalis, are closely associated with the diaphragm in breathing.

At the point where the ribs bend forward they form, save for the first pair, the dorsal angles. These are in vertical alignment with each other, in spite of the varying lengths of the ribs, and are also on a level with and parallel to the dorsal spinous processes of the vertebrae. This arrangement, together with the muscle coverings, gives the appearance of a flat back. The area between the angles forms the gutter of the spine. The gutter of the spine has a considerable depth and in it lie the great longitudinal muscles of the back. These extend from head to pelvis and make a flat contour for the middle region of the back.

In the front, the triangular space bordered by the ends of the ribs, with apex at the sternum, is sometimes called the costal angle. This area outlines the top segment of the wall of the abdominal cavity, which extends higher than we usually imagine, reaching a level opposite the eighth thoracic vertebra. The outer muscles of the abdominal wall run well up over the ribs onto the chest wall. The deepest muscle of the abdomen, the transversalis, runs up on the under side of the ribs, inter-digitates with the diaphragm and functions with that muscle in breathing. (Fig. 32.)

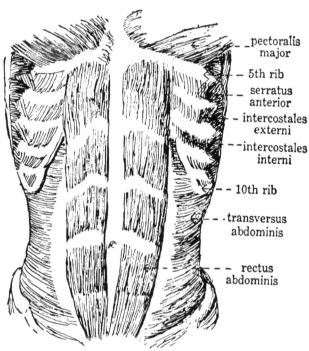

FIG. 32. Transversalis and rectus abdominis muscles, enclosing abdominal cavity at front. (Redrawn after Spalteholz.)

The inner surfaces of the ribs are smooth, and as they are attached to the bodies of the vertebrae on their lateral and dorsal aspects, the bodies themselves project well into the cavity of the chest, making it heart-shaped in transverse section. Due to the pronounced dip of the ribs, any cross section will cut through at least two, and in the lower levels, as many as six ribs.

The sternum is a broad, slightly curved, dagger-shaped bone. It forms part of the front wall of the thorax, and unites the ends of the ribs. In the embryo there are five or six cartilaginous pieces, which unite into the three characteristic parts of the bony adult sternum: the manubrium, the body or corpus, and the xyphoid process.

The sternum is shorter than the thoracic spine, and shows considerable individual variation in its position and general slant. In the adult the top of the manubrium is on a level between the second and third thoracic vertebrae, and the end of the corpus opposite about the ninth or tenth. Its curve and that of the top of the thoracic spine are symmetrical.

The first seven pairs of ribs are attached to the sternum by way of cartilaginous extensions of their ends. The first pair is fused with the cartilage of the manubrium, and the other pairs fit into the sternocostal articulations, the joints being reinforced by capsular and radiating ligaments. This type of attachment lends elasticity to the ribs and permits motion from front to back. The ribs are connected with each other by short ligaments near their heads, and throughout their course by two series of intercostal muscles, the external and internal. These are disposed diagonally in opposite directions between the borders of the ribs, and work alternately during breathing.

The first pair of ribs, attached to the first thoracic vertebra, are short and flat and curve sharply forward to their firm cartilaginous attachments upon the extended corners of the manubrium. They slant so little that they go only through a distance represented by one and a half short, thoracic vertebrae; and their bony parts terminate well to the sides of the sternum at points farther out than those of the second and third pair, and present a broad, flat upper surface throughout. They really form a "collar bone" far more truly than do the clavicles, which, though attached to the manubrium above the first ribs, do not encircle the base of the neck but stretch out in a relatively straight line to either side and give attachments to the scapulae.

The top of the rib-cage is surprisingly narrow in all dimensions, as stated, and it forms but a third of the width of the body at the level of the shoulders. The first pair of ribs have relatively few muscles attached to them, and these act in a vertical plane. The most important are the scaleni, attached to the side and dorsal aspects of the upper cervical vertebrae, balancing and supporting the ribs in relation to head and atlas.

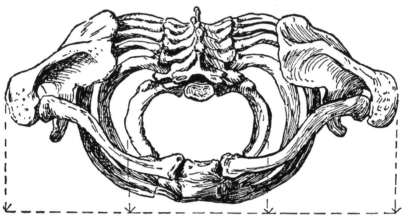

FIG. 33. Top aspect of thorax and shoulder girdle, showing that width of top rib is but one third of entire width of shoulder girdle. (Redrawn after Spalteholz.)

The first pair of ribs are practically immovable at the front and are capable of very limited motion from their articulations with the spine, mainly in an antero-posterior direction. The transverse and the antero-posterior diameters of the thorax are more nearly alike at the back of the first ribs than at any other plane.

The second rib is more slender than and about twice as long as the first. In shape it is more like the lower ribs than like the first. In general curve and slant it follows the line of the first rib quite evenly, so that the two act together in outlining the top of the thoracic cavity. (See Fig. 33.) The third rib resembles the first two in general tendency of curve and horizontal union with the sternum, but the motion of the spinal joint is freer and marks the beginning of an increase in movement at the back, which is notable as we descend the spine. Beginning with the third rib also, the ribs twist on their long axes as they turn to the front at the dorsal angle, so that they present flat surfaces to the side.

THE PELVIS

In the establishment of the upright position the principal change in mechanical functioning came upon the pelvis. It was here that the most important and radical structural adjustments had to be made. In the quadruped the pelvic girdle has the relatively simple supporting function of providing a rigid cross-piece for one end of the spinal girder. To this cross-piece the movable legs are attached, and normally the pelvis need bear only half the weight of the trunk.

In the human being the pelvis has a threefold function. It must receive from the spinal column the entire weight of the head, shoulders and trunk and transmit it to the legs. It must provide means of motion for the trunk upon the legs, and for the legs upon the trunk.

The pelvic problem of weight-bearing, transmission and movement is met by its arched structure. As may be seen in Figure 34, the characteristic design is one of curved and rounded surfaces and columns. The many openings left in the bony wall are covered by ligaments, and serve to make the structure as light as possible without sacrificing its strength. A solid basin, with continuous walls of bone, would be enormously heavy and clumsy.

The weight of the head, shoulders and trunk accumulating through the spine and concentrating upon the fifth lumbar, falls upon the sacrum. The weight-bearing task of the sacrum is so great that its five constituent vertebrae are fused into a single bony mass, and their curve made permanent. The process of fusion is gradual, and is not completed until the twentieth year.

The sacrum with the coccyx completes the axial skeleton. Since our interest is in the mechanical function, rather than the structural anatomy of the skeleton, we consider the pelvis as a whole rather than separating it into its axial and appendicular parts, as represented by the sacrum and the hip-bones or pelvic girdle proper.

Each hip-bone is made up of three portions, distinct in early life and until puberty: the ilium, the ischium and the pubis.

Fused in the adult, they are called the innominate bone. Together these join with the sacrum to make the whole pelvic arch, which is in effect a double arch, functioning as follows: At the

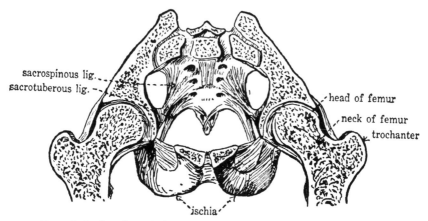

sacrospinous lig.
sacrotuberous lig.

head of femur

neck of femur

trochanter

ischia

FIG. 34. Section through femur and ilia, showing ligamentous bindings.

sacrum the weight is distributed to the two sides, through the sacroiliac joints, and thereafter follows two courses according to whether the person is standing or sitting. When standing the lines of transmission are through the heavy lower parts of the ilia to the acetabula, where the heads of the femora receive them, and they are thereafter passed through the long thigh bones, through the knee-joints, the lower legs, ankles, and feet to the ground. When sitting, the weight, after passing into the ilia, travels through their heavy portions in line with the acetabula, to the lowest points of the ischia, known as the tuberosities of the ischia. These points are the places upon which the whole trunk weight is balanced in the erect sitting posture, and where it is transmitted to the seat of the chair. The Germans recognize this fact by calling the ischia the "sit-bones" (*Sitzbeinen*).

Considered from the ground up, the standing arch is the femoro-ilio-sacral, its sides extending from the acetabula to the sacroiliac joint; and the sitting arch is the ischio-ilio-sacral, extending from the sharp point of the ischium on either side to the sacroiliac joint.

These two arches are the essential weight-bearing portions

of the pelvis, and the sacrum is the keystone for both. All the other parts are reinforcements to the main arches, making the support secure whether the structure is in motion or at rest. One

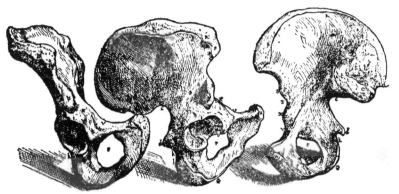

FIG. 35. "Sit on the ischia!" (From Vesalius.)

important reinforcement is contributed by the extensions of the two pubic portions to meet in the front in the powerful symphysis pubis. The pelvic girdle is thus made into a continuous ring, so that the body-load as it travels is distributed around the whole circumference.

The spine, the ilia, the pubis, the ischia and the thighs are bound together by strong ligaments, some sheath-like, some long, some short and round, which cross and interweave in all directions. The ligaments extend between all surfaces, rounding the angles, smoothing the outlines, and making the whole pelvis serve as a great, composite joint. Closely connected with the ligaments in this firm integration are the strong muscles with their tough tendons and their fascial sheaths, which connect and move the bones of the spine, pelvis and legs.

The mechanism of muscular coordination by which one muscle or group operating in a given direction is opposed by another, called the antagonizer, is especially marked in the pelvis. Here the bony parts must be maintained in stable relationship by muscular adjustments, especially as to their angles and their lines of force in thrust-impact and reaction. This is more difficult here than elsewhere because of the accumulated weight and the distance through which it must be guided. The weight of the trunk is carried to the ground through long levers. Antagonistic action here is between groups of muscles and muscle systems rather than between single pairs of muscles.

When the pelvis is in balance, the forces acting through the arches should relate in the same manner to the sacral keystone, whether sitting or standing. The points of rest, the ischia and acetabula, are in vertical alignment. The weight of the trunk on top of the sacrum, as it passes from the keystone through the sides of the arch to the heads of the femora, tends to spread the arch. This tendency is countered by the beam-action of the pubic structures upon the flaring sides of the ilia, and is reinforced by the tie muscles and ligaments inside the arch.

In detailed structure the pelvis is a further series of arches. The wings of the sacrum, formed by the first three fused vertebrae, curve outward, upward and backward in joining the ilia at the sacroiliac joint. The ilia and pubic bones on either side are fused during childhood into closely curved arches to form the acetabula, into which the heads of the femora fit. The femora act as added buttresses to the ilia, which in turn buttress the keystone of the arch. They do this by offering resistance against the weight pressure from above by the thrust of the center of the head of each femur upward against each acetabulum. This is continued through each ilium in lines directed through the sacroiliac joints to the center of the contacting surfaces between the top of the sacrum and the body of the fifth lumbar vertebra.

These lines are oblique lines of upward force, coming through the shafts of the femora from the ground and redirected toward the keystone by tensile forces—muscles and ligaments. They meet and balance the downward compression force, or weight, coming through the joints of the spine and pelvis. They are shown diagrammatically in Figure 36.

With balanced contacts at these joints securing even tonicity of ligaments and muscles about them, the lines of force will counter each other through the sacrolumbar and sacroiliac joints. If the muscles and ligaments are stretched unevenly and the timing system controlling their antagonistic action is disturbed, the weight is received by unprepared structures.

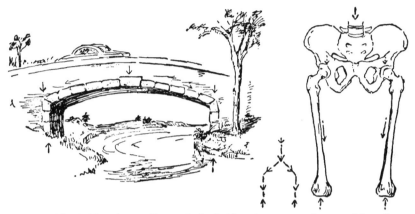

FIG. 36. The bridge that walks, and the bridge that you walk over. Note lines of force in relation to keystone.

The bracing power of the shafts of the femora is lost if the thrusts of the heads are too far forward, as for example when the legs are turned about their long axes in the "toeing-out" position. Under these conditions the counter-thrust to weight is no longer directed through the strong cores of the ilia toward the center of the arch at the keystone, the point where the weight is being delivered from above, but forward or medially against the pubic rami, and thus away from center. This increases the tendency of the pelvic arch to spread at the iliac joints—a dangerous situation. It throws weight strains unevenly upon sacroiliac ligaments which may give way under the strain, with the pain resulting from sacroiliac displacement. Compensatory movement at the fifth lumbar also results from lack of rotary freedom and action in the thigh joints.

By use of tie muscles within the pelvic arch, connecting lumbar vertebrae, sacrum, ilia and femora, we bind this arch together and only a slight effort is demanded to maintain the balance.

Habits once established in form tend to remain automatic in action, unless new education or effort be applied.

Chapter V

DYNAMIC MECHANISMS

PELVIC AND FEMORAL MUSCLES

AFTER REALIZING OUR BONES ALIVE, ACTIVE AND READY TO RESPOND TO A DYNAMIC PURPOSE, WE MUST CONSIDER the machines that move the mass of weight. We must know how organized movement is initiated. This takes place at the base of the upright column. The pelvic muscles are the first to consider, being the largest and strongest and having to control the movement for any change of position of the body mass in space.

About thirty-six muscles are attached to the pelvis. These muscles run in every direction. Many of them extend well up into the trunk and down into the legs, and besides their moving functions, form important supporting parts of the body wall. Here they serve to unite the main units of weight of the skeleton, joining thorax, trunk, legs and even the head, with the pelvis.

Five of the deepest lying muscles or groups are distinguished in the important work of adjusting the pelvis with the spine and maintaining free articulation and balanced movement of the hip joints. These are the psoas major and the psoas minor; the iliacus, the pectineus, the internal and external obturators, and the pyriformis. The two psoas muscles, major and minor, are perhaps the most important of all the muscles in determining the human, or upright, posture, because of their function, relationships and extent. The bulky psoas major lies along the sides of the bodies of the largest vertebrae of the spine, all the way from the twelfth thoracic to the fifth lumbar; it is attached to their transverse processes, and with the quadratus lumborum, forms a prominent part of the lower back abdominal wall. Its

118

fibers arise at the sides of the bodies of the lowest thoracic and first lumbar and from the transverse processes of all lumbar. They pass directly downward and forward over the pelvis,

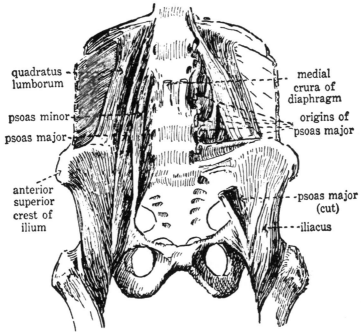

quadratus lumborum

medial crura of diaphragm

psoas minor

origins of psoas major

psoas major

anterior superior crest of ilium

psoas major (cut)

iliacus

FIG. 37. Lumbar muscles from front. Deep anterior support of rotary joint. (Redrawn after Spalteholz.)

where they unite with the iliacus for a common insertion in the femur.

The psoas minor, which represents a separate part of the major, lies on its ventral surface, arising from the bodies of the last thoracic and first lumbar vertebrae. At about the level of the fourth lumbar vertebra its fibers converge into a tendon, which extends like a strap, to insert into the iliac fascia, near the front of the pelvis.

The iliacus arises from the upper half of the anterior surface of the crest of the ilium and the iliac fossa. Its fibers converge downward in a fan-shaped form and unite with the psoas major, forming a common tendon which inserts into the lesser trochanter. Due to this close association, these muscles are referred to as the iliopsoas.

They are completely covered throughout their course by the

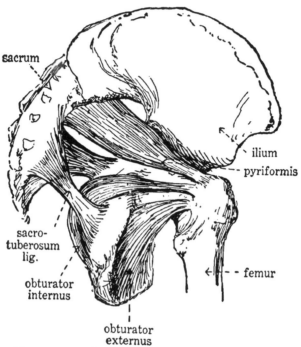

sacrum
ilium
pyriformis
sacro-
tuberosum
lig.
obturator
internus
femur
obturator
externus

FIG. 38. Deep muscles of pelvis. Deep posterior support of rotary joint.

iliac fascia which is attached to the arcuate ligaments of the diaphragm above and to the fascia of the transversalis, and has important connections in the pelvis as part of the breathing apparatus. The psoas minor serves to tense the iliac fascia.

The pectineus arises from the iliopectineal line, on the anterior surface of the ilium, and from the superior pubic ramus— that portion of the pubis which forms, with its mate, the strong, anterior joint of the pelvic girdle called the symphysis. The pectineus inserts on the posterior aspect of the femur, just below the iliopsoas.

The external and internal obturator muscles follow a path opposing that of the iliopsoas group.

The obturator externus, a thick, triangular structure, arises from the anterior surface of the lower half of the obturator membrane (which covers the great obturator foramen lying mesial to the acetabulum) and from the rami of the pubis and

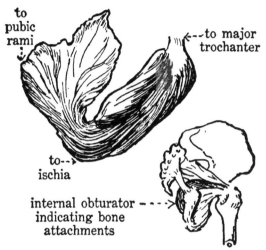

FIG. 39. Internal obturator muscle. (Redrawn after Braus.)

the ischium which bound the lower portion of the foramen. Its fibers pass outward and converge in a rounded tendon, which is inserted into the floor of the digital fossa of the femur just above and in the same plane with the extensive area of insertion for the iliopsoas group.

The internus arises from the inner surface of the rami of the pubis and ischium and from the smooth surface of bone posterior to the acetabulum, and from the whole inner surface of the obturator membrane. Its fibers pass downward and backward, converging into a strong tendon which bends around the border of the ischium near the lesser sciatic foramen, through which it passes outward to be inserted on the inner surface of the greater trochanter, just above the digital fossa. The shape of the internus is extraordinary, as may be seen by Figure 39, in which it is pictured as a whole, removed from the pelvis.

Its action rotates the leg slightly outward, and pulls the front of the pelvis downward. If the psoas and iliacus be stretched, the obturators may pull the pelvis downward to the extent of jeopardizing the support of the load at the fifth lumbar vertebra. A balanced action between the iliopsoas and the obturators keeps the pelvis a working unit between thighs and spine, for weight transfer.

The pyriformis arises from the ventral surface of the sacrum and passes through the great sciatic notch or foramen, to be inserted near the top of the greater trochanter in close association with the internal obturator, supplementing its action in rotating the thigh laterally.

The pelvic floor is made up of two muscles which, acting as a diaphragm, almost completely separate the pelvis from the perineal region, extending across from the pubis and the sides of the ischia to the coccyx. The levator ani and the coccygeus, unlike the other muscles just listed, lie entirely within the pelvis with no outside attachments. In this respect these muscles resemble the diaphragm between the thoracic and abdominal cavities, and the two structures have many similarities in function besides being closely associated in breathing. The pyriformis is above the coccygeus and, extending across the sacrum, forms the posterior wall of the pelvis. The three muscles, the levator ani, coccygeus and pyriformis, are all united by loose connective tissue and are thus continuous.

BALANCING ACTION OF PELVIC MUSCLES

Considered in relation to the pelvis as an area for transferring weight, these muscle groups act together to stabilize the joints. The work of the iliopsoas and pectineus muscle groups is to aid in centering the thrust of the upward lines of force from the femora through the supporting thigh-joints toward the sacroiliac and lumbosacral joints. On the other hand, the contraction of the obturators and pyriformis tends to alter the alignment of the thrust by increasing the obliquity of the pelvis, and to decentralize the thrust by redirecting it forward and away from the keystone.

The action of the iliopsoas and pectineus groups must equal

and oppose that of the obturators and pyriformis if the heads of the femora are to be balanced and steady in the acetabula, and the centralized thrust directed through the pelvis toward the

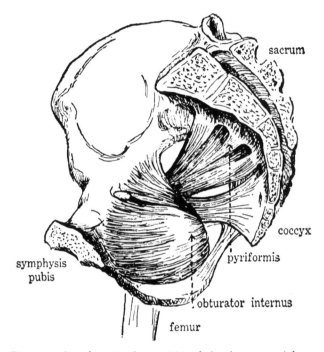

FIG. 40. Deep muscles of pelvis, from within, balancing rotary joint posteriorly. (Redrawn after Spalteholz.)

keystone, the sacrum. These muscles act to keep the joints in a favorable position in relation to the spine quite as much as do the ligaments. If these groups of muscles do not operate to balance each other, the ligaments are weakened and the joints subjected to dangerous strains.

PELVIC LIGAMENTS

The many ligaments on all sides of the joints of the pelvis combine to make this composite joint secure for safe transference of weight. Added to the many structural ligaments binding all joints in this region are the inguinal or Poupart's ligaments, forming the canals through which important nervous and vas-cular structures pass to the lower limbs.

Tough ligaments bind the various portions of the girdle se-curely, not only between and about the joints and their apposed surfaces, but extending in several planes and directions, con-necting more remote borders and surfaces. Three sets of liga-ments, together with the pelvic muscles and fascia, serve to bind the parts and to complete the wall of the pelvis, making it a secure basin of support for the pelvic viscera. The ligaments are: first, those joining the ilium with the sacrum and the fourth and fifth lumbar vertebrae; second, those joining the pubic bones together at the symphysis, also those joining sacrum and ischia; third, the ligamentous membranes that complete the lateral and lower walls in the spaces between the bony parts, such as the obturator foramina and the sciatic notches. The ligaments binding the femora with the several parts of the pelvis are so closely associated with the others as to make them one system.

Balanced support of the spine depends upon the integrity of the pelvic ligaments, particularly the interior and the anterior groups in and about the thigh-joint. Most important of these pelvic and femoral ligaments for insuring the support of the spine are: those about the hip-joint, the pelvic-femoral group, especially those that complete the lower and mesial border and deepen the cavity of the acetabulum, the transverse ligament and the cotyloid, or labrum glenoidale.

The cotyloid is a fibrocartilaginous rim attached to the border of the acetabulum, and to the transverse ligament. Together these ligaments increase the depth of the hip-socket so that its cavity embraces more than half a sphere. This insures a strong connection and at the same time maximum capacity for move-ment at this ball-and-socket joint. The cavity is lined with a synovial membrane that covers the surrounding ligaments.

The capsular ligament, or capsule of the hip, is a strong, fibrous envelope that encloses the joint completely, covering the neck of the femur as far as the trochanters, so that it moves within a flexible tube.

The capsular ligament varies greatly in thickness, and is rather weak in the back, but strong in front where bone is lacking to complete the socket and flexibility is needed. Besides

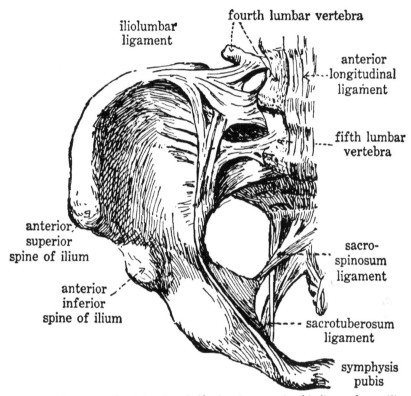

FIG. 41. Ligaments of pelvis, right half, showing anterior bindings of sacroiliac joint. (Redrawn after Spalteholz.)

the distinct bands of the accessory ligaments, there are twisted bands to the back and circular fibers running beneath the longitudinal fibers, which add to the flexibility and strength. Along its course and in its various attachments the capsule is associated with and strengthened by muscular fibers, and also by tendinous and fascial extensions from the deep trunk and pelvic abdominal muscles, particularly the iliopsoas, the rectus abdominis, the gluteus minimus and the obturators.

The ligaments about the lumbosacral joint reinforce both the

attachment of the upper spine to the sacrum and that of the
sacrum to the ilium and ischium, filling in the space between the sacrum and the overhanging ilium and the spaces

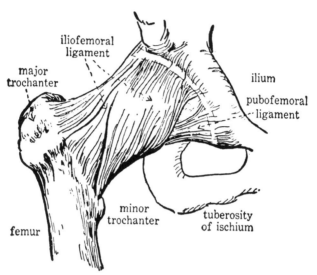

iliofemoral
ligament

major
trochanter

ilium

pubofemoral
ligament

minor
trochanter

tuberosity
of ischium

femur

FIG. 42. Right hip joint from front, with ligaments.

formed by the sacroiliac notches and obturator foramen.
(Fig. 43.)

These ligaments are closely associated with the origins and
passages of muscles to the upper and posterior parts of the
femur, including the pyriformis, the obturators and the biceps.

The two pubic bones are united in the front at the typical
half-joint, known as the symphysis pubis, and by the fibrocartilaginous lamina, reinforced above and below by cross ligaments, the superior and inferior arcuate ligaments.

Less immediately important for our purposes are the ligaments to which are attached the pelvic viscera and the ventral
and abdominal structures, and those through which pass the
vascular and nervous supplies to the pelvis and lower limbs,
such as the inguinal (or Poupart's) ligament, forming the
inguinal canal. However, the ligaments whose work is to bind

the composite pelvic joints to the spine and the legs are intimately associated with these others and have with them mutual structural and functional interactions. (See Fig. 41.)

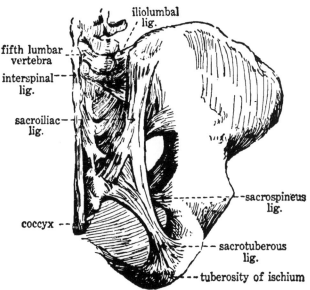

FIG. 43. Ligaments of right half of pelvis, from back. Note posterior bindings of sacroiliac joint. (Redrawn after Spalteholz.)

THE FASCIA OF THE PELVIS

In meeting postural problems, not only are the deep-lying muscles and binding ligaments of abdomen, pelvis and femur important, but also the investing sheaths of connective tissue known as fascia. The various layers of fascia covering the surfaces of the pelvis and enfolding the vascular and lymphatic structures in the femoral triangle and in the lowest portions of the abdomen serve to reinforce the action of the muscles and ligaments.

Fascia constitutes a general interstitial connective-tissue network, traversing all parts of the body, and thickened in various regions to form more or less definite supporting and protective structures for other parts, whether visceral, bony or muscular. The fascial sheets vary greatly in their density, sometimes being quite tenuous or loosely webbed, containing fat, and sometimes forming dense, glittering sheets resembling the expansions of certain tendons, and like them termed aponeuroses. The two layers of fasciae may be distinguished—the superficial and the deep.

The superficial layer, which immediately underlies the skin of the entire body, carries the subcutaneous fat. This superficial layer is connected more or less loosely with the deep fascia, which immediately covers and invests the muscles, and between the muscles becomes continuous with the periosteum enclosing the bone.

Fascial structures, like tendons and ligaments, thicken in areas where extra strength is needed for muscular action, or for support. Fascia, tendons and ligaments, which are all types of tough connective tissue, function together intimately. Their relation is especially close in and about the joints and where muscles are attached for long-range, diversified action, as those which must act (together with small bones) as integral parts of tensile members such as the front wall of the body.

The deep fascia dips in between the muscles of the limbs, forming intermuscular septa, which are so firm that they may serve as the origin of neighboring muscle fibers. Sometimes muscles, such as the crura of the diaphragm, levator ani, and the soleus, take their origin in part from deep fascia, which then becomes thickened along the line of origin to form strong bands termed arcus tendinei. These bands greatly increase the power of the adjoined muscles.

One of the fascial structures significant for posture is the fascia lata, which ensheaths all the muscles of the thigh and covers the gluteal region. The fascia lata begins at the coccyx and sacrum and extends forward along the entire length of the crest of the ilium, thence medially along Poupart's ligament to the body of the pubis; then it passes backward and downward along the inferior ramus of the pubis to the ischium, and is carried over the greater sacrosciatic ligament, and so on back to its starting point. Below, it passes over the knee and becomes continuous with the fascia of the lower leg. At various places the fascia lata is thickened, and one portion, extending from the upper part of the lateral aspect of the thigh to the upper part of the tibia, offers insertion for an important muscle called the

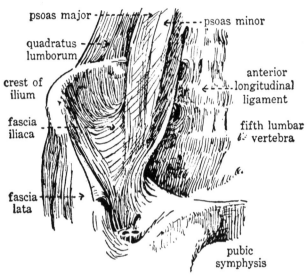

psoas major

psoas minor

quadratus lumborum

crest of ilium

anterior longitudinal ligament

fascia iliaca

fifth lumbar vertebra

fascia lata

pubic symphysis

FIG. 44. Fascia and muscles about the ilium. (Redrawn after Spalteholz.)

tensor fasciae latae. The main function of the tensor fasciae latae is to tighten the fascia lata throughout its entire extent, and it also serves to rotate the thigh slightly inward and to flex it. This muscle is sometimes referred to as the posture muscle. Its effect upon the muscles of the thigh through their sheaths and intermuscular septa in aiding to integrate the action of the thigh with the hip, pelvis and spine is very important.

The tightening of the fascia lata, which is like a jacket about the thigh muscles, prevents any one muscle from overworking to the extent of seriously jeopardizing the safety of the joint.

Another important fascia is the iliac, which covers the entire iliopsoas muscle group from its origin at the thoracic level, through the pelvis and down into the leg. The iliac fascia is near the diaphragm at its upper end, and in the pelvis is closely associated with the pelvic fascia and with the formation of the femoral canal and the femoral ring, while below it becomes continuous with the fascia lata of the leg. The psoas minor muscle inserts by a long strap tendon into the iliac fascia, and serves to tighten it, and thus to integrate the action of the psoas

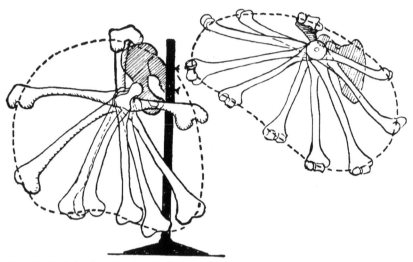

Fig. 45. Radius of revolution of femur and of humerus. (Redrawn after Mollier.)

and iliacus muscles throughout their course. Like the fascia lata, therefore, this fascial structure plays an important part in the coordination of the pelvic and thigh muscles for balanced action in movement and the support and transfer of weight through the pelvis to the legs and feet.

Throughout the body, free circulation of the blood and lymph and better functioning of the various parts depend very largely on deep fascial tonus, as well as upon muscular freedom. Fascial tonus is greatly aided by balance of muscles and bones, since their function as a unit is determined by the proprioceptive mechanism.

In the upright position, the compactness of the body-wall is insured by balanced support of the spine upon the pelvis and of the pelvis upon the legs, and by this only. Balanced support can be obtained only if the integrity of the pelvic ligaments and the anterior common or longitudinal ligaments of the spine is secured by the balanced action of the deep-lying muscles just

described, and by the fascial tonus. A careful study and understanding of the universal joint of the hip in its function as
weight carrier is indispensable to the solution of the organic
and structural difficulties arising from increased lordosis of the
lumbar spine, and the associated visceroptosis.

As we have previously stated: "The power expended by the
leg that kicks a football across a field" . . . must be absorbed
through the universal joint by the equalized support of all the
deep-lying tissues of that articulation; ". . . briefly, the hip
joint is like a wire-spoked bicycle wheel, the head of the femur
being the weight-carrying hub . . . and the soft tissues the
radiating spokes." The equal tension in these radiating, tensile
members balances the femur in the acetabulum in suspension,
"ready to transmit without slack or undue rebound, the antici-
pated stress received or imposed in action."*

THE PELVIS AS A SHOCK ABSORBER

The pelvis acts as a shock absorber against forces coming
from two directions: the downward fall of weight from the
trunk and the upward thrust from the ground as it receives
the impact of the weight. Its rôle as shock absorber depends
upon several mechanical principles: the alternation and combination of substances in the transmitting medium; the distribution and even division of weight; and changes in direction and
plane, with the use of curves and arches and wedge devices.

These principles are all exemplified in other parts of the
skeletal structure, but nowhere so prominently as in the pelvis,
where the need is greatest. The main mechanical factors may
be summarized as follows:

Alternation of substances is provided by an arrangement of
soft and hard tissues, of all grades between fat and bone. Were
it not for the soft, dulling effect of the muscles, fat, fascia,
blood and lymph vessels and the spongy viscera with which the
cavity is packed, and the not inconsiderable fatty covering of

---

* Principles of Posture, with Special Reference to the Mechanics of the Hip-
Joint, by Mabel Elsworth Todd.

the sides and buttocks, the strong, curved and arched bones of the pelvis and lower spine would feel and communicate the effects of weight-shock and rebound.

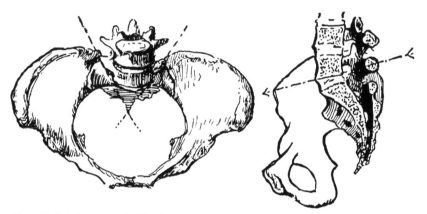

FIG. 46. Pelvis, top and side views. Note pyramidal shape of sacrum and position of fifth lumbar. (Redrawn after Spalteholz.)

Distribution and even division of the weight begins at the level of the fifth lumbar, upon which all the weight of the trunk is concentrated. Down to this point, the weight is transmitted almost entirely through the bodies of the vertebrae, which are held in approximately horizontal planes by trussing ligaments. At the fifth lumbar, however, the transition occurs between the convexity of the lumbar and the concavity of the sacral curves. The body of the fifth lumbar is considerably deeper in front. Its base and the adjacent cartilaginous discs are sloped perceptibly forward and downward from the horizontal plane. The shearing tendency which is inevitably produced at this point is counteracted by the arrangement of the transverse and articular processes. The transverse processes are extended upward and well to the sides, furnishing attachment for ligaments. The processes bearing the inferior-posterior facets are sloped backward, outward and downward at an angle to the perpendicular equal to the forward slope of the lower rim of the body and corresponding to the slope of the sacral facets.

The weight is thus transferred in three planes through three contacting surfaces; that is, the two facets and the body, which between them enclose the strong, blunt triangular wedge formed by the top of the sacrum. The lumbosacral joint has the strong form of one pyramid fitted over another, in itself a way of easy transmission of weight. This means that the fifth lumbar vertebra is more stable than would appear simply from a side view of its place in the curve. The fact also that the entire vertebra is well below the rims of the ilia protects it from side blows and pressures. Often trouble which is assigned to the lumbosacral joint may be found actually to lie between the fourth and fifth lumbar vertebrae, or to be due to ligamentous strain below the joint.

There is an equal division of the weight through the two sides of the pelvis, and thence to the legs. After the weight has divided through the sacroiliac joints, it is received by structures which again are so formed that a section through them would be triangular. The wings of the sacrum curve upward, forward, downward and to the side. The curves and surfaces they outline are continued onto the ilia anteriorly. The ilia flare upward toward their crests, which are on a level well above the fifth lumbar vertebra.

The shape of the acetabula, as formed by the conjoined ilia, ischia and pubes, together with the reinforcing rims of cartilage, is such as to enclose a little more than a hemisphere. These arrangements distribute the weight so that it is communicated evenly during the most extreme range of movement about the femoral heads. Finally, the two upper rami of the pubes unite at the front center in the strong symphysis, whose dense fibrocartilage, and binding and crossing ligamentous fibers above and below, complete the shock-absorbing pelvic ring.

As pointed out by Piersol, "The symphysis, although comparatively unyielding, is in almost the same horizontal plane with the coccyx, the most movable bone that enters into the formation of the pelvis, and with the obturator foramina and the lower part of the great sacro-sciatic foramina. This is in accord with the fact that in no horizontal plane does the pelvis form a complete bony and unyielding ring, but everywhere the resisting bony portion has opposite to it one or more soft and yielding segments, as for example the hypogastric region of the abdomen is opposite the fixed and immovable sacrum. . . ."*

Changes in plane and direction of force are effected in several stages, laterally from the spine through the sacroiliac joint, and then forward on a sloping line through the ilia to the acetabula. Next, the slope is continued forward by the neck of the femur, so that the weight is transferred to the ground, through a plane about 2½ inches in front of the lumbosacral joint, where the weight was delivered from spine to pelvis.

In walking, the whole mechanism acts like a composite spring: the weight is delivered on a curve with considerable give, through two curved arms, onto the round ball tops of the shafts of the femora, upon which it can rock back and forth and sideways, allowing a rebound and recovery of balance between each step.

All these devices, together with the upward pull upon the legs by muscles which arise deep and high in the trunk, serve to absorb shock and retard the momentum of the body-weight as it drops toward the ground. Falling body-weight follows the same principles of accelerated velocity that operate in the case of bodies falling freely through the air.

Conscious advantage may be taken of these principles by so using the muscles, particularly the psoas and iliacus, that they contract just before the load is put on them. This serves to hold the weight of the body and legs so that it is let down gently upon the ground. As already explained, a muscle thus contracting against a load, does so with great efficiency; if not preparing for the load by contracting against it, it cannot lift the weight so far, or carry it so long, as it can if it contracts before assuming the load.

THE LEGS AND FEET

The legs and feet are accessory structures designed to keep the trunk well off the ground and to furnish speed and ease of locomotion. Strength and balance for standing and walking

* Human Anatomy, by George Arthur Piersol, p. 351.

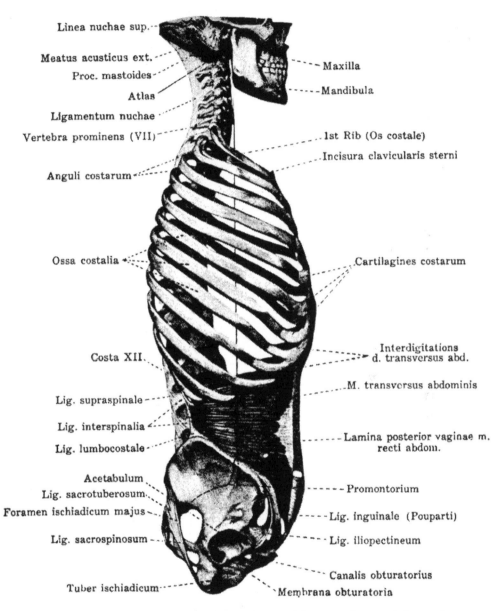

Linea nuchae sup.

Meatus acusticus ext.

Proc. mastoides

Atlas

Ligamentum nuchae

Vertebra prominens (VII)

Anguli costarum

Ossa costalia

Costa XII.

Lig. supraspinale

Lig. interspinalia

Lig. lumbocostale

Acetabulum

Lig. sacrotuberosum

Foramen ischiadicum majus

Lig. sacrospinosum

Tuber ischiadicum

Maxilla

Mandibula

1st Rib (Os costale)

Incisura clavicularis sterni

Cartilagines costarum

Interdigitations
d. transversus abd.

M. transversus abdominis

Lamina posterior vaginae m.
recti abdom.

Promontorium

Lig. inguinale (Pouparti)

Lig. iliopectineum

Canalis obturatorius

Membrana obturatoria

FIG. 47. Trunk from side. Natural position of bones and natural form of muscles as in undistorted body. Front contour of spine and sacrum, shown by dotted line. Note that spine comes to center of body in cervical and lumbar regions. Also that transversalis passes under ribs, to interdigitate with diaphragm. (From Braus.)

[135]

are dependent primarily upon the structures of the trunk and pelvis, and particularly upon those about the hip-joints, where the legs are attached.

In the development of the primate, the legs and feet seem secondary to the arms and hands, since our more immediate ancestors lived in the trees and moved about and supported themselves while climbing largely by the action of the upper limbs. The lower limbs served to balance, and the feet were used to grasp, so that these creatures were four-handed rather than four-footed. This old history is reflected in the prenatal development of the human being, during which the arms are larger and more prominent than the legs, and this priority is continued for some time after birth. But after early babyhood the legs rapidly become stronger and larger than the arms, which are used for support and locomotion only under unusual circumstances.

Mechanically, the work of the legs and feet is to carry the weight from the base of the trunk to the ground. This must be done in such a way that the reaction from the ground will be so directed as to communicate the least amount of shock. This result is accomplished by the substance, shape and number of the component parts, which are characterized by strong elastic tissues and curved, arched and radial structures. There are three main divisions: the upper leg, or thigh, made up of a single shaft, the femur; the lower leg, with the shin and calf bones, known as the tibia and fibula; and the foot, composed of twenty-six bones of varying sizes.

THE THIGH

The femur is the longest bone of the body. At the upper end is a round head on a neck which forms a broad angle with the shaft of about 125 degrees, the junction being heavily reinforced by two protuberances known as the greater and lesser trochanters. The shaft is approximately cylindrical in the middle, and at the lower end expands into two condyles, which articulate with the tibia and form the knee joint.

The point in the acetabulum where the body-weight is trans-ferred from the pelvis to the femur, and the center of the knee where it is transferred from the femur to the tibia, are in perpendicular alignment. The axis of the shaft of the femur which carries the weight is not perpendicular, but is directed diagonally inward from the greater trochanter to the knee. If the weight of the whole is to be centered, and thus balanced eco-nomically, the shaft must be so tied up to the pelvis by muscles and ligaments that the head of the femur is centered in the acetabulum. This is accomplished chiefly from above by the action of the deep-lying pelvic muscles, which are aided by the heavy muscles running along the shaft.

The three masses of powerful muscles of the thigh are sepa-rated from each other by intermuscular septa, which are continu-ations inward of the fascia lata that binds all the thigh muscles together. The fascia lata acts as a controlling agent upon the muscle groups so that they cannot act individually on the femur to shift its axis out of alignment.

As noted before, the tensor fasciae latae, the so-called "pos-ture muscle," aids in this controlling function by drawing the fascia lata tighter upon need, thus pulling the individual muscle groups closer together within their intermuscular septa. This action aids the femur to steer the body-weight back to center from its outward position.

THE LOWER LEG

The framework of the lower leg is formed by the shin and calf bones, the tibia and fibula, and their uniting ligament known as the interosseous membrane. These three structures together operate as a single apparatus so far as weight guidance is concerned. (See Fig. 49.)

The tibia is the real weight bearer of the lower leg, con-tinuing the line of transfer from the femur to the ankle, through which the weight reaches the ground. The fibula is articulated with the tibia by a gliding joint at the upper end and outer surface of the tibia, just below the knee, and at the lower end by a ligamentous joint, somewhat resembling the joint of a safety pin. The Romans, remember, fastened their togas with a "fibula."

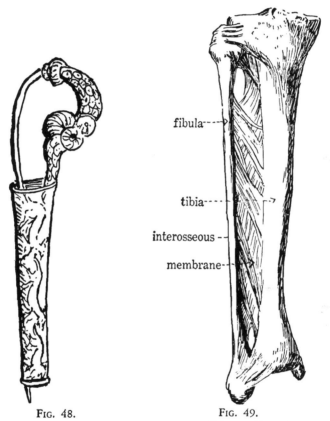

FIG. 48.   FIG. 49.

FIG. 48. Fibula, bronze, seventh century B.C. (Metropolitan Art Museum.)
FIG. 49. Lower leg and interosseous membrane. Note similarity of human fibula to Roman fibula.

In its general direction, the tibia is more nearly vertical than any other bone in the body. It is a long, strong, cylindrical bone, composed of a shaft and two extremities, both having concave, articular surfaces. The upper extremity of the tibia joins with the lower extremity of the femur to form the knee joint, while the lower end articulates with the talus to form the ankle joint.

The fibula is a slender, narrow bone, lateral to the tibia. It bears no weight directly but supplements the tibia in giving elasticity and flexibility to the leg, affording attachment for the

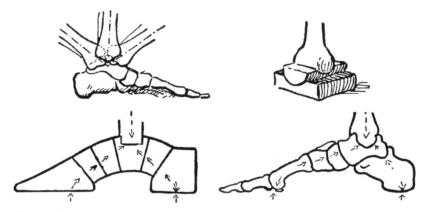

FIG. 50. Diagram suggesting action of forces at ankle joint, with extension and flexion of foot.

interosseous membrane and for important muscles of the leg and foot.

The interosseous membrane is composed of obliquely set fibers running between the borders of the tibia and fibula, and laces the two bones together much as the strings of a snowshoe connect its two sides.

THE ANKLE AND FOOT

The facts that weight is transmitted to the foot at a right angle and that motion and adaptability are required, as well as support for a relatively huge load, necessitate an extremely strong and flexible mechanism, which the arch-like structure of the foot provides. (See Fig. 50.)

The tibia is articulated with the foot at the talus, the large central ankle bone, forming a hinge-joint. Motion is quite free forward and backward, but is strictly limited from side to side by the downward extension of the tibia on the inner surface and of the fibula on the outer. These extensions, the internal and external malleoli, or little hammers, are the most visible parts of the ankle joint.

All weight passes directly to the talus, whence it is distributed to the twenty-five other bones of the foot, which are arranged in a series of arches.

The talus rests upon the heel bone, or calcaneus, which is the largest bone of the foot, and, extending toward the back and front, makes a platform to receive the entire weight of the body and transmit it to the ground. The weight coming through the talus to the calcaneus is distributed through three distinct articular surfaces, sloping in different directions, one to the back and side, and two to the front. The talus is attached by short ligamentous fibers to the four bones with which it is articulated: the tibia, the fibula, the calcaneus and the navicularis, but it has neither muscles nor tendons inserted into it. It is a free bone and is kept in place like any keystone by the pressure of the bones abutting on it, and the slant of the articular surfaces.

Immediately in front of the talus is the navicularis, with three wedge-shaped bones, the cuneiforms, in front of it. In front of the forward projection of the calcaneus is the cuboid, a six-sided bone. All seven bones just described are irregularly shaped blocks and together form the tarsus, or the essential weight-bearing part of the foot. The main longitudinal arch of the foot consists of the calcaneus, forming one side; the talus, forming the keystone; and all the other bones of the tarsus to the front, making up the other side. Radiating from the tarsus are the five metatarsals, long bones with definite heads and ends, to which are attached the phalanges of the toes, two in the big toe and three each in the others. These serve to counter the thrust of weight coming through the bones of the arch.

This extremely brief description barely indicates the intricate structure of the feet, by which fifty-two small bones are enabled not only to support the weight of the entire body, but to move it about with swiftness and assurance.

BALANCE AND STRENGTH OF LEGS AND FEET

The legs, each with its three long bones, are more nearly straight than any other part of the skeleton, but they are not straight, nor does the weight travel through them vertically.

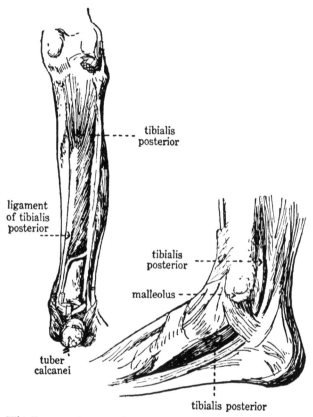

FIG. 51. Tibialis posterior muscle. Note its tendon as it bends under inner maleolus. (Redrawn after Spalteholz.)

The best balance and easiest transfer of weight is secured by keeping the various joints flexible, especially at the knee, and controlling the momentum from above, in thigh, pelvis, and lumbar joints.

Just as the femur is controlled and moved by muscles arising far up the trunk and along the spine, so the bones of the lower leg are controlled by muscles arising well up the femur, or even higher. And the even more delicate bones and joints of the foot are controlled by the long muscles of the leg. Their balanced use reduces strain on all the intervening joints.

Especially important in keeping the axis of weight centered in all the foot bones is the double fan-shaped tibialis posterior. This muscle, the most central of all the leg muscles, arises along both bones of the lower leg, from the inner borders of the tibia and the fibula, and the posterior surface of the interosseous membrane. Its fibers converge into a long and strong tendon that passes downward and around the ankle below the inner malleolus, to insert into the navicularis, with fan-like prolongations to all the other tarsal bones except the talus, and to the bases of the four outer metatarsals. This gives it radial control.

THE SHOULDER GIRDLE AND ARMS

The upper extremities, like the lower, are parts of the appendicular skeleton; that is, they are accessory to the axial or trunk skeleton, which developed long before the ancestors of the amphibian tried to come onto the land. The accessory character is emphasized here because we are accustomed to give the shoulders, arms and hands first place in our thoughts, quite naturally, considering that our effective work and relations with the outside world are carried on through their instrumentality.

The shoulder girdle is a bony, yoke-like arrangement, hung across the top of the thoracic cage. It is not attached directly to the spine at any place; the only bony connection is through the sternum, which is connected with the spinal column by means of the ribs. Developmentally, the shoulders and arms start as folds and projections from the muscular body-wall, and the bony framework forms within the so-called "limb-buds," only gradually extending toward the axial skeleton.

The shoulder girdle is variable in its relation to the axial skeleton, even among the higher vertebrates, and is never connected to it so securely or directly as is the pelvic girdle. For example, in the horse the shoulder blade is in front rather than at the side-back of the thorax.

The girdle serves as a support for the arms, which are fitted into it by ball-and-socket joints. It provides attachments for the many radially disposed muscles by which the arms are moved in all planes. The whole design is such as to enable the arms to move freely and powerfully in a wide range without bringing any pressure to bear on the upper part of the chest where the heart and lungs are situated.

A glance at Figure 52, will show that the shoulder girdle hangs quite free of the rib-cage, through the greater part of its extent. The triangular or shield-shaped scapulae hang at the sides of the chest rather than at the back, the apices pointing downward, and the vertebral borders resting lightly against the rib-cage at the dorsal angles and parallel to them. At the upper, lateral corner of each scapula are two projections curved toward the front, the upper one known as the acromion and the lower as the coracoid process. In the front, at the base of the coracoid, is the glenoid cavity, a shallow, cup-like socket, into which the head of the humerus fits. The glenoid cavity is overhung by the acromion and the coracoid. Also the shoulder joint is further protected on all sides by the heavy muscles and ligaments attached to the scapular projections.

The clavicle, with dissimilar ends and a long, twisted body, extends from the scapula to the sternum. Each clavicle is attached to the sternum by its thick, squarish end at the top of the manubrium, in a strong capsular-ligamentous joint. This joint is provided with an elastic buffer in the form of an articular disc of fibrocartilage, interposed between the cartilaginous end of the clavicle and the manubrium, making it in effect two joints. This arrangement serves to break the shock from blows on shoulder, arm or hand, which otherwise might be communicated to the sternum, and thus to the thoracic cavity. The flat, outer end of each clavicle articulates with the scapula at the acromion through a rather small, oval surface and a weak capsular ligament, allowing considerable movement.

The clavicle furnishes the only bony connection of the shoulders and arms with the trunk. Its mechanical function is to give side support to the shoulder joint for the wide and varied move-

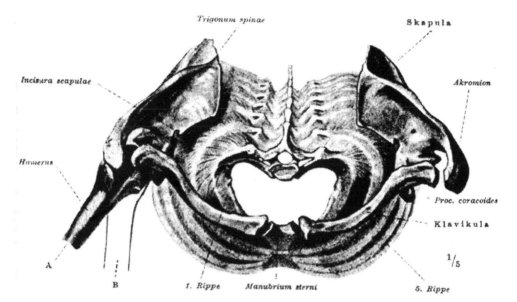

Trigonum spinae

Skapula

Incisura scapulae

Akromion

Humerus

Proc. coracoides

Klavikula

$^1/_5$

A

B

1. Rippe

Manubrium sterni

5. Rippe

Fig. 52. Shoulder girdle from above. Seen from upper entrance of thorax. Natural position of bones. Humerus, raised toward horizontal, is here abducted, through free movement in shoulder joint, from A to B, about 30°. (From Braus.)

The vertebral borders of the scapulae are shown as they balance in parallel planes with the dorsal angles of the ribs. Note the depth of the gutter of the spine and the heart-shaped entrance of the thorax. Large portions of the lungs lie within these dorsal cavities. The entire shoulder girdle is seen as separate from the rib-cage, except at the attachments of the clavicles with the sternum. Observe that the scapula and the clavicle together form a protecting and supporting roof over the shoulder joint.

ments of the arm. It acts like a yard-arm, keeping the shoulder-joint free from the chest, and has a definite though limited action in itself.

The arms are attached to the scapulae by ball-and-socket joints, the heads of the humeri fitting into the glenoid cavities. The glenoid socket is distinctly shallower than the acetabulum, and the capsular ligament is very loose, so that the arms are allowed a freer motion than the thighs.

In the evolution of the higher vertebrates, the clavicle developed with the need for arm movements of more range than that required for simple support and progression, and is today found in its strongest form in those creatures which climb or fly. The protective function of this part of the shoulder mechanism is to keep the scapulae and arms away from the upper chest, where their weight and movements might seriously interfere with the important respiratory, circulatory and nervous structures, within the area enclosed by the first four ribs. The importance of this was stressed in the earlier description of the thorax, the structure of which is also adapted for this protection. The shape, direction and manner of articulation of the clavicle and the nature of the joints and muscular attachments for the arms enhance the protective value of the mechanism at the top of the rib-cage. The arm is removed from the spine by five articulations: at the glenoid, the acromial-clavicular, the clavicular-sternal, between the first rib and sternum, and between the first rib and its vertebra. This is the only bony-articular route between arm and spine. Moreover the direction of the clavicle as it joins the sternum is such as to transmit any shock that passes the first three barriers to the whole length of the sternum, where it can be shared by all the ten pairs of ribs attached to it.

The relative proportions of the tops of the thorax and the shoulder girdle are shown in Figure 52, which pictures the trunk from above. Note that the first ribs occupy just a third of the transverse diameter of the body at the shoulder girdle, and that the shoulder girdle, hanging easily, overlaps the thorax for only a small distance, including not more than a third of the scapula and less than half of the clavicle.

WHEEL-LIKE DISTRIBUTION OF SHOULDER AND ARM MUSCLES

The length of the arms in relation to the small area of articulation at their joints requires a special provision for strength in the attachments. This would be true even if the arms only hung idly from their sockets and were not formed for a wide range of activities and motions. The muscle power must be applied so as to operate through as many arcs as the range and direction of movements require. This is accomplished by a wheel-like design whereby muscles attached through great distances over many surfaces of the skeletal framework converge about the shoulder joint.

Nearly every bone in the trunk, from occiput to pelvis, furnishes surfaces for the attachments of muscles which are also attached to some portion of the shoulder apparatus, either on various surfaces of the scapula or immediately about its joint with the humerus. These shoulder and arm muscles extend in all directions—to the head, around the rib-cage from spine to sternum, through the entire length of the back, are attached to every vertebra from the axis to the sacrum, to the strong muscle bands of the front abdominal wall, and to the pelvis.

It is this wheel-like arrangement of lines of muscle force through all planes which gives such enormous power to the arms and hands, not alone in doing heavy work, in lifting, throwing, carrying and pulling, but also in the control of delicately centered movements of the hands and fingers.

Among the larger and more obvious superficial muscles concerned in furnishing arm and shoulder power, four groups may be selected as illustrations.

The trapezius and the latissimus dorsi muscles together range over the whole area of the back, extending from the center line of the spine downward and upward, from pelvis to occiput, and laterally to the scapulae and the arms; while the pectorals and the serratus muscles converge from the front and sides of the thorax to the scapulae and arms. At their origins and along their courses, these muscles are associated with all the outer muscles of the body-wall. They have many relationships with the inner muscles of the trunk, pelvis and thighs, which are

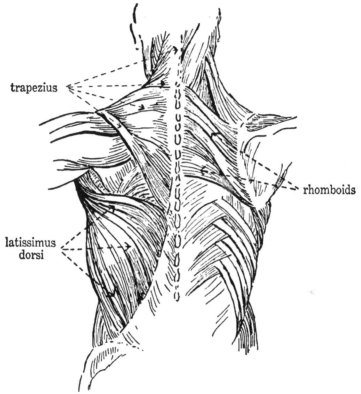

trapezius

rhomboids

latissimus
dorsi

FIG. 53. Executive muscles of the back. Latissimus dorsi is like a hand, enfolding body with thumb ending in arm. (Redrawn after Harrison Allen.)

concerned with the maintenance of the axial framework of support and of the upright carriage. (See Fig. 53.)

The trapezius is sometimes called the "shawl muscle" because of its general double triangular shape and the way in which it covers the neck and shoulders and the middle of the back. It arises from ligaments attached to the skull and all the cervical and thoracic vertebrae. It inserts into the acromion and along the shelf-like dorsal projection called the spine of the scapula. It also inserts into the lateral, or acromial, end of the clavicle. This range of attachments indicates the extent and diversified action of the trapezius. The various portions of the trapezius act to draw the head backward, to pull the scapula toward the midline, and also to rotate it so as to raise its outer end. It is balanced in front by the sterno-cleido-mastoideus muscle, a double suspensory structure between the sternum and clavicle and the head, which serves to draw the head forward and also to rotate it.

The latissimus dorsi has a distribution similar to that of the trapezius in the way in which it arises from the spine and is wrapped around the trunk. It arises in tendinous origins from the dorsal spinous processes of the six lowest thoracic vertebrae (the seventh through the twelfth) and from the intervening interspinous ligaments beneath the origins of the trapezius in the same vertebrae, and from the lumbodorsal fascia, and from the posterior portion of the crest of the ilium. These attachments are supplemented by fleshy digitations from the outer surfaces of the three or four lowest ribs. This makes the muscle enfold much of the heavier portions of the body-wall. Its fibers converge upward and laterally, gradually assuming a horizontal direction at the level of the sixth thoracic, where they pass beneath the muscle bundles of the trapezius. They then travel around the thorax, over the inferior surface of the scapula, and insert by a flat tendon into the axillary aspect of the humerus, just below its head. They are like large hands, enfolding the body wall, with thumbs inserted into the arms.

The placement and function of the latissimus dorsi should be understood and borne in mind, since the muscle has an important effect in the production of strains imposed on the body by arm movements. By intelligent correction, through it, reduction of strains may be accomplished.

The trapezius and the latissimus dorsi muscles overlap at one area of their origins from the lowest six thoracic vertebrae. This overlapping affords a balance in opposition of pull upon the vertebrae to which they are attached, holding them in place. If they balance each other in opposition in this area of common origin, the peripheral action of both is steadied, so that gross

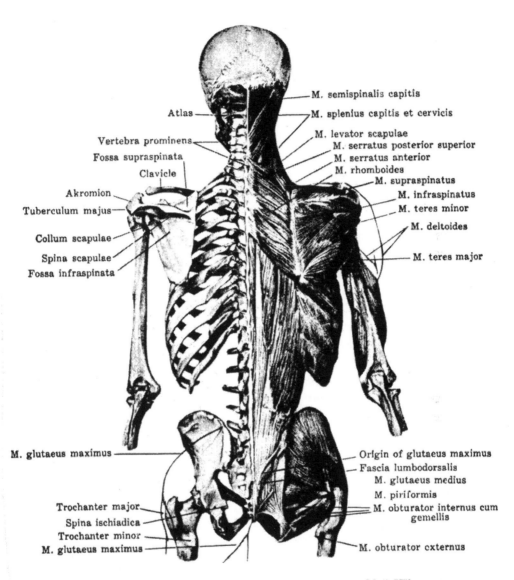

Atlas

Vertebra prominens
Fossa supraspinata
Clavicle

Akromion
Tuberculum majus

Collum scapulae
Spina scapulae
Fossa infraspinata

M. semispinalis capitis
M. splenius capitis et cervicis
M. levator scapulae
M. serratus posterior superior
M. serratus anterior
M. rhomboides
M. supraspinatus
M. infraspinatus
M. teres minor
M. deltoides
M. teres major

M. glutaeus maximus

Trochanter major
Spina ischiadica
Trochanter minor
M. glutaeus maximus

Origin of glutaeus maximus
Fascia lumbodorsalis
M. glutaeus medius
M. piriformis
M. obturator internus cum gemellis
M. obturator externus

FIG. 54. Deep muscles of back, showing several deep shoulder and pelvic muscles. Natural form and position. Serratus posterior inferior and fascia lumbodorsalis are removed. (From Braus.)

activity of either of these muscles does not disturb the spine at the important area of redirection of weight from the thoracic to the lumbar region.

Steadiness of the shoulder and chest regions, even with the most powerful excentric action of the arms, is assured by the way in which muscles operate to support and unite the underlying structures. The muscular pulls on the superimposed structures should be balanced also. The scapulae are supported from the midline of the spine at the lower cervical and upper thoracic vertebrae by the rhomboids, minor and major, that extend in relatively short bands diagonally disposed between the spinous processes and adjoined ligaments and the dorsal side of the vertebral borders of the scapulae. The action of the rhomboids is sling-like, allowing the scapulae to move sidewise freely, while still being supported steadily. Their action is balanced in the front by the serratus anterior, which extends between the anterior surface of the first eight or nine ribs and the ventral side of the vertebral border of the scapulae, and by the pectoralis minor, which extends between the upper ribs (second to fifth) and the coracoid process of the scapulae. The tensile forces of these muscles are balanced by vertical compression forces through the scapulae.

The serratus anterior covers the lateral walls of the thorax, arising by fleshy digitations from the first eight or nine ribs, and runs back to the scapula, where it is attached to the ventral side, along its vertebral border. In general appearance, it resembles a spread hand, reaching around the chest from the shoulder blade, grasping the ribs under the breasts.

The pectoralis minor arises from the anterior surface of the second, third, fourth and fifth ribs and passes upward and laterally to insert into the coracoid process of the scapula. Its action, balanced with that of the rhomboids, releases the larger, more superficial muscles for free and powerful leverage.

The pectoralis major, a large, fan-shaped muscle, lying over the pectoralis minor, is the covering of the whole upper chest wall in front, really constituting what we proudly call our "broad chest." It has three portions: the clavicular, the sternal and the abdominal, arising respectively from the clavicle, from the sternum and cartilages of the first six ribs, and from the upper part of the sheath of the rectus abdominis. All fibers

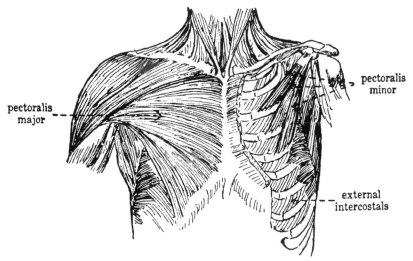

FIG. 55. Front chest muscles. (Redrawn after Toldt.)

converge laterally and insert into the humerus, near the joint. In action it antagonizes the trapezius.

All these radial muscles around the shoulder joint are interrelated in their specific action and also act together with other structures in maintaining the vertical axis of the supporting or axial skeleton. Through their own overlapping, and their connections with the deep-lying muscles of the spine pulling on the opposite side of the vertebrae to which they are attached, these muscles reach in effect throughout the entire longitudinal axis of the body, into the legs.

Through this arrangement, the effect of the movements of the arms is carried into the legs, to the feet, where weight is received and recoil absorbed. In this manner, the stance is made secure by means of integration of action of spine, foot and pelvis, in such activities as throwing a ball or cranking a car. This interrelationship of parts throughout the axial skeleton furnishes strength for renewed and continued activity.

The overlapping of the latissimus dorsi by the trapezius, between the sixth and twelfth thoracic vertebrae, marks the region where the spinal curve is redirected from the thoracic concavity to the lumbar convexity. The upward pull exerted by the trapezius upon the spinous process is balanced by the powerful pull of the psoas muscle on the body of the twelfth thoracic vertebra. In this same area, the crural arch of the diaphragm and the arcuate ligaments offer another opposing force about the connecting structures, since they are attached at the inner surface of the twelfth vertebra and the floating ribs, opposing those attached at the outer surfaces, the trapezius and latissimus dorsi.

If these opposing pulls of deep-lying and superficial muscles are in balance, integrity of the spinal curves is assured. If not balanced, the upward pull on the outer surfaces of these vertebrae produced by shoulder-structure muscles will interfere with the redirection of the thoracic curve, which must be made from the back forward to the lumbar spine at this point. With the axis of the spine secure, recoil from arm movements is absorbed in the pelvis and legs, and no disturbance of body balance in stance is felt.

SHOULDER MECHANICS

If allowed free play, the shoulder girdle gives the best service, as it maintains its balance more effectively in motion. It is suspended, distributing part of its load to the cervical spine and to the head, as its suspensory attachments enable it to do. This accomplishes two things: it helps to give secure balance to the head on the atlas, and at the same time converts what otherwise might be an unfavorable side-load on the spine to a top-load, which is the best type of load for a curved, flexible upright to carry.

The shoulder girdle should adjust itself to every movement of the arms. Never, in motion or at rest, should it be allowed to sink its weight upon the rib-cage at any point. The first four ribs should be easily movable, within their appointed limits, to the side, back and front under this superstructure. The rib

freedom was demonstrated to perfection by Shan Kar's dancing, showing the central movement of the head and spine and
their deep rotation inside the superimposed shoulder structure. This could be accomplished only with flexible ribs under
a free shoulder girdle.

Freedom for all muscular attachments of the clavicles and
scapulae gives breadth to the shoulders and brings the bony
tip of the scapula, known as the acromion, directly above the
median line of the ribs at each side. This balances the action of
the arm and shoulder muscles and distributes their pull equally
in the direction of the spine, sternum, head and hips. This is
accomplished via the suspensory muscles and the latissimus
dorsi.

To repeat, the arm and its muscles are related to each other
somewhat like the hub and the crossed layers of spokes in a
wire wheel. If the action of any of the spokes is impaired by
unequal pulls, the whole mechanism suffers. If the arms hang
free from well-balanced scapulae, so that the acromion is above
the middle line of the ribs, the vertebral borders of the scapulae
will assume their normal, parallel alignment with the dorsal
angles of the ribs. If, on the contrary, the scapulae are held
rigidly up and back, pressing their dorsal borders upon the
rib-cage, as directed by the old military usage, they lose this
alignment. The pull then comes on the deep neck and throat
muscles and unbalances the entire wheel of shoulder and arm
muscles. This interferes with the free motion of the clavicles.
It pulls them backward and upward and presses them upon the
top ribs at the front, just above the connecting cartilages. These
structures, the ribs together with the sternum, must be held up
by muscles from the head to help balance the thorax.

The position of the shoulder girdle is similar to that of the
yoke by which the Hollanders carry their water pails: the arms
swing freely in their sockets in line with the crests of the ilia.
This position allows freedom of motion at both the sternal and
the vertebral ends of the top three pairs of ribs and insures
greater freedom and protection in this portion of the thorax for
the functioning of the blood vessels, especially about the aortic

arch, where the blood starts on its course from the heart through the circulatory mechanism. It is important also to free the apices of the lungs, which are located at the back, in the upper part of

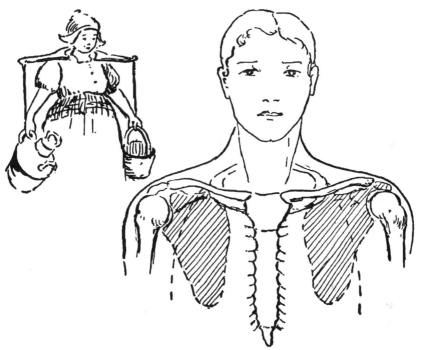

FIG. 56. Shoulder girdle. Rib cage removed. Note yoke-like balance of girdle.

the cavities formed by the first three ribs and between their dorsal angles. These spaces may be crowded by a tilted position of the ribs due to uneven pressure of the scapulae and clavicles.

With this outline of the mechanics of our working skeleton, we can better understand how to use it efficiently in our everyday living. We can see how by allowing it to carry us about our affairs with minimum expenditure of effort, it can continue to fulfill its primary function of protection for the delicate vital organs and processes of our physical and mental life.

To accomplish these aims, a practical philosophy of thinking in relation to structural needs and functions must be encouraged. This furnishes an approach to Structural Hygiene.

Chapter VI

BALANCING FORCES TO STAND ERECT

STANCE

THE STANCE OF THE GOLF OR TENNIS STAR, THE BASEBALL PITCHER, THE BOXER, THE SPRINTER, IDENTIFIES HIM. THESE positions, expressing a given activity, are alert and ready. Preparation for action brings with it an emotional expectation that alters the whole situation from that of passively standing still, as when being fitted by a tailor or waiting for a car. This is hard work; we do not take part in any active way, and as there is no preparation to make, we can do nothing about it. Expectancy is not present, but boredom is, with an accompanying sag of the whole musculature.

But one can, on occasion, with little fatigue, wait for admission to a race track or a theater, and with still less fatigue can stand spellbound watching a play or a game or listening to music. Interest and absorbed attention produce an undertone of excitement that quickens the circulation, heightens the blood pressure, and increases muscular tonus. The venous blood is more speedily returned to the heart, and a fresh supply of blood to the brain decreases the tendency toward faintness, so often experienced in the more passive condition.

The player or fighter stands ready for action, watching his opponent, breathing deeply and steadily, his whole body poised, on the very edge of the unbalance that will mark his take-off at the official command to go.

The baby learning to stand is also playing an exciting game; he is preparing to walk, and by repeated, apparently tireless efforts, keeps on trying until he learns to balance on his two feet. After many bumps, he acquires an upright stability, and with it courage to venture forth, hesitantly but persistently, into that great adventure—walking. How pleased he is when his goal, the waiting knee or hand, is reached! Walking is the first of his great motor skills and the budding of that same spirit of adventure that carries him later into football, baseball and tennis.

Ease in walking depends upon knowledge and practice of the centered posture. The baby learns how to change both his thinking and his doing through trial and error and the use of his imagination. Repetition brings success. In later life any defect in posture will, to the extent of the defect, detract from the ease, grace and efficiency of the movement. For defective posture entails habitually strained muscles and a lack of balance of the bones at the joints. A disturbed kinesthesia and unbalance in the proprioceptive system follow closely in this trail.

The first requisite, therefore, in learning to perfect our carriage for all activities is to understand and to secure a well-integrated position while standing, in which muscles are free from habits of holding weights off center. Neither beautiful walking nor dancing can be grafted into a crooked body. They must grow out of an efficient use of the whole structure, with centered relationships and parts free to respond in mechanical reaction, whether the weights are hanging, sitting or braced.

WEIGHT-BEARING AND DISTRIBUTION IN THE UPRIGHT POSITION

In the upright position, the entire weight of the pelvis and all the parts above it rests or sits on the heads of the femora. Gravity is met effectively when the upward thrust of the legs at the thigh-joints is centered. To insure its being so centered, it is important to understand the manner in which weight is passed through the pelvis to the thigh-joints and the relative functions of the surrounding parts. The legs are the prime movers. They must "get there" slightly in advance of the weight they are to carry; that is, the weights of the trunk and head. This is equally true in standing and in walking. Force and direction of movement must be initiated at the hip-joint, in response to change of head balance, with a follow-through in shoulders, spine and pelvis. Thus a coordinated movement is attained. Free, easy movement of the hip-joints and of the legs is maintained by keeping the muscles of the pelvis active. This is necessary as the whole structure serves as a shock absorber.

The pelvis is fundamentally the base of weight support. An organism once on four legs has lifted itself to two with a resultant change in weight transference in all its joints. This strange adjustment necessitated a great change in the coordination of the muscles as they acted upon the bones.

The animal on all-fours need have little concern with balance. In his reactions to his environment, his every position favors development of the basic muscles used for crouch and spring. These are the lower lumbar, pelvic and thigh groups, and their power and spring-like adjustment result in easy control of body-weights. Control of movements as well as of attitudes of the body lies in these basic structures. The ribs, shoulders and head are thus freed for the quick responses and fine adjustments needed in eating and breathing, in smelling, hearing, feeling, and other sensory functions. At ease, the body has a pose for smelling, a pose for hearing when the ear is attentive, a pose for seeing when the eye is awake, and many poses for starting and guiding the more expansive activities in locomotion.

Man has become absorbed with the upper portions of the body in intellectual pursuits and in the development of skill of hand and speech. This, in addition to false notions regarding appearance or health, has transferred his sense of power from the base to the top of his structure. In thus using the upper part of the body for power reactions he has reversed the animal usage and has to a great extent lost both the fine sensory capacity of the animal and its control of power centered in the lower spinal and pelvic muscles. These are the crouch muscles, which should still be employed for spring or take-off and for shock absorption.

The pelvic zone is the focus for attachments of muscles used for standing, sitting, walking and riding horseback. The deep iliopsoas muscles, which attach the legs to the inner sides of the spine, and the strong abdominal muscles, which fasten to the pelvic rim and run up in front to the ribs and the breastbone, must act together as tensile members to hold the pelvis in position to receive the weight passing to it from the sacrum.

There must be balance between the upward pull of the tensile members in front and the downward compression forces operating through the back. In this short pelvic cantilever these forces must be balanced. We recall that the tensile members and the compression members in a cantilever must be equal and opposite. So if the action of the tensile members of the front body wall and of the front of the spine is not sufficient to equal the compression forces traveling from spine to pelvis, the tensile members at the back of the spine will have to make up this difference. The increased tension in the muscles and ligaments of the posterior aspect of the spine would tend to unseat the load at the sacrum and open up the sides of the pelvic arch at the keystone. These muscles are extensors of the spine; their function is to pull down and back, not up and forward.

The weights of the legs and thorax are pulled together in the pelvis. If we are to manage our bodies intelligently, the terms "ilium," "sacrum," "pubic arch" and "ischium," must become as familiar to us as those of "collarbone," "breastbone" or "jaw-bone" and their relative positions must be understood. Muscles attached to the pelvis from its inside and outside and along its various ridges run up to the neck, out to the arms, down through the thighs to the legs below the knee, and all about and through the abdominal wall. In this way, most of the large muscles of the body are ingeniously drawn together and attached where all can be brought under organized control at the base.

VERTICAL SUPPORTS FOR THE HORIZONTAL BODY

In the four-legged position, as noted before, body-weights hang vertically from the horizontal spine. The weight divides somewhere in the center of the back, and is then transferred, part forward to the forelegs and part backward to the hind legs. The weights supported by the spine rest upon the posterior facets of each vertebra, and at the hind-end the accumulated bulk finally comes upon the posterior facets of the sacrum. The weight-thrust there divides and follows through the pelvic bones on either side to the center of the acetabulum, or thigh-joint,

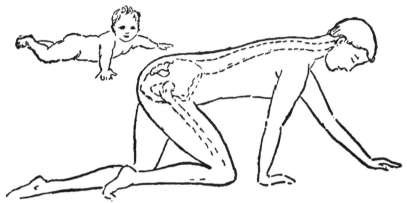

Fig. 57. Four-legged position, using crouch and leg muscles for pulling body backwards, reversing crawl.

and thence to the head of the femur. The horse pulls his load by the strength of his hind quarters; he "pulls," but the pull is actually a push since he does it by pushing his hind legs on the ground and his whole weight forward against the harness. Thighs and hips have the heaviest bones, strongest muscles and fewest articulations.

VERTICAL SUPPORT FOR THE UPRIGHT BODY

In man, the hips and thighs support the heaviest loads, the total of all body-weight resting upon and being moved by them. Thus, as the lion and tiger leap by the power of the strong muscles moving these basic bones, man should also center and move from his base of power.

Anatomists tell us that the hip-joints are 6 or 7 inches apart and well toward the front of the pelvis. But most of us do not commonly think of them that way because our kinesthetic sense does not always agree with our book knowledge, even if we are students of anatomy.

A medical friend used to delight in introducing me to various members of his hospital staff, just for the fun of seeing their confusion when I asked them this particular question: "Doctor, will you do me a favor? Close your eyes and see how quickly you can respond to my command: Raise your hands—thumbs straight—thumbs on hip-joints—quick!" This trick has been tried many times through the years, and unless we had just been talking about skeletal balance, without fail it brought laughter as their thumbs were placed at their sides and then rather sheepishly moved around toward the front when their mistake was realized. Thumbs always landed somewhere in the mid-lateral line of the ilia, ranging variously from the crests down to the posterior level of the greater trochanters of the femora, and never by any chance a hand-span apart at the front of the pelvic girdle where these joints actually are.

Where is the discrepancy—in kinesthesia, in balance of parts, or in thinking? To be sure, sensations of movement are more acute about the greater trochanter, because it is here that the first impulse to movement begins, in the contractions of muscles pulling the thigh away from center. Moreover, the greater trochanter is near the surface and is both palpable and visible. The head of the femur, however, moves imperceptibly, sliding about in its smooth container. Here it is that the weight is supported and transferred.

STRAINED "HIGH CHESTS"

Man, ignorant of the principles underlying bodily economy, has raised his sense of power from the base, and has raised with it his center of gravity. He has formed expensive habits of using organic energy. The result of this may be seen by the way in which the adult habitually reacts to the suggestion to "stand straight." He responds (because of his own conditioned reflexes) by doing various, and often grotesque, things with the upper parts of his body. As before noted, he thrusts back his shoulders, lifts and expands his lower ribs, pulls in his chin, and stiffens his neck.

This strained high-chested position can be produced only by the action of chest and shoulder muscles pulling toward the neck. The contraction of these muscles attached to the outer ends of the ribs, pulls them upward and forward, instead of allowing them to hang easily as they should from the head and from their bony attachments at the thoracic spine.

The mass of chest weight is thus displaced from its alignment with the head and pelvis. The spine must make corresponding adjustments. Mechanically, this would not be of such importance if these upper muscles that are doing the work were themselves attached to the head. In this event the ribs would make a top-load on the spine, via the head, where they could be carried more easily. But, as the working muscles are diagonally disposed at the sides of the neck and upper thorax, the load has merely been lifted higher on the column and is still a sideload, but more unfavorable than before because of its height. This position not only produces bending tendencies in the spine but raises the center of gravity of the mass too high on the supporting structure for easy carriage.

Further bodily unbalance results from trying to get a "high chest" in this way, affecting the entire trunk as follows:

When the lower end of the sternum is drawn forward by the action of raising and expanding the lower ribs, the upper end is depressed. The depression may not be perceptible externally, but it results in unfavorable depression being produced by the bony manubrium upon the first pair of ribs and the soft parts beneath, interfering with the circulation in this important area. Since the lower ribs, being more mobile and longer, have greater leverage than the upper ones, the upper end of the sternum is pressed backward and downward with a force proportional to the lift of the lower end, though little movement is felt at the top. The whole effect is to reduce the antero-posterior diameter of the upper chest, between the manubrium and the first three thoracic vertebrae.

The compactness of the upper abdominal region is lost, and visceral support suffers when the ribs are lifted and spread in front, and the costal angle is widened. The abdominal cavity, topped by the diaphragm, lies well up under the lower ribs, as high as the ventral level of the sixth rib. The ribs and thoracic spine help to form a firm and flexible wall of support for important organs lying in the upper abdominal region and suspended from this part of the spine. These include the liver, stomach, pancreas, spleen and the greater part of the kidneys and transverse colon.

The undesirable changes in chest balance, with their sequels, are produced by the pull of various muscles connecting the shoulders and rib-cage, for example: the arms pull through the latissimus dorsi, the shoulder girdle pulls through the pectoralis, trapezius and rhomboids, and the neck mainly through the trapezius The upper muscles thus combine to carry loads that could and should be carried at the vertebral levels of each pair of ribs, that is, at the twelve levels of their attachments to the thoracic vertebrae.

An extra burden is placed upon the spine by this high side-load situation, since these same weights must pass downward again through the spinal levels from which they have been pulled. The added load places unnecessary strains upon the spine in the upper thoracic and cervical regions and tends to bend it at its weakened points. Since the thorax is held out of alignment in relation to the other main units of body-weight (the head and the pelvis), increased lordosis of lumbar and cervical regions will also result.

The entire upper structure bends forward at the tenth to the twelfth thoracic vertebrae, from the fatigue of holding the chest high and out of alignment, thus throwing added strain upon that section of the spine where the weight must be redirected. From the tenth thoracic to the fourth lumbar, muscles must function to help integrate the curves of the spine to meet the shearing stress incident to the double action of the downcoming load and upward thrust of the supporting bones where the weight is being directed forward upon the lumbar curve. Since the two forces are acting on a slant, they must be made to meet as directly as possible within the bodies of the vertebrae, so that balance of the spine may be retained.

Finally, if the muscles of the lower spine are stretched, the seating of the load upon the sacrum at the fifth lumbar contact is jeopardized, and the obliquity of the pelvis is exaggerated.

Rigidity of the chest produces all these results. Each change of an individual part throws greater responsibility upon an adjoining part. This places muscles under unnecessary strain throughout the structure. To avoid this sequence the body must function so that the compression members at the back and the tensile members at the front balance their action, thus securing a long axis to the spine.

THE DESIRABLE HIGH CHEST

The anterior and posterior walls of the chest are symmetrical, as well as the sides, and this symmetry should prevail in arrangement of parts in the vertical alignment of the structure. While avoiding the stiff, faulty posture, we must not favor a slumped chest, but a symmetrical one. The curve of the dorsal aspect of the sternum and the curve of the ventral aspect of the spine are symmetrical in their structural design. We should take this into account in our thinking.

For balanced symmetry of the upper chest cavity, the manubrium at the top of the sternum must be high and well forward, and the antero-posterior depth of the chest at the level of the first three ribs must be as great as possible. Depth at this level is important for the best functioning of the upper structures of the nervous and vascular systems and of the apices of the lungs situated within the cavity of the dorsal angle of these ribs, in the upper part of those deep spaces on either side of the spine.

The antero-posterior depth can be maintained only by the vertical elevation of the sternum controlled at the top. Pull up the sternum toward the head! The first two pairs of ribs approximate a horizontal position and act as strong, short braces between vertebrae and sternum. These are the only ribs that should be raised together with the sternum to retain the natural symmetry. They are raised mainly by muscles that travel directly to head and neck, and, acting as tensile members, support the top ribs and sternum to balance the compression members, the vertebrae, to which the ribs are attached. This also frees the intercostal muscles of the lower ribs.

The lower, more slanting ribs should have mobility to allow

the intercostal muscles to function freely in breathing. They should not be used to hold a rigid chest. Mobility here will free the spinal vertebrae at the levels of the rib attachments. The

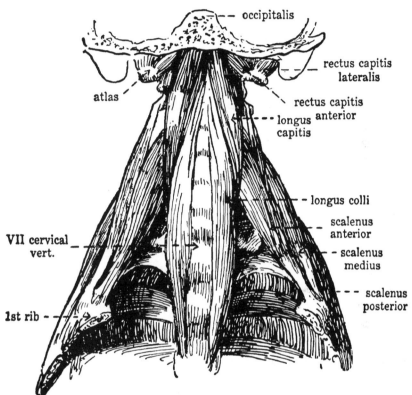

FIG. 58. Deep muscles of neck from front. Vertical spinal group in cervical region corresponds to psoas group in lumbar region. (Redrawn after Spalteholz.)

result is a more complete functioning of all spinal muscles in making small adjustments in response to breathing and in balancing weight.

Imagine your chest a bird-cage, containing a perch too short, from side to side. From the inside, pull in the wires to catch it. At the same time, *expire* through the teeth, like a hissing snake. *Hissing* aids the centering muscles to reduce the lateral diameter of the ribs. This forces the manubrium upward, deepening the cavity at the three top ribs.

By narrowing the lateral diameter of the chest, from arm-pit to arm-pit, the cross-pulls in the spinal muscles in the area of the dorsal angles of the ribs are reduced, the spaces of the gutter of the spine are deepened, and the spinal muscles are freed for individual action. These muscles must act not only longitudinally in large movements requiring trunk extension, but must so function that they will at the same time allow the action of all small parts to aid the four opposing spinal curves successfully to meet gravity and to respond in breathing.

The end-result of narrowing the transverse diameter of the rib-cage is to lift the manubrium and force it forward. The balanced symmetry of the upper chest cavity is thus established, since the curve of the upper thoracic spine is nearly equal to the curve of the upper sternum. The lower ribs, which slant forward at a far greater inclination than the upper three, hang easily from their main support, the spine, a favorable arrangement not only for their own flexibility but for freedom of the diaphragm. Protection of the upper chest contents from mechanical strains is thus insured, and the intercostal muscles may than respond fully in the necessary small movements of breathing, giving them greater play. *"Play,"* remember, not *"hold."*

There is no successive "sitting" or resting of weights from head to pelvic rim through the front of the body, as there is in the back, and as there would be if there were continuous bony connections between the head and upper sternum, and between the lower end of the sternum and the pelvis. There being no bones filling these spaces, the weight of the entire front of the body is finally attached through soft tissues, tensile members, to the ribs and head, and to the vertebrae of the neck. Thus the weight hangs upon the vertebrae of the spine, the compression members, and is ultimately carried through them to the sacrum, the keystone of the pelvic arch.

By balancing the first three ribs between the sternum and the spine, the chest load is more equally distributed upon its suspensory mechanism which attaches it to the spine and head. Aided by the head and neck muscles which connect the ribs and sternum with the skull, via the hyoid, jaw, and mastoid bones, the weight of the chest is brought partially to a top-load. For reasons given before, a top-load is the easiest to carry. This is far from true of a side-load near the top. This top-load is borne

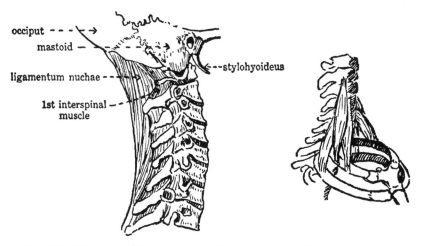

occiput - - -

mastoid —

ligamentum nuchae - -

1st interspinal —
muscle

stylohyoideus

FIG. 59. Side view of ligamentum nuchae, and stilohyoideus attachment for muscle. (Redrawn after Morris.) Side support of top ribs by scaleni muscles. (Redrawn after Mollier.)

finally by means of compression forces which travel via the vertebral bodies, down the spine to the pelvis. The front of the body-wall is composed mostly of tensile members, muscles, fascia and other soft tissues, and in their upward traction throughout the body-wall they should balance the compression members of the spine if the load is to be seated at the base effectively. They do this by a series of cantilevers acting from skull to pelvis. The thoracic cage and shoulder girdle are suspended from the head and neck by a tensile apparatus which includes the sternum, hyoid and mandible, and the weight is carried by the compression members of the spinal column. The pelvis is partly suspended from the thorax by the front-wall abdominal muscles. In these areas, however, the tensile members do no more than support the free ends of the cantilevers; they do not allow these to sag, nor do they pull them up from the horizontal. So the ribs, properly balanced, are neither collapsed nor pulled up, nor is the pelvic rim tilted up or down.

THE SHOULDER LOAD

The shoulders are the ends of a yoke, balanced across the narrow top of the chest cone and extending well beyond it. The only ligamentous connection of the shoulder girdle with the thorax is at the top of the sternum, where the clavicles are attached. Here it must be carefully balanced so that its weight cannot rest upon and depress the first ribs, which are attached just below it at the sides of the manubrium. This balance is achieved by suspensory muscles extending from head and neck to the scapulae in the back, and to the clavicles in front. This balance also is helped greatly by the bisymmetrical shape of the shoulder girdle.

The shoulder girdle is supported in two ways: directly, by suspensory muscles attaching it to the head and to the neck vertebrae, and indirectly via the sternum and the ribs by the compression members of the spine. Mechanical balance between these tensile members and compression members is essential to good functioning in this region.

The many muscles of the upper chest and shoulders used in the special activities of these parts, such as breathing, singing, typing, etc., should be freed insofar as possible from the strain of holding unbalanced bones.

This suspending apparatus has two mechanical advantages. First, the weights of the moving shoulders, arms and rib-cage are distributed over a considerable range of small separate attachments, easing the load and providing for more flexible motion in various directions than would be possible with any other type of support. Second, a considerable portion of the weight is converted into a top-load because it is transferred to the head. Here it is hung from the base of the skull, through many small but strong muscles running from the clavicle and sternum and attached to the hyoid and mandible bones, and to the mastoid and styloid processes. Since these structures are in line with the occipital condyles, the chest and shoulders are balanced with the head. As a result, the head is further stabilized in its balance on the spine, which in turn helps to stabilize the curves of the spine throughout the column. It is by virtue of these muscles, together with the upper jaw muscles and the

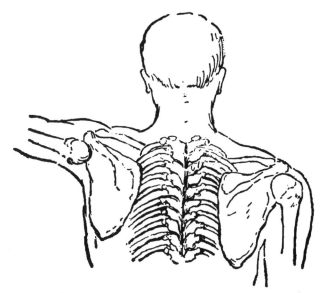

Fig. 60. Relation of shoulder blades to dorsal angles of ribs, when quiet and when in motion.

powerful temporal muscles, that the acrobat is enabled to hang by his teeth.

THE HOOP-SKIRT PATTERN

The type of suspension of the chest and shoulder loads upon the spine may be visualized by thinking of the old-fashioned hoop-skirts. They extended to the ground and consisted of three or four graduated circular hoops of whalebone or flexible metal, which were in turn suspended in an ingenious fashion from the waist by flat cloth bands attached alternately to the hoops, so that each hoop had a certain independence of motion, swaying and dipping with the movements of the lady within. Sometimes panniers were hung across the waist, extending well to each side, over which hung draperies (as often pictured by

Velasquez), repeating the shoulder girdle design in the human body.

The caricature of the hoop-skirt, as worn by the Red and White Queens in "Alice Through the Looking Glass," has its analogy in the stiffly held shoulders and thorax, which can move, not gracefully, but jerkily and "all of a piece."

BALANCING THE CHEST AND PELVIC LOADS

Pelvis and thorax belong together. They supply important parts of the protective body-wall, connected as they are at the back by the lumbar spine and at the sides and front by the abdominal muscles and their tendinous union at the mid-ventral line. The viscera are disposed vertically along the front of the spine, at the very center of the supporting framework, in such a fashion that they can carry on their vital processes without being disturbed by the outer activities of the skeletal structures. The protective wall must not be disturbed unnecessarily, or the placement of the organs at their several levels of support will be jeopardized and their functions possibly interfered with.

If pelvis, spine and ribs are so integrated along the spinal axis by their connecting muscles that the deep-set spinal column can lower all weight under control to the pelvis and pass it through the sacrum and forward to the femora, the body-wall will be able to retain its firmness and straight lines, without weakened, pendulous areas.

If the fourth and fifth lumbar vertebrae tend to sag forward, shear stress is produced between them, and the posterior spinal muscles, the erector spinae group, become tense and pull upon the sacrum in the effort to hold back the slipping load. The erector spinae muscles are extensors of the spine and should not pull in the opposite direction as in the kicking donkey. They should not pull up; they should pull down. All muscles at the front of the spine should pull up to balance the compression members in the spine. The increased lordosis produced by sagging of the pelvic bones at the front stretches the anterior universal ligament, the iliopsoas muscles, the crura of the diaphragm, and the ligaments of the anterior surfaces of the lumbosacral and sacroiliac joints. This sagging is finally communicated to the abdominal wall, and the balance between tensile and compression members is lost.

To balance the structure of the lower spine, it is necessary to maintain the control of the spinal load at the points of redirection of the curves, the most important being from the tenth to the twelfth thoracic and from the fourth lumbar to the area of the first two sacral vertebrae. Here is where the curves redirect the accumulating load.

These facts explain why standing is more difficult than walking. Persistent small but powerful movements must take place in lower spinal, pelvic and thigh joints in reaction to the unbalances caused by movements of the head, upper body, and arms. In fact, as the Red Queen told Alice, in Looking-Glass Land: "Now here, you see, it takes all the running you can do to keep in the same place."

ATTENTION STRAINS

We are seldom entirely idle when standing or sitting. Generally we are using our hands and focussing our eyes on some close activity such as reading, typing, drawing, using a microscope, etc. Such activities, tied up with mental concentration, are largely "unnatural," and have been superimposed by civilization. Hence they produce attitudes of strain, which the body automatically attempts to counteract by persistent movements of the trunk and legs. Without such counterbalancing, sag, shear, and often bending, result. As these tendencies persist, the unconscious attempts of the body to reduce the strains do not always suffice. A knowledge of structural balance from a mechanical point of view is necessary to be able to shift the units of weight more intelligently on the controlling spine. Thus we help nature to help herself.

"DOWN THE BACK" AND "UP THE FRONT"

If the spine is to move the body mechanism economically, all unnecessary pulls upon it by its attached members must be reduced. Then only can it pass the weight under control through the pelvis to the thigh joints. The femora catch the weight as it is delivered and alternately balance it back and forth in movement.

Fig. 61. Active sitting position.

The stiff bones, being compression members because they meet compression stresses successfully, and the muscles, being tensile members because they resist stretching, must balance each other. We should incorporate these facts into our thinking if we wish to keep the spinal axis long and straight and the weight economically disposed.

Put this knowledge into practice. Think *down* the back and *up* the front. Let the spine drag. Picture it extended like the dinosaur's tail, but keep the front wall of the body up. The spine travels the whole length of the back, while the whole front of the body is suspended from the spine and head, directly and indirectly, through connecting bone, muscle and other soft tissues. Thinking "up the front" of the body without lifting any of its bony parts will establish proper traction in the connecting muscles to keep the ends of all bones in the front of the body-wall at proper levels for a balance of weight at their spinal attachments. Thus tensile members at the front balance compression members at the back.

If the thorax and pelvis are in balance and the throat muscles and abdominal wall are firm, the small muscles and ligaments of the spine will maintain such a degree of curvature in each area as will make the whole spinal axis as long as possible. The longer the axis of a flexible, curved structure controlling weight, the greater the speed and power of movement. There is no waste movement of its weights in time-space. Thus all weight is passing downward through the shortest distance possible from top to base. This condition is favored by the reduction of lateral pulls upon the upper spine.

NEW POSITIONS AND NEW FEELINGS

In studying a new idea it is often helpful to change the aspect of an existing situation for one less familiar, so that we may acquire a new set of "feelings" for the truths involved. If, for example, we get down on our hands and knees, or lie on our backs with knees bent and arms resting lightly across the chest, and analyze the relative positions of the several parts of our bodies, we shall get a clearer idea of the mechanical principles involved in our habitual patterns than we could while standing, sitting or lying down in the usual way. We are not diverted by any moral or esthetic preconceptions as to how we ought to look to others, and the relative positions of the parts may be studied from a purely mechanical point of view.

While "standing" on hands and knees, the balance of compression and tensile forces through the body will be more definitely experienced. The relationship of parts may be more easily perceived and a reeducation of kinesthesia encouraged. In the all-fours position, first note the direction of lines of thrust in the rotary joints and feel how the arms shove straight up into the shoulder sockets, and the thighs into the hip sockets.

Reverse the situation by lying on the back with knees bent

and arms held straight up in the air, and allow the arms and legs to "sit" in their sockets. After feeling the weight of the arms settling into their joints, fold them over the chest, still being conscious of the sockets. Then slide the shoulders toward the head, moving them up and down several times, until you feel the clavicles moving with them. A few movements should free the shoulder-blade muscles so that they do not pull up the ribs, as the shoulder blades slide over them.

In each position, two things may be observed: first, the suspensory nature of the shoulder girdle, which is superimposed on the skeleton and not directly attached to the thorax or spine at any point. If there were direct bony attachments between the shoulder girdle and the ribs, the upward and downward thrust of the arms would be felt immediately in the thorax. But there are none. The thorax lies between and beneath the shoulder blades and the ribs should be able to move freely under them.

The second thing to be noted is the direction of the weight-thrust through the supporting joints of the pelvis—the lumbo-sacral, sacroiliac and femoral joints. In the horizontal position, the weight is transferred through the spine by way of the posterior facets of the vertebrae, and not through their bodies as in the upright. Hence the weight is carried at the juncture of the spine and pelvis entirely through the articular facets of the fifth lumbar and sacrum, and thence through the acetabula to the femora in a perpendicular line.

The rotary joints at shoulder and hip offer an excellent opportunity to study both kinesthesia and the principles of balance, since they hold a strategic position in the mechanical and proprioceptive systems. In directing the movements of arms, trunk and legs and controlling the body-weight at the pelvis, their levers must act through more planes than the levers of other joints. And similarly, their muscles move and manipulate external weights through more planes than the muscles about other joints, as in throwing baseballs, kicking footballs, or playing a pipe-organ.

After experiencing these relationships of the arms and legs with the body and recognizing the actual points of contact between them, the mechanical changes in the upright position

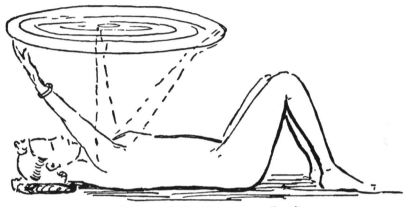

FIG. 62. Arm circling, large to small radius.

can be appreciated more fully. Also the freedom of the shoulder girdle from the body will be sensed more easily.

While lying down, think *through* the body and not *along the outside of it*. Follow the skeleton in your imagination and get a feeling for the position and balance of parts and the points of possible habitual strain. Locate first the two rotary joints in the shoulders, and trace their relation to the associated joints between scapulae and cavicles and between clavicles and sternum; and thence through the connections between sternum and ribs and between ribs and spine to the supporting structures in the spine. The weight of shoulders and arms must travel through these points of bony articulation to reach the spine. The responsibility of holding weight up is shared by the suspensory muscles attached to points still higher on the spine, via the hyoid, mandible and head bones. In the absence of the suspensory apparatus the shoulder girdle would have to be much heavier and their joints more rigid to carry the weight.

To find out where and how deep your joints are, first circle the arms alternately, starting with a large movement, gradually narrowing to a small radius. Imagine the center of the joint at a deep point—about where the knot in the rubber would be that holds the arm into the jointed bisque doll. Continue this until you feel that the impetus of movement lies in the joint

FIG. 63. Weight of thigh and arm dropping back into sockets, with foot flexion and extension.

rather than in the outstretched arm. This centers the muscular action.

Consider the thigh-joints in the same way and do the same thing with each out-stretched leg. But first, find out where your thigh-joints are. Extending the stretched hand across the body at the lower border of the abdomen, taking the bony pelvic rim as a landmark, sink the right thumb into the "break" between the right flexed thigh and the abdomen. This is a point located half-way between the center of the pubic rim and the sharp extension at the front of the hip-bone called the anterior superior spine of the ilium. Extend the middle finger to a similar point on the left side. If the hand is fully stretched, the thumb and middle finger will lie directly over the acetabula —the joints into which the legs fit. The thigh-joints are then experienced as a hand-span apart and at the front of the pelvis, instead of around at the sides of the ilia, or hip-bones, as is the usual faulty observation when standing upright.

After locating the hip-joints, draw both knees up, place the right foot on the left knee, keeping the legs as nearly parallel as possible. Flex the ankle a few times. The weight of the right leg should then be felt to travel through the hip-joint so that the leg seems to sink into the body. Lift the right foot, extending the leg as straight into the air as possible. Move it about in large circles, rotating at the hip-joint and reduce the radius gradually, as you did with the arm. Shake the leg gently, like a palsy, initiating the movement deep in the thigh-joint, until the location of this joint becomes a reality in consciousness. As this is successful, muscles and gravitational forces will be acting in the same direction, toward the thigh-joint. The muscles which had been ex-centering the leg in the activities of the day, will more perfectly re-center it, connecting it more strongly with the lumbar spine and the pelvis, thereby relieving its uneven strains.

Locating the joints in this way, in unusual positions, will bring home an appreciation of the practical value of applying mechanical principles for reduc-

FIG. 64. Sway back. (After Smedley.)

ing strains in the more familiar positions, where habits have dulled the sensory perceptions because adjustments have already been made in nerve and muscle to withstand the strain.

BODY BALANCE AND BREATHING

Changed balance of any one portion of the spine requires compensatory adjustments throughout it. The pulling up of the ribs and fixity of their articulations will stretch the lumbar region in proportion as it crowds the thoracic region. Muscular and ligamentous change of balance of the upper portions of the spine, if accompanied by movement of the rib articulations, will secure a balanced contact of the fourth with the fifth lumbar vertebra, and of the fifth with the sacrum. A lack of coordinated movement of small parts above disturbs the balance of the lumbar muscles below. This especially interferes with the normal functioning of the crura of the diaphragm and of the deep accessory breathing apparatus, including the iliopsoas, transversalis and levator ani.

A surprising number of people think of the diaphragm as a muscle in the wall of the thorax which contracts and expands horizontally in breathing, and which has little or no relation to the other body structures. They are all too prone to accept width of chest as the index of "deep breathing." They are astonished, therefore, to learn that the horizontal part of the diaphragm is a floor for the thoracic cage, upon which the heart and lungs rest, and a ceiling for the abdomen, and that its roots run down the spine at its front aspect almost to the hip-bones. In breathing, its action is up and down, like a piston in a cylinder, deepening the chest cavity instead of broadening it, with every inhalation. The balanced thorax, with freedom of ribs and intercostals, will release the diaphragm, and deep breathing which requires not breadth of chest from side to side, but depth from top to bottom and from front to back, will result. This increases the vertical rather than the transverse diameter of the chest.

The vascular structures of the upper third of the chest are certainly not working to the best mechanical advantage when, through pull of arm and shoulder muscles, the vertical and antero-posterior diameters are reduced and the lateral diameter is increased, as is the case with extreme fixity or rotundity of the chest. This widening may amount to 3 inches more than the width when the ribs hang at their vertebral levels, freely balanced between sternum and spine. The diaphragm is elevated when the lower ribs are lifted and expanded laterally, making its downward excursion more shallow. The dorsal muscles of the lower back then contract to hold the downward traveling load, and the psoas muscles as well as the crura of the diaphragm are stretched.

This vicious circle continues: the obturators (muscles of the pelvis which oppose the action of the psoas to keep the basin balanced) begin to take the greater share of the load within the pelvis, whereas the iliopsoas muscles further weaken their hold. As the origin of the obturators is at the front of the pelvic rim, the pelvis is pulled down by their action. (Figs. 37, 38.) This in turn stretches the abdominal muscles, finally affecting all suspensory muscles at the front. The iliopsoas and obturator-pyriformis groups must pull evenly on the femora if the femora and acetabula are to have balanced contacts.

The psoas muscles have their origins on the sides of the bodies and transverse processes of the lumbar and lower thoracic vertebrae. They travel downward, passing through the pelvis over the rim at the front of the thigh-joint, and attach at the inner side of the femur, after joining with the iliac muscles, those lining the flaring bones of the pelvis, in a common tendon. They insert into the lesser trochanter.

The obturators have their origins on the anterior borders of both the inner and the outer surfaces of the pubic rami, and traveling backward, cover the obturator foramina and pass through the great sciatic notches to insert into the femora just back of, and very close to, the iliopsoas muscles. It may be seen that these two muscles, obturator and psoas, oppose each other and form two diagonal planes of force through the pelvis, which should be equal and opposite. Their point of intersection under a balanced relationship would fall at the gravity line; that is, midway between the axis of the spine and the axes of the legs, if the leg axes were continued upward. This gives a free swinging base for quick adjustments.

The iliopsoas groups have their origins above the back of the joints involved, i.e., the thigh and sacroiliac, and their insertions below and in front of the joints. They thus tend to tighten each of the joints at its front aspect. They can act also to lift the pelvic rim at the front. The obturators, having their origin below in a horizontal plane with the joints involved, and most of their fibers anterior to them, are directed backward where they leave the pelvis for their insertion on the inner side of the femora at the back, and so tend to pull the pelvic rim downward. Thus, as the iliopsoas muscles travel over the pelvis from back to front, and the obturators from front to back, their pulls within the pelvis and at the femur will counterbalance each other. Together these muscles control the weight so that it is transferred through the pelvic joints to the legs with the least possible precipitation or momentum. By this means they bring stability to the lumbo-sacral and to the thigh joints.

THE PELVIC ARCH

The pelvic girdle, having the design of an arch with the sacrum as its keystone, must be reinforced to handle successfully the variable strains that fall upon such a structure when all parts are movable. An arch may be reinforced in three ways: by added buttresses to increase pressure against the keystone; by beams to hold the sides together; or by ties to hold the sides more securely to the keystone or to each other.

In the pelvis, all three methods of reinforcement are employed: the ilia and the femora are buttresses; the pelvic rim is the beam; ties are provided by all muscles and ligaments which originate in the spine and inside the pelvis and insert into the mesial and anterior surfaces of the femora. The principal tie muscles, which bring the beam and the sides more closely together at the front of the keystone to tighten its joinings, are the psoas, iliacus and pectineus. They are tensile members and form a part of the general tensile mechanism which pulls up the front of the body to balance compression forces of the spine at the back. These muscles are attached to the legs and spine, and being able to pull in both directions, their balanced action gives mobility and free swing to the pelvic basin. In this manner, the pelvis hangs between the compression members at the back and the tensile members of the body-wall pulling upward at the front, and makes a pressure like that of the foot in a well-swung cowboy stirrup.

Work done by the tie muscles of the pelvic arch must equal the sum of the compression forces at the lumbosacral and femoral joints. A cantilever is in operation. To balance it, tension must equal compression. When standing, and with alternate steps when walking, these tensile members are aided by the femora thrusting upward into the sockets, and by suction in the joints.

THE FEET AND WEIGHT CONTROL

If when weight is lowered it is controlled centrally by the muscles of the legs, strain is reduced on the feet as they receive it. The controlled weight descending upon the talus, topmost bone of the foot, will then spread evenly over the arch of the tarsus, the main supporting arch of the foot. Only when weight is lowered under control through the knees can the leg muscles, many of which have insertion on the plantar side of the foot, operate to protect the ankle joint from too sudden a precipitation of the load. Weight must be controlled in the pelvis before it can be controlled in the knees; in the knees before it can be controlled in the foot.

On the plantar aspect of the foot, the fibers of the tendons of several of the leg muscles are split and reach finger-like attachments well forward into the toes, which allows flexible movement and controls weight balance in ankle and foot.

It is momentum, due to uncontrolled precipitation of weight, that breaks down the foot arches. This also produces pronated ankles, a condition of spreading of the inner side of the longitudinal arch, which allows the ankle bone to protrude on the inside and throws excess weight onto the great toe. This stretches the inner border of the foot.

Many evils follow in the train of the pronated ankle. The tibialis posterior muscle struggles to prevent this condition, and if it fails, various disturbances ensue, the most serious being impingement upon or stretching of that very important nerve of the foot, the tibialis posterior. Pain and irritation from this may be local, deflected or referred. Excess weight upon the great toe disturbs its balance at bone joinings, producing strains that spread the cuneiforms, resulting in surface irritations, calluses, and sometimes sesamoids. In fact, all bones of the foot may suffer maladjustment when any one joint breaks down under the strain thrown upon it.

These strains should be met intelligently, higher up. The fibers of the muscles whose tendons are in the foot run up at the side, front and back of the leg, and between the leg bones, the tibia and fibula. Their balanced functioning is important especially with the tibialis posterior, the origins of which begin at the back just below the knee and extend along a considerable portion of the surface of these bones and of the interosseous membrane which lies between them. The tibialis posterior muscles are placed on the bones in such positions and with such attachments as to balance with the others for the best reciprocal action to center and guide the controlled weight from the knee to the ball of the foot. The foot has a stirrup-like design, similar to that of the pelvis.

THE "FEEL" OF BALANCE

To test the balance of the foot, stand toeing in, and focus the weight just behind the inner ankle bone. In shifting the weight, do not swing the body backward. At first this will give the feeling of more weight on the heels than on the toes, and of the ankles tending toward flexion. Try to shorten the great toe as though a string fastened to it slipped under the inner malleolus and up the back of the legs, deep under the big calf muscles. Imagine this string pulling the toe back, through the ankle and up, but *without* "*curling*" the toe. Gently rock backward and forward on the ankle, gradually restricting the movement to a half-inch radius. This centers the talus between the leg bones and foot bones, through balanced muscle action.

By repeating this gentle rocking at each joint, ankle, knee and hip, we acquaint ourselves with balance at the individual joints. After rocking at the ankles, center attention on the knees and do the same thing there. Gradually reduce the range of movement to a half-inch radius and try to get a sense of mobility and of the very innermost center of each joint. At the thigh-joints make the pelvic girdle rock on the heads of the femora, with the least possible motion, remembering that the thigh-joints are at the front of the pelvis. When this action is successful, the rim of the pelvis will move slightly up and down, instead of a break occurring just below the waist line in the back. While rocking on the thigh-joint have a sense of squatting with slightly flexed knees. After doing this for a while, walk forward a step or two, imagining that the spine is extended to the floor like the tail of a dinosaur or kangaroo, and walk as though you were climbing, or as if swimming in a sitting position. In such a walk, tension is reduced in the muscles of the back-wall and buttocks and is taken up by the front-wall muscles, where it belongs; that is, the tensile members will balance the compression members of the back. If, on the other hand, the psoas and iliacus, the tie muscles at the front of the pelvis, are stretched, movement of the pelvis will be for the most part in the region of the fifth lumbar. This should not occur.

After standing and rocking, walk about as suggested for a while and then glance in a mirror at your profile: you will see a snugly spanked-in region in the back and you will look taller and straighter. Straightening from below elevates the head, as it lengthens the spinal axis.

A LONG SPINAL AXIS

Analyzed, the pattern of the mechanically efficient posture, whether sitting, standing or walking, implies a long spinal axis and a centered control of the weights it carries. The longer the spinal axis and the more shallow the curves, the shorter the distance through which the weights must be moved. The spinal axis is the resultant of the weight and movement of the intrinsic spinal structures (muscles, ligaments and bones) designed in four opposing curves to give the spine its supporting strength.

By making the lumbar spine straighter from below, that is, producing a more uniform curve, the head is elevated. It is futile to attempt to lengthen the axis of the spine by expanding or pulling up the chest. This shortens the axis by unbalancing the weights on the spinal curves, crowding the thoracic and cervical vertebrae, and stretching those in the lumbar region so that the lower portion sags. The crowded vertebrae in the upper region have to go somewhere, so they protrude, and an ugly bulge at the back of the neck or at the shoulders results. This sometimes takes the form of so-called round shoulders.

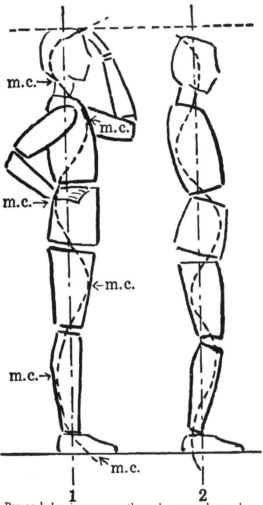

FIG. 65. 1. Power balancing power through opposed muscle centers. Muscle centers coordinate across line of gravity in movement when bones are balanced. 2. Bones opposing bones. When bones are unbalanced, weight opposes weight across line of gravity, thus throwing muscle centers under tension.

For more perfect control, we should use the strong crouch and spring muscles of the lumbar and pelvic regions, both to transfer weight effectively from spine to legs through the pelvis and to catch the recoil from legs to spine. Recall that action and reaction persist from foot to head in bodily movements. Use of these base muscles integrates the lumbar spine, the strongest and heaviest portion, and the motor control center of the entire column. In all movement the lumbar curve keeps nearer the gravity line, which passes through the center of the body mass, than any of the other curves except the cervical, upon which the head is centered. A flexible upright which, like the spine, carries unevenly disposed weights, must be curved, and the curve must touch the gravity line at two or more points.

Because many persons fail to realize how deepset the spine is, it is well to emphasize the fact again, that all vertebrae become increasingly larger and thicker toward the base, and in the lumbar region they are very large and deep and extend well forward into the body cavity. (Fig. 66.) Sink the thumbs into the sides just over the crests of the ilia: if they could be extended through the body they would graze the front of the lumbar spine. We thus see that the lumbar spine at its deepest, extends through one-half of the trunk at this level. Even in the chest, the thoracic spine extends deeply toward the center, due to the peculiar shape and adjustment of the ribs at the sides of the vertebrae. Large portions of the lungs lie behind the front borders of these vertebrae, as shown in a cross-section of the chest.

Try in imagination to locate the front of your spine instead of remembering only the little projections of its vertebrae that you can feel externally at the back. These projections mark the tips of the dorsal spinous processes, which are developed for muscle attachments. The weight is supported through the deeper parts, the bodies of the vertebrae.

To review balanced standing, the ideal way of carrying ourselves is, as we have seen, to pile up the weights of the body with the gravity axis passing through the centers of the three main bulks of weight (head, thorax, and pelvis), all to be balanced with as little output of muscular energy as possible, allowing the bones to do their full share of the work. Ambition for structural balance rather than notions about appearance should guide our efforts in seeking better posture. Our success depends ultimately on our knowledge of where and how our

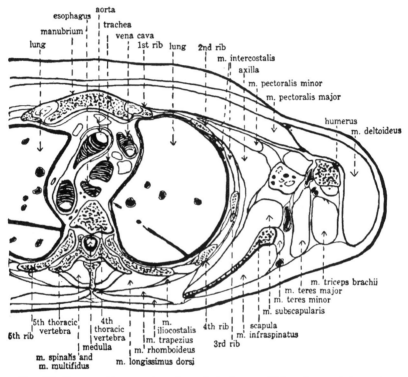

Fig. 66. Cross section passing through body at middle of manubrium. Cuts through first, second, third, fourth and vertebral ends of fifth ribs. (From Eychlesheimer and Schoemacher.)

weights sit, hang, or are braced, and on the degree to which we can realize the meaning and feeling of balance. This again depends on our kinesthetic sensitivity. To encourage this, begin with the feet and note the most favorable alignment about each joint.

First, think upward through the body, trying to get a keen sense of balanced adjustment at each joint: ankles, knees, thighs, through the pelvis to the spine. Make no effort to move the parts. The less conscious motion, the quicker the adjustment at the center. Try this experiment several times with increasing consciousness of a real balance at the bony contacts. Imagination will effect the responses. Next, try the rocking motion at each joint as described before, first at ankle, then at knee, then at hip. If the weight is not balanced mechanically at the joint, you will find that you cannot rock, but can only move by shoving the parts about with a distinct effort of the muscles and a break in the lower spine.

Another experiment in standing is to place the feet so that they are directed straight forward, with the inner borders parallel and 5 or 6 inches apart. Imagine all parts drawing together toward the center of the ankle joint, like a duck, pulling its foot out of a mud puddle. Feel the pull up the leg as high as the thigh joint. This should give you an appreciation of the long arch of the foot, and the integration and mobility of its many parts. The sum of the action of all these centered lines of force in the foot lifts the main longitudinal arch, preparing it to receive weight from above and impact from below. The muscles in the sole of the foot act as ties to reinforce the arch and should be firm across the bottom of the foot.

At the ankle we have an even more complex situation for transfer of weight than at the pelvis, since there are twenty-six bones in each foot to be adjusted. Shock absorption is made possible by all forces being drawn together to integrate the talus, the keystone of the tarsus.

The toes should receive the weight-thrust equally so that they may aid in redirecting the moving load or adjusting the foot to the ground for security of tread. For a well-balanced foot, toes and metatarsals must have individual movement, since their mechanical function is to adapt the pressures between the down-coming load and the ground. Their purpose is to shift the weight if it becomes too concentrated at any one point on the tarsus. In the process of standing and even more in walking, the toes often have to change their pressure through the metatarsals against the cuneiform and cuboid bones to balance the talus.

The knees should be flexed just sufficiently for free play of the surrounding muscles and restricting ligaments. This allows the centering of weights in these hinge-joints, where there is little possibility of lateral adjustment. Weight is passing through very long levers between pelvis and foot. The long thigh muscles and deep short muscles at the back of the knee must be free to guide it through the joint or excess strain will fall upon the ligaments.

PELVIC EQUILIBRIUM AND THE TRUNK AXES

The pelvis should swing freely between the spinal axis and the leg axes, the latter of which lie not in continuous, but in parallel planes. These axes are the resultants of the mechanical and organic forces acting through the joints and the connecting levers to effect balanced contacts and seating of the loads. Gravity, bones, muscles, ligaments, fascia, are all involved in keeping compression and tensile forces effecting a balance.

Imagine one ventral plane lying between the axes of the legs and extended upward through the thigh joints, and a second plane, marked by the axis of the spine, continued downward. These two planes should be parallel to the plane marked by the line of gravity which bisects the body vertically through the centers of the three main units of weight. These three imaginary upright planes are produced by actual forces. Keeping them parallel and close together will bring all joints of connecting parts into the best mechanical relationship for a balanced structure. With the structure thus balanced in the upright position, the compression forces at the back and the tensile forces at the front will be equal and opposing, and the center of gravity will lie somewhere in the mid-plane of the body. In dynamic equilibrium, when a body is stable, any motion of its parts will raise its center of gravity and offer leverage for organized movement. The spaces between these planes allow for this leverage. And especially is this true of the space lying between the base of the spine and the thigh joints. This is the spring-board for action.

By mechanical definition, a body is in stable equilibrium when any movement from its position will raise its center of gravity. It is in unstable equilibrium when any movement will lower its center of gravity, that is when it cannot prevent itself from tumbling down, without help from an outside force.

In standing, imagine that you keep within the compass of the three planes just described, but without rigidity. In other words, keep as small around as you can without bulging any part. Feel that the lower trunk is behind the legs, and that the upper thigh is in the lead. Feel the spine extending and dragging on the floor. Have a consciousness of the thigh-joints being in planes in front of the sharp spines of the hip bone; and with an acute sense of the leg axes marking a plane that is separate, in front of, and discontinuous with the planes of the other two axes, the spinal and the gravitational.

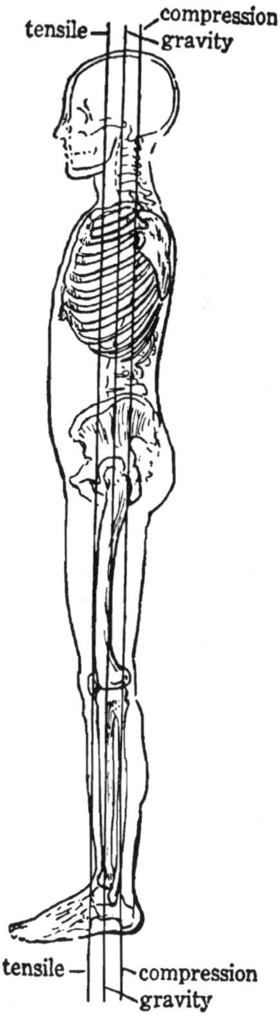

THORAX, SHOULDERS AND HEAD

Thorax and pelvis should be well integrated by the use of the lumbar-pelvic muscles and the muscles of the abdominal wall. By keeping these two structures as close together as possible without bending the upright spinal axis, we secure better placement for the viscera, and favor a balanced action between the diaphragm and the lower accessory muscles of breathing, partic-

FIG. 67. Lines of force: tensile, gravity, compression.

ularly the transversalis abdominis, the psoas and the levator ani. This insures a deeper excursion of the diaphragm, because of a more effective contraction of the lumbar and crural portions, which is supplemented by the contraction of the lower accessory muscles of breathing. Tension in the rib muscles is relieved, and breathing becomes vertical or *tubular* in character.

The integration of thorax with pelvis is possible only when the rib structure is relieved from crosspulls produced by the action of muscles of arm and shoulder, and when the thorax hangs easily suspended from the head between the spine and the sternum, its compression and tensile members. Especially important in securing this easy support of the thorax is the position of the first three pairs of ribs and the upright support of the manubrium. These ribs should be balanced without rigidity between the top vertebrae of the thoracic spine and the top of the sternum, as they serve as braces for the support of the whole thoracic cage on the spine. To insure this easy balance the antero-posterior diameter of the upper chest must be as great as possible, and the thoracic spine must be protected from unnecessary lateral pulls. The top of the sternum, the manubrium, should be directed up and forward during inspiration. The whole alignment of parts will be favored by lessening the transverse diameter of the lower chest, or by allowing the lower ribs to hang easily from their vertebral attachments instead of consciously lifting them.

The shoulder girdle should be balanced on the top of the sternum by the clavicles, and suspended from the neck and head by its own muscular suspensory mechanism. Neither clavicles nor scapulae will then be allowed to rest upon or press against the upper ribs, but their weight will be equally divided between the suspensory members. The attachments of these tensile members are distributed so evenly around the skull and neck that the weight of the shoulder girdle and arms is ultimately carried to the spine, through whose compression members it then passes, in such a way as to stabilize the placement of the head upon the spine. With the girdle in this balanced position the acromions, tips of the shoulders, will hang easily, and in line with the lobes of the ears, and the arms will lie along the median line of the side body-wall, or in the same plane as the line of gravity.

The head is the top-load on the spine. When the main units below are in balance, it will rock easily on its support, cradled as it is upon the broad base of the atlas. It is further stabilized by the little pinion tooth of the axis, which holds and limits its motion. A little nodding motion, like that of the Mandarin doll, continued for a few moments, will give one a feeling of freedom in the neck muscles and make clearer to consciousness the fact of how deeply centered is the support of the head upon the spine. Gently up-reaching the head will increase the kinesthesia in this region, providing the forehead and chin hang in the same vertical plane. Getting a feeling for these pictures in the imagination will raise the head to a straighter position and bring it into line with the axis of the supporting cervical spine.

Analyze these points carefully as suggested, and try to sense the feeling of mechanical balance throughout the whole structure. The terms used to describe the feelings may seem childish, but thinking about them and setting up the bones to accord with the pictures will eventually open the neuromuscular pathways and the habit of ease in standing will be acquired.

As we shall see in the next chapter, walking is easier by far, but it will be made a more economical procedure if the structure is habituated at the same time to balance in standing.

Chapter VII

BALANCED FORCES IN WALKING

"THE PHYSIOLOGY OF WALKING"

Oliver Wendell Holmes, writing in 1883 on "the physiology of walking," has furnished, prophetically, our introduction to ways of easy, balanced walking, and hence balanced bodily movements of all kinds:

The two accomplishments common to all mankind are walking and talking. Simple as they seem, they are yet acquired with vast labor, and very rarely understood in any clear way by those who practice them with perfect ease and unconscious skill.

Talking seems the hardest to comprehend. Yet it has been clearly explained and successfully imitated by artificial contrivances. . . .

But no man has been able to make a figure that can *walk*. Of all the automata imitating men or animals moving, there is not one in which the legs are the true sources of motion. So said the Webers* more than twenty years ago, and it is true now as then.

. . . We wish to give our readers as clear an idea as possible of that wonderful art of balanced vertical progression which they have practiced, as *M. Jourdain* talked prose, for so many years, without knowing what a marvellous accomplishment they had mastered. We shall have to begin with a few simple anatomical data.

The foot is arched both longitudinally and transversely, so as to give it elasticity, and thus break the sudden shock when the weight of the body is thrown upon it. The ankle-joint is a loose hinge, and the great muscles of the calf can straighten the foot out so far that practiced dancers walk on the tips of their toes. The knee is another hinge-joint, which allows the leg to bend freely, but not to be carried beyond a straight line in the other direction. Its further forward movement is checked by two very powerful cords in the interior of the joint, which cross each other like the letter X, and are hence called the *crucial ligaments*. The upper ends of the thigh-bones are almost globes, which are received into the deep cup-like cavities of the haunch-bones. They are

* Traité de la Mécanique des Organes de la Locomotion. Trans. from the German in the Encyclopédie Anatomique. Paris, 1843.

tied to these last so loosely that, if their ligaments alone held them, they would be half out of their sockets in many positions of the lower limbs. But here comes in a simple and admirable contrivance. The smooth,

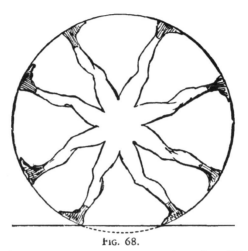

FIG. 68.

Figs. 68-72 are from drawings by Darley, made for Oliver Wendell Holmes's "Physiology of Walking."

rounded head of the thigh-bone, moist with glairy fluid, fits so perfectly into the smooth, rounded cavity which received it, that it holds firmly by *suction*, or atmospheric pressure. It takes a hard pull to draw it out after all the ligaments are cut, and then it comes with a smack like a tight cork from a bottle. Holding in this way by the close apposition of two polished surfaces, the lower extremity swings freely forward and backward like a *pendulum*, if we give it a chance, as is shown by standing on a chair upon the other limb, and moving the pendent one out of the vertical line. The force with which it swings depends upon its weight, and this is much greater than we might at first suppose; for our limbs not only carry themselves, but our bodies also, with a sense of lightness rather than of weight, when we are in good condition. Accident sometimes makes us aware how heavy our limbs are. An officer, whose arm was shattered by a ball in one of our late battles, told us that the dead weight of the helpless member seemed to drag him down to the earth; he could hardly carry it; it "weighed a ton," to his feeling, as he said.

In ordinary walking a man's lower extremity swings essentially by its own weight, requiring little muscular effort to help it. So heavy a body easily overcomes all impediments from clothing, even in the sex least favored in its costume. But if a man's legs are pendulums, then a short man's legs will swing quicker than a tall man's, and he will take more steps to the minute, other things being equal. Thus there is a natural rhythm to a man's walk, depending on the length of his legs, which beat more or less rapidly as they are longer or shorter, like

FIG. 69.   FIG. 70.

metronomes differently adjusted, or the pendulums of different time-keepers. Commodore Nutt is to M. Bihin in this respect as a little, fast-ticking mantel-clock is to an old-fashioned, solemn-clicking, upright timepiece.

The mathematical formulae in which the Messrs. Weber embody their results would hardly be instructive to most of our readers. The figures of their Atlas would serve our purpose better, had we not the means of coming nearer to the truth than even their careful studies enabled them to do. We have selected a number of instantaneous stereoscopic views of the streets and public places of Paris and of New York, each of them showing numerous walking figures, among which some may be found in every stage of the complex act we are studying. Mr. Darley has had the kindness to leave his higher tasks to transfer several of these to our pages, so that the reader may be sure that he looks upon an exact copy of real human individuals in the act of walking.

The first subject is caught with his legs stretched in a stride, the remarkable length of which arrests our attention. The sole of the right foot is almost vertical. By the action of the muscles of the calf it has *rolled off* from the ground like a portion of the tire of a wheel, the heel rising first, and thus the body, already advancing with all its acquired velocity, and inclined forward, has been pushed along and, as it were, *tipped over*, so as to fall upon the other foot, now ready to receive its weight. [Fig. 69.]

FIG. 71.   FIG. 72.

In the second figure, the right leg is bending at the knee, so as to lift the foot from the ground, in order that it may swing forward. [Fig. 70.]

The next stage of movement is shown in the *left* leg of Figure 3 [71]. This leg is seen suspended in air, a little beyond the middle of the arc through which it swings, and before it has straightened itself, which it will presently do, as shown in the next figure.

The foot has now swung forward, and tending to swing back again, the limb being straightened and the body tipped forward, the heel strikes the ground. The angle which the sole of the foot forms with the ground increases with the length of the stride; and as this last surprised us, so the extent of this angle astonishes us in many of the figures in this among the rest. [Fig. 72.]

The heel strikes the ground with great force, as the wear of our boots and shoes in that part shows us. But the projecting heel of the human foot is the arm of a lever, having the ankle-joint as its fulcrum, and, as it strikes the ground, brings the sole of the foot down flat upon it, as shown in Figure 1 [69]. At the same time the weight of the limb and body is thrown upon the foot, by the joint effect of muscular action and acquired velocity, and the other foot is now ready to rise from the ground and repeat the process we have traced in its fellow.

No artist would have dared to draw a walking figure in attitudes like some of these. The swinging limb is so much shortened that the toe never by any accident scrapes the ground, if this is tolerably even. In cases of partial paralysis, the scraping of the toe, as the patient walks, is one of the characteristic marks of imperfect muscular action.

Walking, then, is a perpetual falling with a perpetual self-recovery. It is a most complex, violent, and perilous operation, which we divest of its extreme danger only by continual practice from a very early period of life. We find how complex it is when we attempt to analyze it, and we see that we never understood it thoroughly until the time of the instantaneous photograph. We learn how violent it is, when we walk against a post or a door in the dark. We discover how dangerous it is, when we slip or trip and come down, perhaps breaking or dislocating our limbs, or overlook the last step of a flight of stairs, and discover with what headlong violence we have been hurling ourselves forward.

Two curious facts are easily proved. First, a man is shorter when he is walking than when at rest. We have found a very simple way of showing this by having a rod or yardstick placed horizontally so as to touch the top of the head forcibly, as we stand under it. In walking rapidly beneath it, even if the eyes are shut, to avoid involuntary stooping, the top of the head will not even graze the rod. The other fact is, that one side of a man always tends to outwalk the other side, so that no person can walk far in a straight line, if he is blindfolded.

The somewhat singular illustration at the head of our article carries out an idea which has only been partially alluded to by others. Man is a *wheel*, with two spokes, his legs, and two fragments of a tire, his feet. He *rolls* successively on each of these fragments from the heel to the toe. If he had spokes enough, he would go round and round as the boys do when they "make a wheel" with their four limbs for its spokes. But having only two available for ordinary locomotion, each of these has to be taken up as soon as it has been used, and carried forward to be used again, and so alternately with the pair. The peculiarity of biped-walking is, that the centre of gravity is shifted from one leg to the other, and the one not employed can shorten itself so as to swing forward, passing by that which supports the body.

This is what no automaton can do . . .*

More than half a century later, Dr. Holmes' description is still fresh and vital, and his pictures, taken from photographs

* We are indebted to the Houghton Mifflin Company for this quotation, and for the use of the plates by Mr. Darley, the illustrator for Charles Dickens. The selection, as made, was not from the first edition of the article, which must have appeared about 1883, but from a volume entitled "Selections from the Breakfast-Table Series, and Pages from an Old Volume of Life," p. 290 ff., published in the Modern Classics Series.

made when the instantaneous process was news, make one think what good use he would have made of the movies.

The Autocrat ended his piece with the adage "Solvitur ambulando." The problem of structural balance, like other problems, can be solved while walking. Let us look closely into the mechanics of this most familiar daily activity, which makes the ground pattern for all skillful and beautiful body motions, whether in the dance or in the active sports, running or jumping.

EASY WALKING

Standing, as we have seen, involves maintaining our equilibrium in one place. In walking we meet many of the problems of standing, plus the added one of locomotion. Walking is nevertheless an easier process than continued standing still, as we have learned by experience, because its movements are rhythmic and adapted to the native requirements of our muscles for alternate activity and rest.

The balance of the iliopsoas muscles with their antagonizers, the obturators, keeps the thigh-joints well integrated and the pelvis supported. This centers the upward thrust of each leg as, in alternate action, it receives the body-weight. The diagonal lines of force passing upward through the femora and the ilia, at the thigh-joints must be so directed toward the center of the sacroiliac joint and the sacrum as to keep this keystone securely placed or buttressed to serve the pelvic arch, and thus to direct the weight from the fifth lumbar vertebra to the thigh-joints successfully. As Dr. Holmes pointed out, the free leg in stepping forward must be made shorter than the other to escape the ground. This continuous automatic adjustment is effected mainly by the ligaments of the thigh-joint acting with the tendons of the deep-lying iliopsoas at the center and the lesser gluteals at the side.

The pelvis, considered as a short cantilever bridge, moves constantly as the weight comes upon it from the spine and is passed through it to the legs. Its movement as a whole is a composite of several movements as the legs alternately shorten and lengthen in traveling forward.

A mechanical engineer was asked how he would describe in simple mechanical terms the movement of the pelvis in the act of walking. After consideration, he said that it was "a combination of undulatory motions in three dimensions, the resultant of which described a spiral like that followed by a point on the helix of a screw-conveyor." Pressed for explanation, he elaborated:

"Sand or grain, in being processed, is poured into a hollow cylinder, on the inner surface of which there is a fixed screw with a thread upon it called the 'helix.' The helix extends like a blade from the surface of the screw throughout its length. The cylinder rotates, and as it moves the grain is shoved ahead by the turning blade, which does not itself move forward, but seems to, as it describes a spiral curve with each rotation of the cylinder. If a point marking the center of gravity of the weight of the whole body could be observed as it passes through the pelvis on its way to the ground, it would be seen to follow a path like that of a point on the edge of the blade of a helix."

In the body, this resultant spiral movement is brought about by the tipping and tilting of the pelvis from side to side and from back to front as it rotates alternately on each femoral head. If we consider the body-weight as constantly moving through the pelvic joints from spine to thigh, as the grain moves forward through the conveyor, we shall get the idea.

GRAVITY AND WALKING

The light tread, the buoyant walk, result from control of the body-weight as it is transferred from spine to legs through the rolling pelvis. This in turn is aided by keeping the hip-joints close up toward the center, so that the heads of the femora are not swung outward but remain balanced to receive the reacting support from the ground. It is by virtue of the wheel-like arrangement of the muscles about the thigh-joint that this can be done.

In walking, it is helpful to remember that gravity is affecting our action in two ways: in down-thrust and in equal up-thrust due to resistance by the ground to the pressure of each foot. In this way we are prevented from sinking into the center of the earth, as the ground is pushing us up in proportion to the weight and momentum of each step. Thinking of this fact has an amusing way of making the earth seem to work for us. It brings about a coordination of the antagonizing muscles managing the tumbling weights about the joints so as to tighten the anterior aspects of the bone joinings where shearing might easily take place. To control weight, shearing at joints must be avoided.

Control of the cumulative weight is accomplished by the deep lower and inner back and pelvic muscles, which reach well up into the thorax and down into the legs. The most important muscle group, the iliopsoas, is actually supported by the strongest and largest portions of the spine and from the broad areas of the hip bones. These structures are attached to each vertebra of the lumbar spine and to the lowest thoracic. The leg thus swings from the largest and strongest portion of the spine, and by the deepest trunk muscles. These muscles have the greatest range of attachments. All the muscles around the pelvis help to support the weight, of course, but the iliopsoas group both centers and supports it.

To appreciate the significance of this, one must note the points where the weights fall forward, important among them being the contacts between the fifth lumbar vertebra and the pelvis, and between the pelvis and the femora. Here is where the greatest amount of "tumbling," or precipitation of weight, takes place. If this is not retarded at the start by the deep-lying muscles, the force of accelerated momentum will add to the already complicated problem. Weight dropped from a height gains momentum as it falls. This makes a proportionately greater strain on the receiving structure, the degree of which may be measured in foot-pounds in ratio to the distance dropped. Momentum is handled by muscles being prepared for the load. If a 50-pound weight is lowered under control until it rests on someone's toes, there is little shock; but who would like it if the same weight were dropped suddenly on his toes from the same height? Stepping down inadvertently from a curb is another illustration of the same principle.

In walking the leg bones are being acted upon in three mechanical ways: by weight, by pulleys, and by momentum introduced by movement. A balance between these forces must be found or one or the other will hastily increase its advantage and unbalance the trio. For example, weight may pass through a given bone and, as long as the muscle pulleys keep it balanced, momentum will be under control even though there be an increase in speed. But if the muscles fail to keep the balance, momentum gains and unseats the load, and bone tends to slide. This is what happens when one starts to fall and then quickly recovers oneself—the shock may be greater than the effect of the fall would have been. If one does fall after this attempt, the result may be severe. An elderly person may even break a hip bone in a slight fall by trying to save himself, while the baby, who gives way at once, is seldom hurt. Actors and acrobats learn to fall under control, giving way at each joint until the fall is complete. Nature's technique, the successive falling forward and recovery, the process involved in walking, is thus utilized.

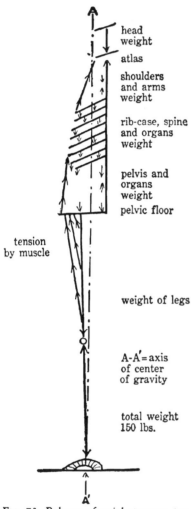

head
weight

atlas

shoulders
and arms
weight

rib-case, spine
and organs
weight

pelvis and
organs
weight

pelvic floor

tension
by muscle

weight of legs

A-A'=axis
of center
of gravity

total weight
150 lbs.

FIG. 73. Balance of axial stresses: tension in front, compression in back.

To get the feeling of what this means, try the old trick of falling backward into some one's arms. There is just enough control of the spine to keep it from collapsing, and yet it is not stiff. This fall is better described as sinking.

It is the inner thigh muscles and the deep-lying pelvic and lumbar muscles, rather than the outer groups, which center the joints, bring the body-weight under control, and prevent momentum from getting the advantage. The front aspect of all joints transferring weight must be tightened up to keep the keystone secure. This reduces materially the strain on knees and feet.

To experience this and the accompanying buoyancy, when next walking through a long tunnel, such as from the Grand Central Station in New York to the Roosevelt Hotel, note the click of the heels and the echo from the walls. Then try to boost the pelvis from the front, up toward the lumbar spine, feeling "thick-set," but without stretching, bending, sagging or protruding any part of your body-wall. Now note the change in sound and echo of the heels. If the legs and pelvis are well integrated with the front of the spine, and the legs are swinging from the deep lumbar spine within, a very noticeable change in buoyancy and in sound will be experienced. This effects a reduction of momentum at the joints, and the pounding of the heels will be much lighter and the echo correspondingly reduced. What happens is that your weight is being lowered under control, and buoyancy secured by balance and control of the weight through the muscular and ligamentous integrity of all joints, especially the lumbosacral, the thigh, knee and ankle.

The foot is conditioned by what happens to it from above, as well as by its impact with the floor. When walking, amuse yourself by thinking of your upright trunk as sitting in the carriage of the pelvis and of the legs as horses in advance. Keep the horses ahead of the load, the thighs ahead of the abdomen. Don't put the cart before the horse.

The action of all centering muscles works for economy of control in that no effort is being wasted by holding parts out of alignment, that is, away from center. In movement, however, the weights must depart from center and return again. So long as they keep moving under control there is little strain. Strain comes when the bones are held out of alignment by the muscles.

Ex-centering, on the other hand, is the work of the larger superficial muscles of hip and thigh, which direct the swing of the legs outward, through their arcs of movement. Their first act is *ex-centering*, or no organized movement could take place. The time-space relation of toppling and recovering weights determines the rhythm of organized movement.

Economy of energy requires a long spinal axis parallel and as close as possible to the line of gravity. The line of gravity, passing through the center of gravity, marks the placement of the separate body weights in relation to the earth, and also in relation to the axis of the spine.

The more nearly the line of gravity and the parallel axis of the spine by which the weight is controlled approximate each other, and the lower the center of gravity of the whole, the greater the economy in carrying and controlling the load.

TIMING AND THE TAKE-OFF

In walking, the weight is successively tumbling forward through all the body joints and being quickly met by the centering muscles to control it, and then the advancing leg swinging forward to support it. The femur must move slightly in advance of the pelvic weight that it is to receive. The time element here is important. The leg must get there just before the pelvis if the weight is to be successfully managed by the balanced reciprocal muscle groups around the thigh-joints. The alternate leg must be ready just in time to catch the tumbling weights again. The sensation of walking is so familiar that one does not realize this. But change the familiar to the unusual situation, and add a handicap to the joints, as for example by stepping into the strong current of a trout stream, and you will realize it immediately. Your legs must get there first if you are to keep upright. Let us repeat the imagery of the three planes.

The axes of the supporting legs are in front of and parallel to the line of gravity. If we should imagine these axes continued upward through the acetabula and the body, they would pass through the breasts and cheek bones; whereas, if the axis of the spine, through which the body weight must pass into the pelvis, were continued downward, it would pass through the lower border of the sacrum and rest on the floor behind the plane of the heels, like the third leg of a tripod. If the imaginary lines in the front were extended medially and the axis of the spine on either side laterally until planes were formed, as has been previously stated, we should have two upright parallel planes, between which we may imagine a third, also parallel to these, if all forces were balanced. The third plane would be the plane of gravity, produced by the laterally extended line of gravity.

The best balanced upright position is that in which these three planes are parallel to each other, and their forces in balanced action. Control of these planes of force depends largely upon reducing lateral pulls in the thoracic region, as discussed in the preceding chapter, and in the integration of the reciprocal muscle groups in the lumbar-pelvic-thigh region.

In walking, as in standing, the smaller the distance between the plane formed by the upward thrusts of the legs and the plane of the axis of the spine, the more centered and balanced will be the pulls of the controlling muscles and ligaments for reduction of momentum throughout the body.

In the transfer of the body-weight to the supporting legs, it is passed through five pelvic joints: the lumbosacral, sacroiliac, and thigh-joints, the planes of which are not in vertical alignment; hence, the necessity for balance of ligaments and muscles controlling these joints. It is the very fact that these planes are not in alignment but have spaces between them that makes the difference between a static and a dynamic situation. Organized movement is possible only when loss of balance of the mass, or shift of the center of gravity, may be initiated from within the mass and recovery instigated through the same mechanism. Leverage and opposition of parts are indispensable requirements. If there were no space allowed between the line of gravity of the mass and the axis of the curved structure that controls the load and the axes of the legs which receive the load, we should have no springboard for movement. In other words, the distance between the lumbosacral joint and the thigh-joints provides a leverage for organized movement.

Man is dynamic, not static. He maintains his equilibrium by means of forces acting through various planes, and the adjustment of his many parts to these forces in time-space. As noted by Richet, the French physiologist, his systems are just enough unstable for the "act of living" to maintain stability.

With all parts working together for the whole and employing principles of leverage and of mutual opposition as a means of "take-off," all movements follow through successfully in orderly and unobstructed fashion.

The supporting leg in walking, through its balanced joints, must transfer weight to the arch of the foot. Here the weight must be properly placed upon the talus, the keystone of the arch. This is done by the tibia, with the aid of the fibula and the controlling muscles, most of which are on the side and back of the leg, and have their insertion through diverging fibers of their strong tendons to various small bones on the plantar aspect of the foot.

The balanced use of these leg muscles acts in such a way at these points of attachment as to tend to hold together the small bones of the longitudinal arch, the tarsus. Their action is very like that of the string of a bow. They hold the two ends of the arch together and aid the forces through the arch to converge toward the keystone. The upward thrust from the impact of the foot and ground is thus centered and directed through the talus to meet the weight coming down through the axis of the leg. Many small parts are involved in centering the foot to receive weight and to absorb shock. These parts are drawn together at the talus by muscles and ligaments of both foot and leg in such a way as to place the weight under balanced control, upon the talus. If the leg weight-thrust is met and controlled at the center of the talus, at the knee and at the acetabulum, it follows that the rotary joint of the thigh will have freedom of movement in all its planes, and body-weight will never progress faster than the legs that carry it.

Thought of the upward thrust of the ground helps to keep these joints free. Add the ground to your bones in your imagination as working factors in bodily economy.

THE THIGH-JOINTS

The thigh-joints are "the hub of the universe" for our personal world. They must have every muscle fiber of their arcs free to respond to the multiple responsibilities thrown upon them from all directions as lines of force converge toward the hub from the many possible angles of impact.

The first act of walking is to fall; the next is to catch the falling weight; and the third is the continuation of the other two acts in alternation and in rhythm, until the decision to reorganize the pattern of movement is made. But the response by the structure to such a decision from within could never be consummated with precision if it were not for the distance in the pelvis between the vertical planes of the sacrum and the femora. It is this distance, although only 2 or 3 inches, that makes possible the cantilever action of the pelvis.

The weight delivered to the sacrum at the back is transferred to the legs at the front, where the thigh-joints, acting like wheels with their hub-like centers, transfer the body-weight to the moving supports. These joints, with their many diverging muscles and ligamentous fibers forming spokes, act to distribute, guide and absorb the shocks coming toward them through their expansive arc of movement, and offer a great variety of leverage for starting new movements.

It is by virtue of the character of these universal joints and their spatial relation to the axis of the spine that coordination in organized movements is effected. Therefore, as pointed out in an earlier article, the hip-joints are the important focal points in postural education.*

We have likened the supporting function of the bony pelvis to a cantilever bridge, but there are the differences that the power is applied from within through nervous stimuli, and that

* Principles of Posture, with Special Reference to the Mechanics of the Hip-Joint.

all parts are movable and in constant mutual readjustment. The upward thrust of the femora and the thrust of the spine at the sacrum where the fifth lumbar vertebra delivers the accumulated

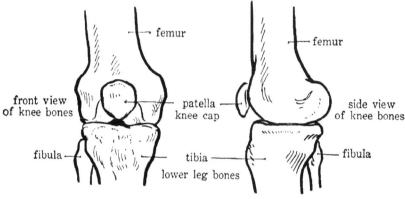

front view of knee bones — femur — patella knee cap — side view of knee bones — fibula — tibia — lower leg bones — fibula

FIG. 74. Knee joints.

weight of the body to the pelvis make a continuous adjustment necessary between the tensile and compression members, that is, between muscles, ligaments and bones.

If the legs in alternate action go forward in time to receive the weight, the weight is then controlled centrally, through hip and knee to ankle joint.

KNEES

The knee is the largest joint in the body. Its size insures stability in spite of various mechanical disadvantages. Due to the length of levers meeting at this point, it has the least possibility of adjustment laterally. The knee can meet the vertical weight-thrust only by broader bone surfaces and a peculiar design for the attachment of its tough, restricting ligaments. But the knee is unfitted for meeting stresses from slantwise thrusts of weight, such as occur when one slips on a banana peel. This is because there are·no bones at the side for lateral muscle attachments through which it might recover balance.

Moreover, the knees are subject to almost unbroken momentum of the moving weights, so far as direction of weight-thrust is concerned. This is due to the way in which the joint has straightened in the upright position. In the animal, the body-weight is redirected successively through the joints of the hind legs, which have a spring-like design at hip, knee and ankle. In the upright posture the weight is transmitted through the long bone of the femur in a plane practically vertical and parallel to the direction of the spine. This increases the chance for shock on the knee. One saving element is offered by the fact that the femur does slant medially to meet the tibia at the knee; this fact, and the fact that it is so deeply buried in muscles with close-knit fascial sheaths, serve to counteract the effect of the action of the long bony levers which it connects.

LOWER LEGS AND ANKLES

The arrangement of the lower bones of the leg makes up somewhat for the mechanical disadvantages of the knee and can take up a good portion of the shock incident upon it from the long thigh-bone above.

The interosseus membrane, a tough meshwork of ligament, laces together the tibia and fibula, lying between them along their entire inner vertical borders. As noted before, it appears very much like the lacings of a snow-shoe and acts in the same manner, as a shock absorber to distribute the force of impact over large surfaces. One of the most important posture muscles in the body, the tibialis posterior, is closely connected with the action and integration of this membrane, and with the plantar fascia of the foot.

If the weight is controlled at each stage by allowing the upper muscles their sling-like action, it will pass with relative ease through the lower bones to the ankle and foot. Thereafter, responsibility for support will spread evenly from the talus, the keystone of the supporting arch of the foot, to the metatarsals and toes. This reduces strain on all small parts of the foot and prevents pronation of ankles.

The pronated ankle, as noted before, spreads the inner side of the longitudinal arch, lowers the arch, and allows the ankle bone to protrude. Each change occasions another, and so the vicious circle continues. Eventually the muscle tendons on the plantar aspect of the tarsus, which belong to the long muscles of the sides and back of the leg arising just below the knee joint, become irritated and strained. Through their reciprocal action, these muscles safely guide and control the weight of the body through the relatively slender leg bones which must carry it to the arches of the feet. Serious maladjustment in their teamwork produces real trouble. Through disturbed reflexes, pain may be either local or referred to remote points, even as far as the neck or head. All body tissues persevere in fighting strains. It is often difficult to determine which member will yield to the strain first—nerve, muscle, or bone. Ultimately the nerve does the crying.

The alignment of the ankle bones is as dependent upon the muscles above as on those below. The body is a unit, and each part depends upon its fellow, no part being fixed. Muscles act together upon their bony levers to effect balance. They should be freed for this purpose. Their response must meet the two main necessities: mechanical reaction and muscular coordination. The one involves the principle that action and reaction are equal and opposite, and the other that through the mechanism of reciprocal muscle action, organized movement is possible. One is a universal principle of pure mechanics; the other, a biological principle of the living organism. These two principles must be coincident in time-space-movement for smooth balance and controlled action.

Examples of swift, easy walkers occur to all of us, the Indian, with "pard-like tread," being the familiar classic. The cat climbs a stairway noiselessly, his weights propelled from the rear. But note how noisy he is going downstairs when he cannot control the weights because his unaccustomed front feet must bear them first. At night, walking is easier and quieter than by day. This is because, undistracted by sight, the body falls into the ancient, unlearned patterns of movement in which the mechanics are blocked less by self-conscious constraints, and the primary reflexes may carry through.

THE GAME OF WALKING

Treat walking as a game. At some appointed time, at least once a day, let a group of motivating pictures pass clearly through the consciousness. Get the feeling of release from fixed habits of holding special parts in particular positions, as you fall into the patterns of the pictures. Following are a few suggestions for the appropriate imagery:

While walking, imagine as suggested before, a dinosaur tail dragging from the end of your spine, and your legs trying to run away from it. Again, imagine as you walk that you are kicking the autumn leaves in a field or wading through the current of a stream.

As the axis of the spine should be long, imagine that your head is reaching up toward a hook in the sky, and like Bluebeard's wives, you are hanging by the hair. This should give a feeling of stretch to the back of your neck and to the lower spine, but without raising the chest. This thought of stretching lengthens the axis of the spine.

The spine functions best when its axis is long. The opposing curves are then closely set to the axis with the intrinsic tensile and compression forces balanced. With this long axis the weight will be traveling in the most direct line possible through the spine. Also with a long spinal axis the body-wall tensile members at the front will be doing their share of work to keep the weight balanced.

The spine can lengthen its axis only downward. The head, a load of 15 or more pounds, has nothing above on which to pull, so it cannot lengthen the spine upward. The spinal axis is lengthened and the spine integrated by the compression and tensile forces, balancing at each curve. As the weight of each segment settles upon the next, all small muscles and ligaments at this level balance, by their tensile forces, the compression forces in the bones. The effect of this action of the soft tissues is to integrate the curves, drawing them closer to the spinal axis. The end-result would be a longer axis and less energy expenditure at each segment through which the weight must travel from top to bottom. It travels in a more direct line between two points.

FIG. 75. Hanging in Japanese parasol.

The head is thus elevated, as the lower spine pulls under to control it, and the extensors of the spine pull down. The added tensile forces of the body-wall aid in this control. The weight of the head may then travel in a straight line to the ground, but the chain of events that makes this happen is initiated in the spine as the thought of reaching up with the head engages all the appropriate reflexes—the extensors pulling down, the front body-wall pulling up and the lateral diameter of the upper chest reducing. Thus all vertical lines lengthen.

Another picture for balanced walking is to imagine yourself sitting on a third leg, dropped from the end of the spine (like the cane with the folding handle seat used at the polo field) and that your real legs are trying to run away from you.

Imagine yourself hanging from a tree, in the form of an open Japanese parasol, with toes dangling on the ground and head above the spread parasol. Fold down the parasol around the spine and, in imagination, draw up the pelvis and legs vertically towards the head, so that the closing folds of the parasol come down around them.

Or, like a frightened turtle, stop a moment and shorten the legs as though drawing them under a shell toward the center of the body. This procedure, which is accomplished by the deep pelvic and spinal muscles, will center the legs toward the spine, ready for renewed and balanced movement.

The pelvis and the thorax belong together and should be so well integrated by the inner pelvic muscles and the abdominal wall that the whole trunk may seem to be a cylindrical unit, like those of primitive dolls and animal toys. This organic unit within the body is continuous and should not be stretched apart in front. It cannot be stretched in the back.

Continue to walk with the thought of a bicycle chain clicking down the back over each vertebra as it travels, then turning and clicking up the front, carrying each bony point closer to the next one, until it reaches the hyoid bone (Adam's apple) when it turns and starts down the back again. Keep this going for several rounds and see how light your feet become!

The actual process involved in bicycle riding is one which unifies the whole body and is worthy of our consideration. The trunk and arms and legs are directly involved in moving and controlling the movement of the bicycle, so that the bicycle and the rider become in effect one machine for locomotion, employing several similar mechanical devices for transferring and multiplying power. Another form of unified action is horseback riding, the index of its excellence being that "rider and horse seem one." However, the mechanics in this case are different and not so enlightening as to the human body mechanics as in the case of bicycle riding.

Let us carry our analogy further by reviewing what happens

mechanically, when riding a chain-wheeled bicycle. Your feet are *walking* on the pedals, and your ischia (the extreme lower portions of the innominate bones) are *sitting* on the seat, which is just the right width to accommodate them. As you pedal, you are moving a large sprocket wheel, over which a block chain passes to a small sprocket wheel, attached to the rear wheel of the bicycle, which is held down by your weight through the seat above it. The motive power furnished by the muscles of your thighs and lower trunk propels the whole bicycle and yourself forward. You can progress with ease and speed because the muscular force is multiplied through the mechanism of the pedals, the sprocket wheels and chain, and is controlled in its application directly at the back wheel. That is, the power is precisely centered, and not dissipated by lost motions away from center.

While the bicycle moves forward on a horizontal axis, your body is acting in much the same fashion at right angles to it. In fact, your machinery and the bicycle's are parts of the same locomotor mechanism, both operating by the same mechanical principles, with active and passive phases, and the application of compression and tensile forces. Thus the larger sprocket wheel turns forward by the active drive of your foot on the pedals (compression force), and the chain is pulled forward by the large sprocket wheel and pulled back by the small sprocket wheel (tensile force). As one foot on the pedal passes the lowest horizontal point in its circular motion about the center, the whole leg relaxes. It is carried back and up by its own weight and momentum, and the drive of the other foot, until it returns to the top to restart the cycle, when the leg, thigh and pelvic muscles contract again for the downward push. As one foot is up the other is down, so the motion of the whole mechanism is continuously forward in the same line; each leg is alternately active and passive, as in walking.

So, while walking, *sit* in the pelvis as though you were on the bicycle seat, and feel the compression forces in your back carrying the weight *into* the seat; and imagine that the pavement has a little give, or response, to your feet, as the pedals have; and as you apply your power in walking, think *up* the front of your body to keep the tensile members integrated.

The balancing power between the compression members in the back and the tensile members in front is like the bicycle chain. Should something happen to make either portion of the chain relax or contract more than the other, it could not be moved forward, around, back, and up over the little wheel, and forward again smoothly; and its power for multiplying the muscular force from your body would be lost. So with the body-strength. The weight comes down the back, and the power, gaining in force as the weight accumulates toward the pelvic arch, would unbalance the structure if it were not balanced and checked by the lifting strength at the front of the spine and of the front muscle-wall connecting the pelvis with the thorax, the neck and the head. The lifting strength of the front wall is lost if the members are stretched. Compensations elsewhere in the body must then take place.

So it is not purely a fantastic analogy that is suggested between the body and the bicycle. Power, in the form of compression force, comes down the back and turns forward through the pelvis, and in the form of tensile force it travels upward again from pelvis to the top of the chain, through sternum, hyoid, mandible, to the base of the skull, and down the spine again. This keeps the whole machine steady, so that the drive of the muscle force, added to the weight, can be continued into the legs and provide the strength to swing them in walking or running, to drive the bicycle ahead or kick a football.

RÔLE OF THE EYES IN WALKING

The final game suggested is one that had best be played where strangers cannot see you, and where you can stop quickly and rest, as it may make you dizzy: Lay a tape on the ground for a guide, then with an opera glass or field glass look down at your feet through the large end, and see how straight you can walk. You will find it very hard to keep on the tape so long as you keep looking at your feet through the glasses. The reason is that the primary reflexes between your eye muscles and the rest of your proprioceptive reflexes, in the semicircular canals and otoliths in the ears, or in your leg and thigh muscles, are thrown out of gear by the different-appearing distances between your head and the floor. You cannot believe your senses, and you stagger more or less drunkenly, the amount being dependent upon your sensibility to these impressions.

Unless disturbed by some such extraordinary change in the sequence of impressions as in this last game, or as in trying to walk toward an object while looking at its reflection in a mirror, your native reflexes are pretty well geared for walking straight in the desired direction. But fatigue will set in rapidly unless the balances are maintained.

It is safe to assume that the dynamic rhythms will carry through in walking if the forehead, the upper chest at the manubrium, and the front of the thighs are kept persistently in the lead. This keeps the back straight and the lumbar-pelvic-thigh muscles in command of the weight.

When you finish with these pictures, you will find that you are no longer walking with your chest and neck, but that your center of gravity has lowered and your pelvis and thighs are easily carrying your spine and its adjoined weight forward. You walk with a lighter tread and a high head. Hissing through the teeth while walking aids in these games. It may sound silly, but it *works*.

Chapter VIII

BREATHING

RHYTHMS

TO BREATHE IS LIFE. WITHOUT BREATH WE DIE. TO BREATHE RHYTHMICALLY IS HEALTH BUT THERE ARE AS MANY possible maladjustments in the breathing mechanism as there are in the arrangement and use of the bony system. The near-normal human being employs many of these and the neurotic most of them.

The diaphragm and its associates, both nervous and muscular, reach into the deepest recesses of the individual. At present, the diaphragm is the least understood of all the vital agents of human living. It is tied up with every living function, from the psychic to the structural, and within its nervous mechanism sends out ramifications to the remotest points of the sphere of living. Like the equator, it is the dividing line of two great halves of being: the conscious and the unconscious, the voluntary and the involuntary, the skeletal and the visceral. Through a deeper study of the unconscious we unlock more of its mysteries.

The secrets of the function of breathing are vast and much research must be done before we can understand the intricate connections of the diaphragm, in their relation to all expressions of life, physical, mental and emotional. In this mechanism must reside the accurate time-keeper of the changing rhythms of the various systems involved in living.

In the study of human strains produced by the activities of daily living, it is important for us to realize that locomotion and breathing developed together. We must also remember that dangers were greater on land than in water, coming from more

217

directions—up, down and all about. In a park in Los Angeles, there is a bed of quicksand from which (it is reported) the bones of prehistoric animals have been recovered. This is just one of the many types of danger that had to be faced unexpectedly on land, which would never have been encountered in the water.

To meet the land hazards, a highly integrated, delicate and intricate development of nerve reflexes and musculature must keep the organism acquainted with the needs, and supplied with the means to meet them. Stimuli must be switched to and from the different systems which make up the bodily economy. The organism must be protected and at the same time, powers must be projected to meet these dangers.

Therefore a mechanism must be supplied for both these purposes. We have means provided to meet every conceivable emergency; the mechanisms of locomotion and respiration, and the nervous and glandular devices that afford protection to the vital functions of the viscera during strenuous, accelerated activities.

CHANGES IN BREATHING

It is a long step in the evolution of the living creature from gills, in which gas exchange is made at the surface of the body, to lungs through which this exchange is made within the body.

In man, and other air-breathing vertebrates, the lungs afford large surfaces for gas interchange by means of their billions of tiny air sacs. These sacs are supplied with a fine meshwork of capillaries, arranged just beneath their surfaces. In respiration, the rapid circulation of blood in the capillaries and pressure of air in the air sacs effect an exchange of the gases, oxygen and carbon-dioxide. Oxygen is taken from the air and drawn into the blood through the air sacs. Carbon dioxide, one of the waste products of the body, is at the same time drawn into the air sacs from the blood, to be eliminated at once in exhalation. This entire process, inhalation and exhalation, and exchange of gases in the lung sacs, is called "external respiration"—by Lavoisier, "primary breathing."

The oxygen which has been taken into the blood must then be prepared for distribution to the myriad cells throughout the body which are clamoring for it. This preparation is made by the hemoglobin of the blood. In this we find another of the balances essential to life, that of blood balance.

The upkeep of bodily cells depends upon blood balance. One of the important constituents for blood balance is hemoglobin, contained in the red corpuscles, the oxygen carriers. With serious reduction of the red corpuscles oxygen has no means of reaching the body cells. If the hemoglobin is seriously reduced, the cells of the entire body are facing death by suffocation.

The exchange of oxygen contained in the red corpuscles with carbon dioxide contained in the body cells is called "internal respiration." It is effected through the cell-wall and the capillaries in the same manner as it is through the walls of the lung sacs and their capillaries. Lavoisier, who first described it, called this phase "secondary breathing." These two functions of respiration take place simultaneously. Rhythmic, dynamic adjustment of bodily tissues is the outcome, and in the functioning of this dual breathing mechanism we may observe again our bodily structures attaining balance between the two phases of living: activity and rest.

The extensive mechanics of breathing must be more fully studied before we can understand the meaning of metabolic balance, and maladjustments produced by or causing muscular hypertension. These problems are tied with problems of the primary patterns of movement necessitated by breathing air, walking on hard surfaces, and surviving in the face of new dangers.

RHYTHMIC COORDINATION

Coordination of breathing rhythms and skeletal rhythms must be continued as the animal prepares for the unusual. Responses must be accelerated and with as little interference as possible with the vegetative organism. In extreme emotion, anger or fear, for example, the central nervous system does many things—

plugs in on many switchboards unused in quiet living; through the action of the glands the skeletal muscles are prepared to fight or run; through the autonomic, the vegetative system is inhibited for protection of vital processes. All stimulation and energy are poured into the skeletal muscles which will then act with maximum power and speed to meet the emergency. In this mechanism lies the reserve strength for the athlete; the "second wind" for the runner. The power that we unconsciously call upon to do the deeds that are ever after looked upon as "superhuman," is in no wise superhuman, but merely beyond the capacity of the conscious self. We have examples of the operation of this life-saving device in the great deeds of any age, in physical prowess and in outstanding mental achievements.

The body is unstable or it would not have survived. It is just enough unstable to make possible the constant struggle for equilibrium between its parts. When the animal developed to meet the hazards of living on land, mechanisms evolved for both function and structure: to meet the need of locomotion over hard surfaces, to take oxygen from air instead of from water, and to relay it to the deep recesses of the body. With reduced pressures on body areas, new sensory adjustments and new structures developed to meet the new needs. Without going into extensive detail, we find in the proprioceptive system and in the body materials, all that is needed for bodily coordination and for subtle and speedy adjustment to meet these changes on land. The bony structure and the neuromuscular unit are designed to make the necessary adjustments of balance and rhythm in locomotion. The breathing apparatus and the timing mechanism relating breathing rhythms to skeletal rhythms are developed to meet the need for getting oxygen to all the deep body cells, burning up in the activities of living; and this is done with complete harmony between the rhythms of the two systems. In addition, another provision must be made by nature simultaneously, to protect the visceral organism from the strains produced by the other two acting mechanisms. Also when in such extreme emotional drives as those involved in fighting or escaping, no demand must be made from visceral organs, their activities must be inhibited. These needs are met through action of the glands and the sympathetic nervous system, regulating the rhythms of the vital parts. No animal has time to stop for diarrhea in the midst of a fight.

These patterns of response are unlearned and primary. They are all that we have upon which to base our understanding of the struggle for equilibrium, physical, mental or emotional, and may guide us to possible methods for regaining equilibrium after it is lost.

The parts composing the systems operating in these rhythmic balances to be studied are: skeletal balance, already discussed in this text; respiratory balance, now being considered; emotional balance, which must be understood as affecting both these as well as the visceral rhythms.

THE DIAPHRAGM

The diaphragm is the most active agent in breathing. It is a muscular structure which forms the floor of the thoracic cage and the roof of the abdominal cavity. Its outer rim of muscle fibers, attached on the inner side of the rib-cage, arises from the lower border of the rib-cage in front, on the sides, and from the lumbar spine in the back. This muscular rim converges upon a middle tendinous sheet, shaped like a double cupola, called the centrum tendineum. The whole structure is in the shape of a lop-sided mushroom with its stem nearer to the back margin than to the front. The heart rests on the top of the diaphragm, and the liver, stomach and spleen are immediately beneath its under surface. All of these viscera are in close contact with it and even directly connected with its tissues.

The diaphragm, then, is so situated and attached to parts of the skeleton and to parts of the viscera, as to be able to function in close relationship with both the visceral rhythms and the skeletal rhythms, is affected by them and has an effect upon them.

Through deepening of the thoracic cavity, the movement of

the diaphragm affects the rhythms of the thoracic viscera. By stimulating peristalsis and pressure upon other abdominal viscera, it affects the digestive rhythms; and through internal respiration and the associated muscle attachments of its long fibers, it affects the rhythms of the skeletal musculature. So it is closely tied to the organic rhythms and to the skeletal rhythms.

It is the only muscle having such a strategic position between the rhythms of the two systems. To a degree, it responds to voluntary directions—but only to a degree. One may hold one's breath for but a limited time, usually less than a minute. One may voluntarily starve by denying oneself food; it is physically impossible for one to starve voluntarily for the want of oxygen.

REST ALTERNATING WORK

Next to the heart, the diaphragm is the most continuously active of all body structures. It does not become fatigued, partly, because like the heart, its rest periods are longer than its working periods; that is, the phase of relaxation is longer than that of contraction. Expiration normally lasts from 1.3 to 1.4 times the length of inspiration, and there is, moreover, a slight pause after expiration.

Like the "rest" that the musician employs in composition, to enhance and amplify appreciation of musical tone quality and variation in phrasing, so Nature employs frequent rest periods. It is as though Nature must reestablish the potential energy balance before allowing it to be employed again in kinetic form. In all such rest periods, we find that some part of the adjoining body musculature is reinforced automatically as a product of this rhythm in movement.

The movements of the diaphragm illustrate especially well the principle of coordination of muscles, as they alternate in action and rest, so important a feature in the economy of bodily activities. In the case of the diaphragm, as it relaxes during expiration, the tone of the abdominal muscles is augmented; while during inspiration, their tone is inhibited. Also, the individual muscle fibers of the whole diaphragm work in relays

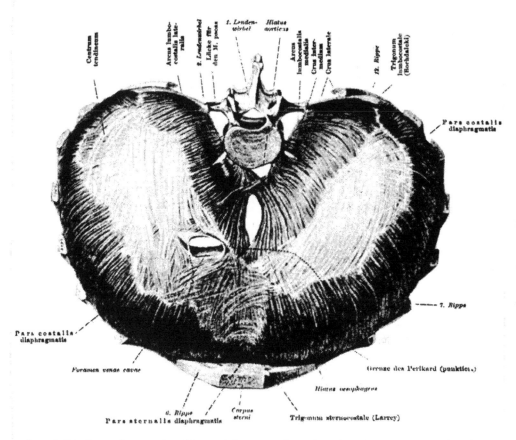

FIG. 76. Diaphragm in natural position and form, seen from thoracic cavity. Note curve of surface at circumference, indicating dome shape of upper surface of centrum tendineum. Esophagus passes through meaty portion of muscle, thus allowing diaphragm to act upon wall of esophagus in its up and down stroke. Blood vessels, aorta and vena cava pass through that part of diaphragm where less action takes place. Arcuate ligament protects aorta from ever being affected by action of diaphragm and vena cava only in deep breathing, when diaphragm aids return of blood to heart. (From Braus.)

[223]

during the contraction periods: potential energy into kinetic—kinetic back to potential again.

Reciprocal action between the diaphragm and the abdominal muscles is so marked that where there is a loss of tone in the abdominal muscles, as in a condition of visceroptosis, with accompanying increased lordosis of the lumbar spine and increased obliquity of the pelvis, the action of the diaphragm may be seriously disturbed. As the tone of the iliopsoas muscles is lost in this state of maladjustment, the weight that should be carried through the lumbar vertebrae is dragging upon all muscles attached to these vertebrae and to the pelvis. The iliopsoas, the quadratus lumborum and the abdominal obliques are stretched. We could, in this case, continue to analyze unbalanced muscles throughout the structure, as with the unbalance of weight, carried through the bones, muscular unbalance must inevitably follow. When this unbalance takes place at the base, free motion and reciprocal action between the supporting muscles are lost. The whole structure would lean forward and topple if the extensors of the back did not increase their pulls upon the skull and sacrum to keep the spine erect. It is a hard load to manage, and it is small wonder that such backs get stiff and tired.

If the pelvis is balanced, swinging easily between spine and legs, the extensors of the trunk are free from strain and can aid in lengthening the rib-cage. On the other hand, if these dorsal spinal muscles are pulling upward on the pelvis to compensate for an increase of pelvic obliquity (due to the failure of deep-lying pelvic muscles to balance the load between spine and legs) the muscles of the back will be unable to function freely in the thoracic region. Under these conditions, normal lengthening of the rib-cage in breathing cannot take place, as it does when lying down, as in sleep.

TRUNK EXTENSORS AND TRUNK FLEXORS

It may be well at this point to review the action of trunk extensors and flexors, to picture their balances more clearly, in controlling and moving the spinal structure.

Considering the whole spine and trunk as a unit, with muscles capable of moving it in various directions, as to bend it over or straighten it out, we find the muscles distributed to the back or front according to their general function. All muscles which tend to straighten the back have their complementary muscles tending to bend it toward the front, and any motion between the extremes of bending and extension is effected by a mutual adjustment in action of the two sets. The spine, lying between these two planes of action, is moved back and forth at its various levels, that is at its separate vertebrae, the degree being dependent on the position of any given vertebra in the curve of its region, and the limitations made on its motion by its attachments to adjoining parts. The movability of the several vertebrae is quite various. In some areas, as in the upper chest, they are only slightly movable, the whole arrangement of side processes and attachments being designed to maintain a relatively stable and symmetrical cavity within, for the upper thoracic viscera. Extreme flexion or extension of the trunk does not vitally affect this area. Another limitation on local motion of the spinal segments is the necessity for assuring a steady route for the transference of weight through them to the pelvis.

So far as location along the spine is concerned, the muscle groups dorsal to the lateral processes of the vertebrae belong in the extensor class, including the longitudinal muscles lying in the gutter of the spine and extending from head to pelvis; and associated muscles as far forward as the mid-lateral line of the side wall of the body. The flexors of the trunk are those muscles attached at the front of the spine, which would, upon contracting, bend the body forward. When these two sets of muscles are in balanced action, they aid breathing by lengthening the thoracic spine and integrating the lumbar spine, upon whose integrity the diaphragm depends for support.

ANATOMY OF THE DIAPHRAGM

The regular rhythmic movements of breathing, which last from the moment of birth to the very end of life, are those of the diaphragm. The active fibers of the diaphragm are of dif-

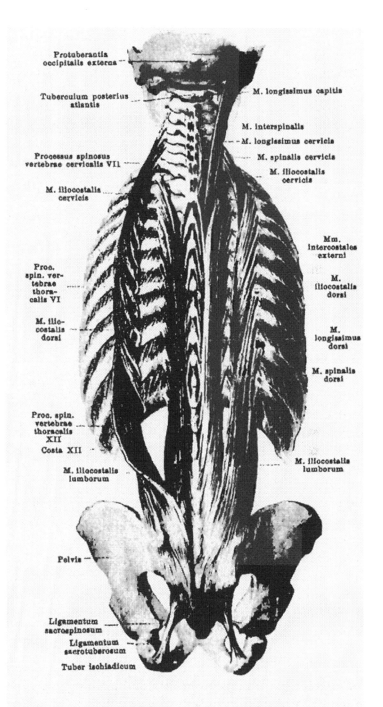

FIG. 77. Trunk extensors of back. (From Spalteholz.)

[227]

ferent lengths and directions, and the effect of their contractions varies accordingly. Three groups are distinguished by their place of origin: the sternal, the costal and the lumbar portions.

The sternal portion of the diaphragm, which is the shortest, arises as two bands from the back of the lowest section of the sternum, and runs up and back to insert into the middle front of the centrum tendineum.

The costal portions arise at origins of the transversalis, from the borders of the cartilages of the six lower ribs as they slope away from the sternum in the costal angle. These fibers pass upward and backward and insert into the sides of the centrum tendineum, and make up the largest portion of the contractile rim. (See Fig. 78.)

The lumbar portion consists of two sets of fibers. The first set arises from two fascial structures known as the arcuate ligaments, which stretch between the first lumbar vertebra and the twelfth ribs, arching successively over the heavy bands of the greater psoas and quadratus lumborum muscles. These fibers pass upward and forward, forming the rim of the diaphragm at the back. The second set of lumbar fibers is in the form of two relatively long muscle bands, known as crura, which complete the inner margins of the arcuate ligaments and arise from the anterior and lateral surfaces of the first four lumbar vertebrae. The crura are the longest fibers of the diaphragm muscle, and act to pull the diaphragm down, inserting into the middle of the back of the centrum tendineum.

Because of their shape and position, the action of the crura is more easily comprehended than that of the other muscle fibers of the diaphragm. It is their contraction that is most definitely involved in the pulling downward of the top of the dome of the diaphragm. Their action can also be most readily interfered with by any unfavorable pressure upon them, such as may be exerted by the lumbar spine when the curve is exaggerated by unbalanced conditions.

In shape, the diaphragm is a double dome, the larger one being on the right, into which the liver fits, while the stomach and spleen lie under the smaller left dome. The heart rests on the upper surface of the diaphragm, the pericardium being continuous with the middle part of the centrum tendineum. This part of the centrum tendineum where the heart lies is the

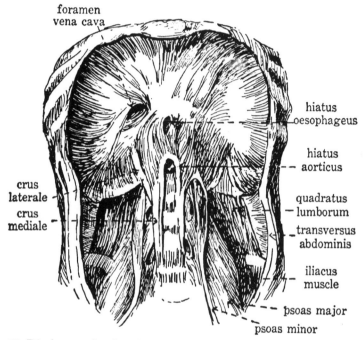

FIG. 78. Diaphragm, showing close association of psoas and quadratus lumborum muscles with crura.

least contractile and moves less during breathing than the two domes.

The diaphragm is penetrated by a number of structures, including the esophagus, the great aorta, the vena cava, the thoracic duct and various nerves. Some of these are so placed that the muscular fibers press upon them during contractions, and others are scarcely affected by the movements of the diaphragm. Thus, the esophagus penetrates a most active area between the fibers of the crura, which surround it in a sphincter-like fashion, and can thus exert pressure upon it. This opening is called the hiatus œsophageus, and the vagus nerve and the arteries and veins supplying the esophagus also pass through it.

Below, and to the back of this opening, is another called the hiatus aorticus, which is formed by the two crural bands as they pass upward from the lumbar vertebrae, and is arched by a tendinous band, the median arcuate ligament. Through the hiatus aorticus pass the great aorta, main arterial trunk line for the whole body below the thorax, and the thoracic duct, which is the main channel for the lymphatic circulation. This aperture is so located that the fibers of the crura in contracting cannot lessen it, in fact cannot affect it in any way. The vena cava passes through the centrum tendineum, and in shallow breathing very little if any motion takes place here. In deep inspiration, however, all parts of the diaphragm move, even that part attached to cardiac fibers. Thus venous circulation is aided by deep diaphragm action. Increased action of all basic muscles accessory to breathing: quadratus lumborum, transversalis, iliopsoas, levator ani and coccygeus, even down to the thigh muscles, is another aid to that overworked organ, the heart. Their action drains the venous blood from the fatigued muscles and returns it to the lungs for aeration, thence back to the heart. This action removes toxins from tense muscles, thus enabling arterial blood to be distributed to their cells more easily.

FUNCTION OF DIAPHRAGM

Mechanically, deep breathing increases the space around the upper heart structures within the area of the first three ribs. Wide and too full breathing brings into play the upper accessory muscles, before the diaphragm has made its fullest possible vertical excursion. The result of this type of breathing, if carried to extreme, is to tense all muscles of the shoulder structure, neck and jaw, and to reduce the longitudinal diameter of the chest cavity by increasing the horizontal diameter. If vertical depth is attained, to the full extent of the stretch of the thoracic spine, the expansion horizontally will accompany it in extended breathing. This latter function should be secondary. The strain in the muscles about the clavicle, upper scapulae and top ribs interferes with the circulatory structures at the important top area of the heart, if high, spherical breathing is encouraged.

Breathing is automatic. It is controlled by the medulla oblongata, a lower part of the brain. Its automatic action is initiated the moment the blood, passing through the medulla, reports too great a load of carbon dioxide. But breathing may be influenced by emotional states and bodily movements, both voluntary and involuntary. The rhythms of the diaphragm, during sleep, are slow and regular, but in emergencies, increase in speed and force in respiratory movements.

ACTION OF DIAPHRAGM

The action of the diaphragm, effected by the contractions of the muscle fibers in its rim and stem, as we have seen, is to lower the centrum tendineum, and thus lengthen the cavity about the lungs, which hang suspended in the rib-cage from above. At the same time that the surface of the diaphragm is lowered by the contracting of its crura, the ribs and sternum are lifted and the thoracic spine lengthened by the action of the intercostal and spinal muscles. The diameter of the chest from front to back also is increased; in this way the cavity may be enlarged in all dimensions.

By this action of the intercostal muscles, the distance between the ribs is increased. At the same time, the extensor muscles of the spine should be free from strains of structural unbalance, to allow their free movement between the vertebrae. To maintain the symmetry of the thoracic wall in the deepening of its cavity, incident to breathing, the spaces between the ribs in the back must increase to equal the increase of the spaces between the ribs in front of the thoracic cage. As by far the greater number of lung sacs lie behind the plane of the front border of the spine, a free action of skeletal parts in this region is necessary for balanced breathing.

INTERRELATED STRUCTURES

During inspiration, the air rushes into the myriad sacs of the lungs when the space about the pleura is enlarged. When the diaphragm relaxes, after this lung expansion, the ribs and sternum lower by their own weight, the sacs collapse, and air is expelled.

In these motions, all parts of the thorax are involved to some degree, but the muscular contractions of the diaphragm are the most definite, so that quiet breathing is practically confined to the diaphragm. Accompanying this, however, is action of the intercostals and the extensor muscles of the back, which aid in lengthening the breathing cage. If muscles of the shoulder girdle are holding the ribs fixed and too spherical, this lengthening is impossible, and wide breathing rather than deep breathing will take place. As breathing becomes more active, other muscles are engaged, one accessory group following another, beginning with the lower. The muscles to be added in close succession are the psoas, followed by the transversalis and the quadratus lumborum, which complete the inner muscular lining of the body-wall. All these muscles are in close association with the diaphragm through fascial structures or with interdigitating fibers. (See Fig. 78.) Accelerated breathing may involve all trunk muscles extending down as far as the levator ani and coccygeus muscles which form the pelvic diaphragm. It may also involve muscles as far up as those connecting chest and head, such as the sterno-cleido-mastoideus, and in extreme activity, even muscles of the legs, arms and jaw may be included. All body muscles can assist in breathing when the need is great, but in primary patterns of movement upper accessory muscles are the last to be called upon.

The diaphragm is lowered only from 1 to 1.25 cm., or about half an inch, in quiet breathing, and only a little more in active breathing. If this seems a small distance, remember that the whole diaphragm extends over a very large area, and that the distance it moves vertically multiplies many times into the cubic content of the cavity. The diameter of the large surface, extending horizontally across the entire body cavity, in the lower thorax, would be from 12 to 15 inches. To lower such a bulk even a short distance from its circumferential attachments offers quite a problem to the muscular structures of the crural arch and adjoined trunk muscles. Gravity, however, favors the short, stocky, radiating fibers of the crural arch for their task. They are favored also by the arrangements of ligaments and muscles of the lumbar region, which through fascial and muscular connections increase the power of the radial pull downward.

The crura of the diaphragm, which are the active agents in drawing it downward in inspiration, are closely associated in their attachments to the lumbar spine with the iliopsoas and quadratus lumborum muscles, which, as we have noted, are in turn importantly occupied in the support of the trunk on the pelvis and the transfer of weights through the spine to the pelvis and legs. Breathing and skeletal support in this region are closely interrelated. If the lumbar spine is unduly curved, the anterior longitudinal ligament, and thus the crura, are stretched, weakening the action of the psoas and quadratus lumborum. The weight of the trunk is thrown forward, bringing added strain to the spinal curves, with the effect of changing the axes of the crura and limiting the range and power of their piston-like action.

The transversalis abdominis, interdigitating as it does with the diaphragm and attaching to the ribs, pelvis and spinal column by the lumbar fascia, functions as a structural and balancing muscle to help maintain the cylindrical design of the body-wall. Its fibers run horizontally about the body, so that it may be accurately described as a "belly-band" muscle. Its origins and insertions are deep-set into the bony rims to which it is attached, under the ribs and under the deep borders of the pubis and ilia. It is a muscle associated closely with the diaphragm and with the pelvic and lumbar regions, through its connections with the deep fascia and the iliopsoas and quadratus lumborum muscles above and the levator ani below. Thus acting together with the very important fascial sheaths, it connects the two diaphragms, the thoracic and the pelvic.

If free from the strain of maladjustments in the adjoining bony parts, the transversalis aids in supporting the visceral structures and functions as an active part of the breathing apparatus. But this favorable action can be interfered with if the

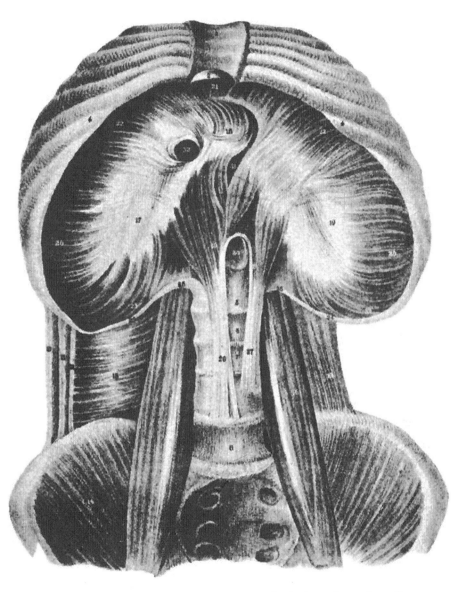

FIG. 79. Diaphragm: 1, Sternum; 3 and 4, beginning of costal cartilages; 8, fifth lumbar vertebra; 9, crests of ilia; 13, transversalis muscle; 14, quadratus muscle; 15, great psoas; 25, ligamentum arcuatum; 26, 27, 28, 29, crura of diaphragm; 30, aorta aperture; 31, esophageal aperture; 32, vena cava aperture. (From Quain and Wilson.)

rib-cage is held out of easy balance, as when an attempt is made to broaden it laterally for "full breathing," or to hold it high and rigid to follow a false concept of desirable posture. Under these circumstances, there is little if any interplay between the ribs, in the back. The chest is held up laterally or moved as a fixed spherical mass, while the muscles attached to the shoulder girdle and neck, through their contractions, are carrying loads which should be distributed to the various vertebral levels of each individual pair of ribs.

When we are holding our chests up with the back of the neck the whole body suffers. The shoulders are held back so that their free movements are checked, as are those of the arms. The function of the respiratory system is interfered with by limitation of the diaphragm; and because the lumbar spine, in an effort to compensate for the unbalanced load at the top, is curved more deeply forward and the sacrum inclined more acutely, the balanced action of the deep body-wall muscles of the back, abdomen and pelvis is greatly hampered.

Centering the weights in accord with the principles of mechanical balance secures a firm body-wall, with weight and side strains removed from the inner structures. As a consequence, maximum protection is afforded for both the dorsal canal with its precious contents, the central nervous system, and the ventral canal, with heart, lungs, alimentary canal, kidneys and the great veins and arteries. If a hollow cylinder, one-third the width of the shoulders, were dropped through the body from head to pelvis, it would enclose most of the important viscera—all the vital parts. For the first quarter of its length this cylinder would include the strong walls of the laryngeal cartilages and the spine. For its second quarter, it would be surrounded by the walls of the rib-cage. Its last half would contain the massive lumbar spine, its strong supporting curve extending to the center of the cylinder, the base of which would be enclosed by the bony pelvic girdle. From the lumbar vertebrae, in this strong, centrally disposed spinal base, the diaphragm gets its purchase and may be aided in its ceaseless task by the balance of all these structures. Especially is the secondary phase of breathing, that of internal respiration, aided by the balance and activity of the lower accessory muscles.

DEEP CONTROL OF BODY MOVEMENT

Motions of the body as a whole are mainly controlled by the lumbar and deep pelvic muscles. These muscles, as we have seen, reach up into the upper parts of the body, even to the arms and head, and down into the legs.

The animal walks, runs, springs, by means of power in his haunches. The forelegs are used primarily for balance and control of direction. With this biological inheritance, man should make more conscious use of his muscles in the pelvic and lumbar base, since it is by these muscles that the most skillful, as well as the strongest, movements are controlled. In throwing a ball, it is the strength of the muscles in the back, pelvis and thigh that makes the powerful pitcher, not alone the strength of shoulder and arm.

Coordination of the spine as a unit is greatly affected by the method of control of its more flexible parts. Full use of the deep-lying muscles of the pelvis and of the lower back in breathing is necessary to insure this coordination. At the same time there must be free movement of the vertebral joints and of the rib joinings in the thoracic spine. This freedom may be attained by consciously realizing a flexible, upper structure in easy balance and movement. Keep the top end of the sternum up and out and the lower end hanging freely downward. This releases the shoulder girdle. Kinesthetic perception in this area is not easy, but should be encouraged. We should associate the shoulder girdle, in our imagination, more closely with the head than with the chest, if we are to center the upper weights successfully on the spine. This converts a side-load into the more easily balanced top-load. In the primary patterns of movement, the thorax and pelvis work together, with breathing rhythms adjusted to the coordinated whole, while shoulders and arms follow the dictates of the head.

The support of the weight of the shoulder girdle, as noted

before, depends peculiarly on suspension. This can be realized best by following the bones, scapulae and clavicles, through their joinings to sternum, thence through ribs to spine—their

FIG. 80. "Winding up" for power and aim.

ultimate support, and through their suspensory muscles and attachments to the skull and the neck. One may do this by the few direct muscles running from skull and cervical verte-brae to clavicle and scapula and by the more numerous indirect attachments through the front structures of the neck and head, the hyoid, mandible and skull.

Each rib hangs at a particular vertebral level, and its weight, with that of the soft attached tissues, is supported by the vertebra with which it is articulated. By this arrangement, the load of the chest is quite evenly distributed over the thoracic spine. The sternum gives balancing support, through the cartilages of the ribs, to the entire rib-cage. It supports this weight from the skull as described.

The intercostal muscles and other muscular attachments at the spine and sternum can function freely only if the thorax hangs in easy balance between spine, sternum and head. The ribs are connected with other parts of the trunk and with the appendages, arms and legs, through the great systems of the back, pelvic, abdominal and shoulder-girdle muscles. Due to this, they are affected by large and wide movements peripherally, as well as by the deeper action of the central and lumbar muscle tracts.

Mobility of the ribs must be maintained at both sternal and vertebral extremities, to insure full excursion of the diaphragm and greater freedom for action of the intercostal muscles at the dorsal angles of the ribs, thereby securing a larger cavity for the lungs at the back. The action of the intercostal muscles at the dorsal angle of the ribs, with mobility at the ventral ends, will bring free action of the body-wall in breathing. The spine extends slightly to accommodate the diaphragmatic pull. Its flexibility is increased if the iliopsoas muscles are properly integrating the lumbar spine and the pelvis in balanced relationship. The transversalis, the iliopsoas muscles, and the quadratus lumborum can then aid the diaphragm in its downward excursions.

Since the crura are the active and primary agents in respiration, shallow breathing results from the reverse of these conditions, due to fixity and top-heavy situations. The effect of this is not fully evident until increase of muscular activity, as walking or carrying weights, throws greater responsibility upon the breathing apparatus, because of the more rapid burning of blood sugar in the muscles. In this event, the upper accessory muscles already called upon must increase their work and the diaphragm cannot pull against this tension. The extreme of such tension is the high, tight breathing of hysteria.

CHEMICAL BALANCE

The virtue of "full breathing" has been very much over-estimated. In the tidal air of quiet breathing there is all the oxygen needed for the use of the individual under ordinary circumstances. There is always oxygen as well as carbon dioxide exhaled from the lungs. This has been measured, under stated conditions of temperature and humidity, and found to compare as follows: oxygen contained in inspired air, 20.95 vols. per cent; expired air 16.4 vols. per cent; while carbon dioxide inspired was 0.04 vol. per cent; and expired, 4.1 vols. per cent.*

The amount of residual air present in the lungs is sufficient to keep the oxygen balance. Their content is about three quarts. When a greater amount of oxygen is needed for the body cells, as in extreme activity, there is deeper and faster breathing, not wider, "fuller" breathing, unless hysteria is present. When we gasp at a sudden shock, the ribs become rounder and stiffer. But the deep breathing in response to the physical and chemical needs of the inner cells of the body is vertical breathing.

These chemical balances Nature takes care of, and the individual need not concern himself with "filling the lungs." His task is to see that as many of his body muscles are free to act in breathing as may be consistent with his occupation. Deep action and not "full" action is the important thing.

BALANCED SUPPORT FOR THE THORAX

The balanced support of the thorax depends primarily upon the adjustment of the fourth and fifth lumbar vertebrae on the sacrum.

If the lower trunk and pelvic muscles are not interfered with by a stiff thoracic spine and its chain of effects, these are the first to act with the diaphragm; and only when the need becomes much greater are the upper accessory muscles of breathing called upon. If, however, the lower accessory muscles, the transversalis, iliopsoas, and levator ani cannot act freely, the upper accessory muscles are forced into action immediately. These upper shoulder muscles have their own independent work to do, in dealing with the environment in various ways, and should be called upon for extra respiratory work only as a last resort.

* Principles of Human Physiology, by Ernest H. Starling, 1936.

Local rigidities in and about the upper chest are thus seen to be handicaps to the coordination of the whole skeletal apparatus, including the appendicular portions, with increased pressure and added strain thrown upon the respiratory and vascular systems. With a balanced, curved spine, supported pelvis and free rib-cage, the powerful iliopsoas group, the levator ani, the transversalis and other lumbar muscles can aid the diaphragm immediately in its piston stroke in such increased activities as jumping or running. This will keep the thoracic and cervical spines and the shoulder girdle free for response in guiding the movements of the head and arms. In this process the center of gravity is lowered, pressure is removed from the vital systems within, and more of the unlearned patterns are engaged, thus providing normal rhythm between breathing and moving.

DIAPHRAGM AND SPINAL CURVES

The twelfth thoracic vertebra has a strategic position between the upper and lower parts of the trunk, as its dorsal spinous process is the lowest attachment for the trapezius muscle, and the sides of its body the first, or highest, origin of the great psoas. To it also the diaphragm is attached. The spinous process of the twelfth thoracic is long, though not quite as long as those of the lumbars, which it resembles in shape and direction. The trapezius is the great multiple muscle that aids in holding the spine, head, shoulder, arm and upper ribs in erect alignment and mutual adjustment. The iliopsoas is the muscle-group that chiefly holds together and moves the legs, pelvis and lumbar spine as a coordinated unit. Any pull, therefore, from above or below, powerfully affects the twelfth thoracic and compensations must be instantly established. If the iliopsoas muscles do not hold it firmly at the front, the twelfth thoracic is pulled up and back by the trapezius, during expansive arm and shoulder movements. This threatens both the thoracic and lumbar curves. It jeopardizes the redirection of weight between them and changes the action of the spine. Through this structural unbalance the action of the crural arch and its adjoined muscles and fascial sheets is changed in breathing. There is every reason for frequent trouble in this part of the spine. Some disturbances may come even from diaphragmatic irritation. They are often manifested by referred pains, either higher up or lower down. The areas of greatest weakness are the transitions between curves.

INTERDEPENDENT RHYTHMS

Both heart and breathing mechanisms in emergencies must increase their speed and force of movements, or sufficient oxygen is not carried to the burning muscle cells. In strenuous exercise, they must have about a quart with every inhalation. This is twice the amount needed in quiet breathing.

In primary patterns of movement, in the absence of structural fixities superimposed by man, the breathing apparatus and the locomotive apparatus interrelate, aiding one another. This must be so, since locomotion and breathing developed movement and form together.

The rhythms underlying all primary patterns of movement overlap each other in harmony and without interference. If this were not so, a man in the upright position could not meet gravity, endure momentum, breathe, pump the blood, think and feel, all in the same breath.

A man or a tiger, fighting, must have coordination of his skeletal parts in centering and ex-centering movements or his stance could not be maintained. This involves a perfect mechanism for determining time-space-movement with power to hold. In addition, it involves a continuity of glandular and nervous functioning to supply the persistent needs of the working mechanism, and this must be done without interfering with the mechanical rhythms necessary to adjust effectively weight and power levers in proper timing to survive. At the same time, the vegetative functioning must be protected from destruction by this drastic behavior.

During this struggle, oxygen must be supplied quickly to the muscles, and they must be relieved of their waste products. The muscle is the living engine, working for the survival of the individual. It must be guarded and aided by all other parts of the organism. It is rapidly burning its fuel; it needs oxygen for the purpose; its ash must be removed. The heart, the lungs, the diaphragm, nerves, glands, muscles, bones, all play their individual parts in the working unit.

TESTING BODILY RHYTHMS

To better acquaint yourself with the rhythms of your own diaphragm under various conditions, begin by making a few observations of its behavior under some stated conditions. Choose unusual positions in which to do this, so that gravity passes through your body in different axes from those in ordinary postures of living; such positions as lying down on the floor or standing on all-fours. While on all-fours, hold one arm extended, then shift and hold the opposite arm and leg extended, and perhaps while in this position touch the top of your head to the floor. The efforts of the body in balancing and the changes in breathing will have a relation to one another. As you lose your balance, you will catch your breath and vice versa.

If one wishes to develop kinesthesia in anything as vital to oneself as learning how one's own breathing rhythms change under emotion and movement, one must play somewhat the same game upon oneself that the early modern French painters played upon the public. They used distortion, overemphasis, weird shadows and various devices to bring to light other qualities of the subject which were so familiar as to go unnoticed. They distorted the shape of a peach, of a bird, of a man, to introduce an appreciation and feeling for color, texture or other qualities. And they were many times successful in making us more sensitive to relationships than we had been before.

To develop kinesthesia by placing your body in unused and unusual positions and noting changes made quietly but persistently by your inner mechanisms is one way to find a better balance for your own bodily forces. Test your kinesthesia in the following ways:

Lie on the back on the floor, with knees bent and drawn up,

feet resting on the floor, arms folded over the chest. This position provides a broad base of support, instead of the usual narrow one to which you are accustomed. Also in this position, gravity is working through your body from front to back, instead of from head to foot, so that the weights fall in a different relationship to each vertebra of the spine. The pull upon habitually strained muscles is lessened, and it is consequently easier to release tense muscles than when the body is in the customary position.

In this position the diaphragm may adjust its rhythms to "tubular," longitudinal breathing instead of wide, full breathing. Hiss the breath out between the teeth until no more can be expired. After forced expiration note where the bones of your back rest upon the floor, at head, at shoulders, at hips and at the end of the spine.

After discovering where there is greatest pressure upon the floor, experiment with forced expiration. Blow all the breath out through the nose until you cannot possibly exhale any more. Do not take a breath first. The lungs contain about three quarts of air all the time and you can safely expire about three pints of this without regard to the tidal air, that which comes and goes in ordinary breathing. As you expire with considerable pressure you will find that there are certain parts of the body wall which tense more than others at the extreme end of your ability to expel. When blowing the air through the nose, this spot of greatest tension you probably will find located in the upper part of the abdominal wall near the costal arch. After about three of these efforts are made, resting until comfortable breathing is re-established between expirations, note possible changes of bone pressures upon the floor. During these rest periods do not take an unusually full, active breath.

Next, try blowing the breath with slow but forced expiration, through the lips as though blowing out a candle. When the last gasp is reached you may note that the very tense spot in the abdomen is lower down and covers a larger area than when blowing through the nose, although not quite so tense.

After assuring yourself through repetitions that these differences in location and pressure are discernible, try a third method. Blow the breath through the teeth with lips relaxed and with lips and tongue in no way interfering. With teeth loosely set and tongue relaxed *"hiss"* the breath out, prolong the hissing to the extent of your residual air expiration, and note that the body has grown slightly smaller around under the arms and all about the body-wall. A reduction of about 3 inches in lateral diameter is possible, but you will feel no tight "plate" of contraction in the abdomen. Note again, after repeating and a few rest periods, where your bones are now hitting the floor. These motions and pressures will vary in different persons, and in the same person at times according to his physical, mental and emotional tensions. While these readjustments may seem so small as to be scarcely noticeable, they actually produce far-reaching changes throughout the coordinating bodily systems.

Chapter IX

THE PROPRIOCEPTIVE SYSTEM

MOVEMENT RESPONSE IS A COMBINATION OF REFLEXES. THE UNLEARNED PATTERN CONSISTS IN RECEPTION OF a stimulus, preparation by the body for movement, and action responses consummated. Stimulation of the brain cells appears as motion in the body. This may not be apparent and it may be wholly unconscious, but it is taking place nevertheless. The part or parts moving, and the direction they take may, however, fall to the lot of conscious decision. Accuracy and speed are determined by the proprioceptive system. Stimuli from the environment and stimuli from the thinking are correlated and relayed as motion in the body.

Determination of weight balance, for example, is in the head, effected through the proprioceptive system. In preparing to jump a hurdle, internal preparation is made, and tensions in the pelvis are increased to receive the added poundage from the shock of landing. Greater depth of breathing also accompanies this preparation and the centers of gravity and of breathing are lowered for safety, speed and power.

Biological, chemical and mechanical forces are the determinant factors in these activities of the human being. About 90 per cent of our behavior resides in these forces and is unconscious. About 10 per cent of our movements are considered to be under our direct control.

The neurological basis for the reactions between bodily structures must be established so that correlation of stimuli for adequate responses may be made. Visual judgments, judgments from the semicircular canals, from the skin and in fact from all parts of the body, are important to these reactions.

Through the proprioceptive mechanism our security in space is maintained.

We have only the old association mechanism on which to build. This mechanism developed to meet the hazards of a complex environment and has an adequate equipment for its use. We have a framework of weight levers, supplied with active power levers, all parts working in opposition, to effect organized movements; a fine communicating system, with power to take, to distribute and to give messages; an organism to supply fuel for the burning engines and oxygen to keep the fires going; a transportation system to carry all these materials to the remotest and deepest parts of the living mechanism, and to recover and dispose of the waste products of the muscles, the engines of living.

This equipment has met and countered gravity, inertia, momentum, temperature changes and pressures of life on land, and has survived.

Reviewing in detail, bones support weight and serve muscles for attachments, and together they effect movement. Muscles are arranged in pairs and work intelligently through rest and activity phases; this occurs between fiber bundles within each muscle and in the rhythms of the muscle antagonizers. Nerve ends receive stimuli from the outside world, carry them through nerve fibers, relay them through central neurones. Here a collection of memories of past experiences is correlated with incoming stimuli. The outgoing stimuli are then directed toward the surface, where the appropriate response to the environment is made. This involves many nerve stimuli and myriad muscle twitches, but it has been a successful mechanism or survival would not have been possible.

MOBILIZATION FOR MOVEMENT

In making a single movement of the simplest kind, energy must be transformed to work for mobilized action. Weights must be managed in our irregular segmented structure for organized movement. To do this, each part must move freely, in opposition to each other, across a median line, which becomes a line of force as it measures the opposing forces operating through it. This is the line of direction of movement. Weights must be managed with just the amount of energy to meet the time-space-movement for the particular action. If speed, momentum, dexterity are added, as in the "life-saving situation," more power must pour through the opposing muscles for acceleration, possibly continuing over a prolonged time. This involves many things besides muscles and bones. It involves a storehouse of energy and a rapid supply of oxygen and no time to stop to get either. Muscles and forces must be kept at the height of activity.

Breathing and moving rhythms must be coincident in the function for survival if the fighting animal is to hold his stance. He must not give way to his enemy. His bony structure must balance and move with as little waste motion as possible. Head, arms and shoulders must be dextrous and mobile. In short, the animal must hold his ground, fight his battle, and, at the same time, automatically meet all bodily demands which would include an adequate supply of oxygen to his working cells. To accomplish this, the breathing rhythms must be able to harmonize so perfectly with the locomotion rhythms that the mechanisms for locomotion and the mechanisms for breathing may serve the common purpose for survival. Muscle cells burn rapidly, and must have a continuous supply of oxygen to burn. The nerve mechanisms for breathing rhythms and locomotion rhythms therefore must be very closely tied.

According to Macleod,* "Nerves of the vasosympathetic, vasomotor and respiratory centers alter their activity in muscular effort." Macleod concluded that: "The stimuli which first act on the centers are derived from the cerebral cortex. They are believed to irradiate onto the medullary centers from the motor pathways along which impulses are passing, on their way down from the cortex to the spinal cord. The most weighty evidence favoring this belief is that increase in the rate of

* Physiology, by John J. R. Macleod.

the pulse and respiration may occur at the moment a muscular effort is attempted, before there is any time for hormones to become developed, or for reflexes from the muscles themselves to be set up. Moreover, the degree of alteration of the medullary centers is not at first proportional to the actual amount of work done." If a person expects that great effort will be required for a piece of work, the pulse and respiration will increase simultaneously with the starting of the work, even though it turns out to be a more trivial task than he expected. Preparation initiates with expectation. If one's imagination habitually makes mountains out of mole hills, one may be flooded with unused energy most of one's life.

Macleod describes respiratory innervation thus: "Afferent nerve fibers going to the respiratory centers may conveniently be divided into two groups—those coming from the respiratory organs and those coming from the other parts of the body." He also concludes that "the vagus contains two kinds of afferent fibers to the respiratory center, one kind stimulating inspiration and the other stimulating expiration." The question of how they become excited in the lungs is discussed, and conclusions made that the mechanical distention and collapse of the alveoli (lung sacs) occurring in respiration offer the stimulus. In addition to the effect upon breathing of afferent nerves coming from all portions of the body, reporting temperature changes, pressure changes, irritations, from both within and without, the carotid sinus, as well as hormones in the blood, influences respiration.

THE IMPORTANCE OF EXPIRATION

We find in active expiration the renewal of vigorous and deep inspiration. In the inherent quality of muscle lies a principle whereby the stretching of muscle tissue prepares it for its next contraction. This fact, coupled with the fact that in internal respiration oxygen is taken into the body cells in the expiratory phase of the breathing rhythms, leads us to analyze the lower structures of the body at that moment when contraction of the diphragm ceases. The diaphragm is stretched as exhalation takes place, due to the collapse of the ribs and the drag of the spine and pelvis in response to gravity pull. During this rest period of the tensile members of the thoracic wall, the intercostals are stretched, and because of the same factor, that is, gravity, acting on the ribs.

In respiratory movements the crural arch of the diaphragm, the iliopsoas, the levator ani, the quadratus, the transversalis, the pectineus and their associated fascial sheets connecting with upper thigh muscles, are integrated for use in the breathing apparatus. This power apparatus, accessory to the diaphragm, has its most active phase during expiration. These are the muscles which enable the animal to hold his stance when fighting, or with which he presses the ground to spring him forward when running. The muscles of crouch, in spine and pelvis, and those of expiration, have a unified functional rhythm. They both must serve the purposes of each at the same time in the "life-saving situation."

The nervous connections for forced expiration have, to my knowledge, never been worked out in detail in laboratory procedure. It is understood, however, that there is such a mechanism for control, as in forced expiration the action ceases to be one of a merely passive phase, as it appears to be in quiet breathing. Also, following the most forcible voluntary inspiration a passive, not active, expiration occurs. All agree that such a mechanism is in the medulla oblongata with connections through association fibers with other portions of the brain.

Most of the motor nuclei of the central nervous system are but reflex centers, the motor discharges at the surface being dependent upon impulses received by other neurones by way of the sensory paths.

Any of the sensory nerves of the body may affect the speed and force of the respiratory rhythms. This fact may be demonstrated easily. Almost everyone has experienced sudden changes in breathing rhythms from a dash of cold water on the back of the neck, the sight of an accident, or from hearing sudden sounds or groans. In various emotional states, also, changes may be observed in the respiratory rhythms. According to

Howell,* "We must assume, therefore, that this center (respiratory) is in connection with the sensory fibers of perhaps all of the cranial and spinal nerves, and is influenced also by intraspinal paths, passing from cerebrum to medulla, paths which are efferent as regards the cerebrum, but afferent as regards the medulla." He speaks of the nerve fibers which effect either increased stimulation or increased depression as "respiratory pressor" and "respiratory depressor" fibers.

He notes as well that "a cutaneous fiber which through its central chain of neurones eventually ends in the cortex cerebri and gives us the sensation of pain, may by collateral connections affect also the medullary center and produce effects upon the heart, blood vessels and respiration."

DIAPHRAGM INNERVATION

The phrenic nerve, originating from the fourth and fifth cervical, innervates the diaphragm. Other nerves innervating the respiratory apparatus are the brachial plexes supplying the upper accessory muscles—those of the shoulders and neck; the intercostals innervating the muscles of the thorax and abdomen; and branches of the lumbar plexus supplying fibers to the lower pelvic and thigh muscles, the lower accessory group, which are augmented in the expiratory movements and used vigorously for both respiration and weight-holding purposes in extreme activity, as in the fighting situation already mentioned.

All of these accessory muscles belong to the voluntary apparatus. And although under ordinary conditions breathing rhythms are entirely involuntary (inspiration, rest, expiration), and controlled in the medulla oblongata, in unusual situations these accessory muscles come into play, as well as act and react upon the structure, through the proprioceptive system, to maintain balance.

It is the effective stimuli of the sensory fibers of the vagus that maintain the normal respiratory rhythm. Experiments have shown that any disturbance of the vagus immediately affects these rhythms of the respiratory center.

* A Text-Book of Physiology, by William H. Howell.

For inspiratory rhythms, the accessory apparatus aiding the diaphragm for the intake, even in quiet breathing (in addition to those which have been mentioned already in the upper accessory group) comprises the smaller muscles connected with the air passages. These are the muscles controlling the size of the glottis (with each inspiration the glottis is widened by abduction of the vocal cords) and those of the laryngeal cartilages, upon whose tone the balanced action of larynx, pharynx and nasal passages depends. The muscles of the larynx receive innervation from the vagus, and it is important also to note that the facial nerves send branches to the muscles of the nose.

BALANCED FORCES IN EMERGENCIES

Through association mechanisms the entire tensile structure of the body is toned, breathing rhythms are made ready for renewed and continuous action when emergency calls; and expiration must follow inspiration in vigorous and rapid succession, all without disturbance of bodily balance in movement.

The compression members of the back, the spinal vertebrae, must be balanced by the tensile members of the front of the body-wall if stance and movement are to be adequate to the emergency. The chemical demands must be taken care of at the same time by the breathing apparatus. The diaphragm harnesses as many muscles to its aid as are available, and the fighting tensile members are augmented in power as the weight or ballast at the base increases. If the tensile members demand more power, the trunk extensors add ballast by pulling down, lowering the center of gravity. We never see a fighting animal with his tail high in the air. In the charging animal, however, this is not true. The principles of the low-swung automobile are clearly demonstrated in the old fighting patterns, a low center of gravity and a deeper breathing center to support the outward thrust of head, jaw and arms in dexterous movement are necessary responses in the living economy. The deep muscular mechanism (the lumbar and pelvic muscles) in extreme activity pulls well under and extends the forward line of the sacral curve. Static contractions of the

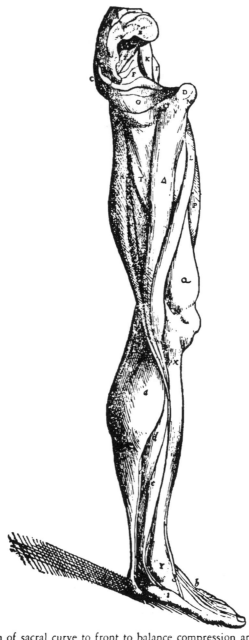

FIG. 81. Return of sacral curve to front to balance compression and tensile forces
at thigh-joint. (From Vesalius.)

trunk extensors upon groups of spinal vertebrae, which may have become fixed in bad positions, are released, and these spinal muscles then pull downward as is their normal function. Thus their force is added to gravity pull, and balances the projections of the upper body forward in movement. Ballast must be increased to support the forward drive and this must be produced along the compression members of the back.

The nerve mechanisms employed in forced expiration seem to be a part of the emergency mechanism used in preparation for fight or flight. The posture of the return of the curve of the lower spine toward the front is the pose of most animals and even birds when preparing for attack.

To balance bodily forces, think down the back and up the front. Let the spine drag, but keep the front of the body up. The vertebrae *sit* the full length of the back, while the whole front of the body is *suspended* from the spine and head, directly and indirectly, through connecting bone, muscle and other soft tissues. Thinking up the front of the body without lifting any of its bony parts will maintain proper traction in the connecting muscles to keep the ends of all bones in the front of the body-wall at proper levels for a balance of weight at their spinal attachments. Thus the work of the tensile members at the front balances the work of the compression members at the back.

If the thorax and pelvis are in balance and the throat muscles and abdominal wall are firm, the small muscles and ligaments of the spine will maintain such a degree of curvature in each area as to make the whole spinal axis as long as possible. Thus all weight is passing downward through the shortest distance from top to base.

As the muscles of forced expiration engage, and the trunk extensors pull down the back, tonicity of all front body-wall muscles is augmented, including those lifting the manubrium and controlling the laryngeal cartilages. This is seen in the pose of many animals such as the cat and the snake when hissing. The exaggerated pose of forced expiration accompanies these sounds of hissing and of guttural intonation of the growl of other animals, and even in the raucous scolding note of the frightened bird. This pose, often assumed in the warning call, is a part of a mechanism for protection of the young, and therefore part of the survival mechanism.

SECOND WIND

The reemployment of these unlearned patterns is undoubtedly the main factor in the so-called "second wind." The habitual posture fixities must be fatigued out of existence before the individual can *feel* his second wind.

Second wind indicates the complete exhaustion of all those muscles being used to pull the weight of the body up. After these muscles refuse to do any more, their fibers settle, with the bones to which they are attached, in any direction in which the weight seems to be bending, as gravity has the advantage upon this cessation of struggle. When the upper accessory muscles of breathing and support cease their struggle, the case seems hopeless. Here the character of purpose in the individual comes into service. If he will place all his faith and concentration in his legs and even though haltingly, jerkily, keep them advancing just enough to stay under the load, the lower accessory muscles will begin to increase their aid to the diaphragm. As soon as their action in breathing and in locomotion has established its primary connections in rhythm, the second wind gives new life and courage to go on. This reestablished rhythm is the old, original, unlearned pattern of movement firmly developed in the four-footed animal when he learned to meet gravity through a hard surface and to breathe air.

To understand compression and tensile balance and normal tonicity in muscle fibers, we should acquaint ourselves with the mechanism controlling expiration and the function it holds in the fighting apparatus. Expiration, which in quiet breathing is called the "passive phase," is by no means a passive phase in the fighting animal. It appears to contain the first reaction to the glandular and nervous preparation for danger, as seen in the behavior of frightened beasts and birds, in sounding the warning cry.

POSTURE AND SPEECH

In responding to the unusual, the first act of an animal with young is the sounded note and bodily attitude of alarm. In that moment of warning, physiological balances have changed. The hormones have touched off the mechanisms for shutting certain systems and opening others for the supreme effort required for protection of the young, if the danger or enemy is formidable. Preparation is being made by the body for the possible struggle. Fight or escape may be necessary and there is no time to be lost.

In the history of this alarm mechanism for survival lie the answers to many of our queries today about hypertension, its causes and cures. In fact so closely associated is the speech rhythm with the rhythms of bodily movement in locomotion and the timing of breathing rhythms accompanying it, that students of problems of the neurotic take cognizance of these factors even more than they may realize. Success is determined more or less by these often unconscious observations. Speech rhythms are always disturbed by deep emotional conflicts.

ELEMENTS OF SPEECH

The intricate art of speech involves the employment of three different mechanisms, the lungs, the larynx and the cavities of the pharynx, mouth and nose. According to Starling,* "the neurological basis of language must be regarded as co-extensive with the sensory centers, and with the whole region of lower association. As Bolton points out, 'a word, such as mouse,' at once sets in effect processes of association which pass to every projection sphere with the solitary exception of the gustatory, and even this might be aroused in a person who has eaten a fried mouse in the hope of thereby recovering from an attack of whooping cough."

The aspirates and sibilants in the elements of speech seem nearest of all to the guttural primary sounds of alarm heard in the animal. These animal sounds occur on the explosive expira-

* Human Physiology, by Ernest H. Starling, 1936 ed.

tory movements accompanied by a characteristic body pose. Expiration is prolonged when sound is being produced.

The aspirates are produced by the passage of a simple blast of air through a narrow opening, which may be at the throat, as in *H*, between tongue and teeth as in *th*, or between lips and teeth as *ph* or *F*.

The sibilants, which may be voiceless as *S*, or accompanied by phonation as *Z*, consist of continuous noises produced by a narrowing of the path of air between the tongue and the hard palate. They are similar in production therefore to the aspirates.

In these elements of speech, *H* is produced most nearly like the low, guttural growl or the hiss of the alarmed animal. In cases of certain types of speech difficulties, it has been found that lists of words beginning with *H* such as "Hupmobile," to be spoken with the explosive breath on the first syllable, offer an effective technique. The theory is that it ties the speech, breathing and posture rhythms back to the old associations in the central mechanism for meeting the unusual and preparing for defense. It deepens the breathing rhythms and lowers the center of gravity—economy devices.

For the same reason, in movements taught for the reestablishment of bone balance at joints, hissing is a valuable adjunct, with, however, a very long time rhythm and without breath explosion at the beginning of expiration. Thus it aims to reestablish a tie between the long rhythms of locomotion and the deep respiration used by the unconditioned animal.

CONDITIONED REFLEXES IN BREATHING

The human being has stretched himself up and out, and partially lost the deep central controls for the unifying of breathing and movement, used by all animals in defense and escape. But by exaggeration and practice he can acquire again the old, unlearned patterns in the harmonious action between these two functions, breathing and locomotion. Because expiration is the passive phase of respiration in quiet living, there will be fewer unnatural conditioned reflexes to break down in tying these mechanisms together, if emphasis is laid in reconditioning on the expiratory phase, rather than the inspiratory.

When breathing is employed as an aid to health, most often the oxygen intake for the benefit of the lungs and blood is stressed. Except, however, under very unusual or pathological conditions, it would be impossible for the blood to *not* get all the oxygen it needs from the lung sacs, even in the most quiet breathing.

The importance to health is not the amount of oxygen taken into the lungs, but the amount and extent of gas exchange made in the muscle cells of the body. Therefore the number of muscles employed is more important than the amount of air inspired. (Recall that the exchange of gases is made on the expiratory phase.) Internal breathing is important as it is the phase of breathing to which we can voluntarily bring greatest aid. This can be done by a better balance of bones, by the freeing of more muscles from "holding," thereby allowing them to act as an accompaniment in breathing. In other words, we should breathe all over!

As noted, Sherrington found that there was inhibition of tone in abdominal muscles during inspiration, and their tone during expiration was augmented. In the "passive phase" of the diaphragm action, during expiration, increased tonicity of the abdominal wall prepares the lower muscular mechanism for its next action—either in jumping or breathing. This movement of expiration, carried to greater extreme, produces the pattern noted in the warning cry of bird and beast. We are, then, employing a primary pattern to free the musculature for further organized action. In the study of extremes, we often find a basis for interpretations of normal behavior. Repeated assembling of its forces for the unusual, habituates the body to act more freely in ordinary living.

ANATOMY OF SPEECH ORGANS

In the speech connections will be found the coordinating units that lead us back to the primary patterns before man disturbed them by false "education."

The larynx, in which sound is produced, is formed by four cartilages: the cricoid, the thyroid and the two arytenoids. The cricoid lies directly over the ring of the trachea, like a signet

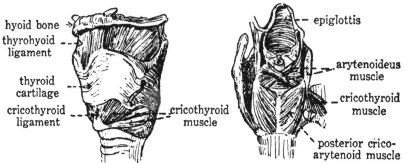

hyoid bone
thyrohyoid ligament

thyroid cartilage

cricothyroid ligament

cricothyroid muscle

epiglottis

arytenoideus muscle

cricothyroid muscle

posterior crico-arytenoid muscle

FIG. 82. Ligaments and muscles of respiration and voice in larynx. (Redrawn after Toldt.)

ring with the plate-like part directed toward the back. The thyroid cartilage consists of two parts, jointed in front, forming the "Adam's apple." The back of this cartilage has four processes, the superior being attached by ligaments to the hyoid bone, while its inferior process articulates with the posterior lateral portions of the cricoid. Free movement is permitted between these two cartilages. Movements of the thyroid upon the cricoid are also possible.

The two arytenoid cartilages are pyramidal in shape and their bases articulate with portions of the cricoid cartilage; the anterior angle of this base is the vocal process. The two vocal cords are the thyro-arytenoid ligaments stretched from the thyroid cartilage to the arytenoid cartilage. The space between these cords is the glottis.

The exterior angle of the base of the arytenoid cartilage is its muscular process. When in rotation on a vertical axis, this muscular process may face backward and inward, or conversely.

Position and tension of the vocal cords are effected by the intrinsic muscles of the larynx. Four of the muscles are important in these actions: the cricothyroid, the posterior-crico-arytenoid and the thyro-arytenoid, consisting of two portions: the musculus thyro-epiglotticus and the musculus vocalis.

It is not my purpose here to cover the field of voice production; that would take another volume. But I wish to call attention to the intricacy of this structure as an intrinsic mechanism serving sound reactions, and to note that it is attached to important structures used in the locomotion mechanism and in the breathing mechanism. It not only forms a part of the speech and breathing apparatus, but also of the tensile supporting wall of the front of the body. Nerves and muscles of the three systems—breathing, speech and locomotion—must interact. The structural connections of tensile support are demonstrated where a man hangs by his teeth, as does the trapeze performer. And so we find that the structure of the mechanism for speech and breathing serves also, in its cartilaginous, ligamentous, bony and muscular traction, as a part of the *tensile posture mechanism* of the entire body. This is due to the extension of its attachments to the axial skeleton.

We see the mutual effects of voice and breathing mechanisms in such acts as sneezing, coughing, groaning, gasping, the startled hiss or cry of bird or beast, and in the song of the prima donna. Appropriate bodily attitudes accompany these various extremes of behavior.

In quiet living, the expiratory phase is a passive one, but its individual character, when separated from the respiratory rhythms is notable. According to Howell, only under certain conditions do we have active and rhythmical expirations. These may be engaged in quite independently of the respiratory rhythms, as in laughing, coughing, defecation, micturition and parturition.* In the expiratory phase lies renewal of vigor, through some hidden form of muscular release.

* A Text-Book of Physiology, by William H. Howell, 1920.

Chapter X

PHYSIOLOGICAL BALANCES AND UNBALANCES

MAN'S STABILITY

C OMPLETE RELAXATION WOULD BE DEATH. IN COMPLETE BALANCE THE HUMAN STRUCTURE WOULD BE DEVOID OF activity. Living we shall never attain either. But unless we struggle toward these ideals, balance and rest, and acquire a knowledge of principles underlying the balance of bodily materials and forces, there is no way of dealing intelligently with the extreme imbalances, emotional and physical, of living.

Our object is that of preserving that fine bodily "instability" mentioned before, where available energy hangs in the balance, ready to be converted at an instant into its working form, movement.

"The living being is stable — it must be so in order not to be destroyed, dissolved, disintegrated by the colossal forces, often adverse, which surround it. By an apparent contradiction, it maintains its stability only if it is excitable and capable of modifying itself according to external stimuli and adjusting the response to the stimulation. In a sense, it is stable because it is modifiable; the slight instability is the necessary condition for the true stability of the organism."*

Due to the fact that the organism is modifiable, benefits as well as disturbances may be imposed equally by the individual, according to his ignorance or intelligence in making use of his mechanism. Just as the power of man in this machine age has been multiplied many times by the very machines which he has created, so could he multiply his own useful power by applying equal intelligence to his own machine. Through ignorance, however, he continues to initiate many unnecessary

* Charles R. Richet, Physiologie. Paris, Alcan, 1893.

strains, with various and far-reaching results upon his inner balances.

Fatigue is a common experience. Physical fatigue is caused by the accumulation of waste products, due to metabolic action in living cells. Work or strain has brought the chemical and physical balances of the cell to an unbalanced condition in which sarcolactic acid and other breakdown products are present. The behavior of the cell is thus affected and the working rhythms of the muscle become less and less dependable, and muscular hypertension exists.

Fatigued muscles may be stiff and slow of response or may be too rapid in response and jerky in action. Under certain phases of fatigue, performance is accelerated as a result of acid stimulation. Breakdown products in the cell may be the cause of fatigue or the cause may be of nervous origin. The neurones may themselves suffer from overwork, overstimulation. The smooth muscles of the organism may also enter into the picture of fatigue and usually do, if physical fatigue is prolonged or if psychic factors are introduced.

The several kinds of fatigue all partake of the same general characteristic pattern. Balances are lost in the neuromuscular machinery; balanced rhythms of rest and activity periods within tissues may fail, coordination between parts is disturbed and the rate of accomplishment is not dependable. As movements become jerky or irregular, so also does the product of movement, work, become impaired.

In mental fatigue the span of attention is impaired and accuracy in details is lost. In emotional fatigue, irregularities in response and imbalance in rhythm exist. A varying degree of instability is observed in emotional responses or may be expressed in complete lassitude.

Many factors qualify these reactions. Changes in muscle function are found in prolonged mental and nervous strains, coincident with reaction changes in the neurones. All are familiar with the nervous or mental fatigue experienced after hours of close mental application, with little or no muscular exercise.

Disturbed physiological functioning exists in less obvious forms of fatigue. For example, in those who are always complaining of that "tired feeling," balances in muscle cells often do not show evidence of impairment; nevertheless this is a very real handicap and the resulting disturbances are unquestioned. Inefficient functioning appears in the individual suffering from this type of maladjustment, which is so often considered to be "in the imagination" only, but which has very definite repercussions throughout the entire being. There are changes within the organism effected by itself, which serve to inhibit its continued activity. Both quality and quantity of work are impaired almost as by malice aforethought. Muscular coordination is lacking and accidents occur. Sometimes, if the accident is severe enough or far-reaching in its personal effects, it corrects the inertia of the habit, temporarily. The habit of the "feeling of fatigue" is to be discouraged if one is to remain on the safe side of emotional and mental balance. However, this habit is started often under very real systemic disturbances, such as a tired feeling resulting from unbalances in organic functioning, sometimes extending throughout the whole body. Toxic conditions arise, reducing accomplishments in daily output of energy, and worry finishes the picture of depression, and starts the "inertia of acceptance." This in the extreme becomes the neuromuscular weakness in certain types of fatigue in which organic functioning is impaired, due to psychic disturbances, however, instead of real bodily illness. In the early stages of this phase of fatigue, findings in tissue changes are negative.

All these states of fatigue have periods in which warnings are sounded and if these are observed, bodily harm may be avoided. In this particular type of fatigue, the state of "inertia of acceptance" with attendant excuses for non-accomplishment, either true or false, is the "red-flag."

A certain degree of fatigue accompanies all bodily activity. If this remains within normal limits, it is not unpleasant. There

is satisfaction in the anticipation of rest, and luxurious enjoy-
ment of rest when the opportunity offers. When, however, rest
brings little or no relief unless it can be prolonged over unreasonable periods of time, as for instance, when one is as tired
after sleeping or eating as before, there are hypertensions in
the body which should be analyzed, studied and corrected before
the exhaustion or chronic stage of fatigue sets in. The energy
reserve is perhaps being tapped seriously. Exhaustion will
inevitably result if one experiences fatigue of the real sort over
too long a period without interruption and correction. Fatigue
is a subject upon which an entire book could be written. Some
of the main features only can be touched upon here.

CHRONIC FATIGUE

Chronic fatigue always contains a factor not to be found in
normal physical fatigue, the psychophysical. In this instance,
emotional unbalance and the reduction in mental achievement
form a part of the "feelings of fatigue" affecting the physical
ability to carry on without constant reminder that one is "so
tired." There often is added to this type of fatigue a kind of
emotional longing for something else, that never arrives. This
subjective aspect, when a part of chronic fatigue, undoubtedly
is due to confused sensations from the muscles of the body,
both smooth and striated.

CONFUSION STRAINS

Inability to interpret the sensations coming from the afore-
mentioned unbalances is one cause of the continuance of this
fatigue. Confusions result.

Strains are caused when there are confusions in decisions.
If the "stop and go" signals of the traffic control system were
flashed on and off irregularly or at the same time, there would
be interruptions in the timing of movement of traffic, and
serious blocks would occur through this loss of rhythm. Unless
a clear and well-ordered direction is given at the proper time,
orderly functioning ceases and chaos begins. Balance of opposing lines of force is lost. The same may be true in the case of

the individual, a damming-up of the neuromuscular forces due to these unbalances—unbalances with consequent stress, strain and wasteful tension.

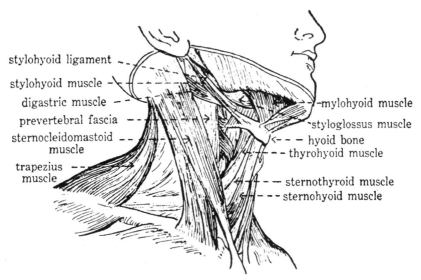

stylohyoid ligament

stylohyoid muscle

digastric muscle

prevertebral fascia

sternocleidomastoid muscle

trapezius muscle

mylohyoid muscle

styloglossus muscle

hyoid bone

thyrohyoid muscle

sternothyroid muscle

sternohyoid muscle

FIG. 83. Suspensory muscles of neck.

When it has really arrived, this subjective chronic fatigue is not all imagination, as some would have us think. It is fatiguing to neurones to always handle confused messages and this fatigue of the nerve centers may react unfavorably upon muscle cells, and either hypertension or hypotension reduce blood supply and vigor. Whether hypotension or hypertension, and whether general or specific, seems to be greatly influenced by the degree of conflict between two alternatives: the desire to accomplish and the unconscious desire to *not* accomplish.

There may be hypertension produced by uncertainty in muscular responses to confused orders. Psychophysical fatigue requires much study and should be dealt with more technically than is possible here. There are many variables behind neuromuscular tension and its opposite, flaccidity. The study of the release of these conditions carries us into the diversified but also related subjects of biochemistry, mechanics, psychology, and their governing principles. To venture an opinion on the causes of fatigue unbalances and of possible means to aid recovery of physiological balance is courageous. We know that many of these unbalances are experienced daily by all active individuals and all of them by many. The causes of hypertension and the ills growing out of them are very obscure and deserve the most careful and thoughtful attention.

There is no attempt here to deal at length with physiological findings in the various types of fatigue. When we have discovered the secrets of fatigue our knowledge of the unconscious will be greater than it is today. Only the more obvious notations are made here to enable a theoretical discussion of various approaches to the subject, and to note some clinical findings resulting from years of dealing with fatigue problems in their many phases of expression.

The subject is introduced into this book to project two phases of relaxation which seem important and which may promise greater results in the clinical field if more extended research is done along these lines: first, the relation that the balance of bodily parts has to fatigue, and second, the relation that breathing rhythms and locomotion rhythms have to each other and to the problem of hypertension.

Many chronic strains come from conventional postures or accompany worry and intense mental application. Man alone can be afraid all the time—of what has happened, of what is happening, of what may happen. He thus interferes with the wise workings of the body. How much and in what ways hypertension (static muscular contractions) interferes with the circulation of the blood we cannot say. But by intelligent adjustments of bodily balance and release of tensions and inhibitions, improvements in circulation and in regulating blood pressure can be achieved.

As we have seen in the unconscious functions of bodily tissues, rest is paired with work, as noted in heart and diaphragm action. This alternation, activity with rest, is varied in its rhythms, according to the mechanical and physiological service of the individual part to the organism as a whole. Rhythm, including its rest phase, is evident and may be studied in all bodily materials. Human materials and metals alike suffer fatigue. Every mechanic understands that rest is beneficial to his machine. In the human machine there are more factors to weigh in the balance. In the study of bodily fatigue, the living forces as well as those of the mechanical and chemical are added to our problem. An effort to understand these three expressions of force in the human being is essential to make the study of fatigue productive in a tangible and practical way. Every thought, every emotion has its instant muscular response, however slight, and equally there can be no muscular strain without its resultant mental effect.

During long mental strains, one is merely aware of a persistent growing and apparently unreasonable bodily fatigue, with no perception of its causes.

MENTAL FOCUS

Paying attention is hard work and the amount of fatigue and of recovery in nerve and muscle is greatly influenced by the emotional elements in the subject attended. One may attend to two strongly habituated activities at once and the body manages very well. One may knit and read or talk, and all goes smoothly until reading matter or conversation takes a personal turn, then emotional factors enter and a stitch is dropped. One may drive his automobile and discuss politics; if the traffic lights are working normally all goes well. Conditioned reflexes may work together or separately with no distress symptoms, but if a traffic jam occurs confusions arise, activities must be separated or accidents may occur. If the driver has been away from the city for a year the confusions will be more acute, but after a week of daily practice he would probably perform as well as before.

Starling says of the conditioned reflex: "Endless numbers of conditioned reflexes can be based upon one unconditioned reflex."* One unlearned pattern may form the basis upon which several variations may be built. Salivation reflex reinforces

* Principles of Human Physiology, by Ernest H. Starling, 1936 ed.

and is reinforced by sound; when both are applied together, a greater effect may be produced than by either alone. We also note that if a conditioned reflex "decays" through disuse it

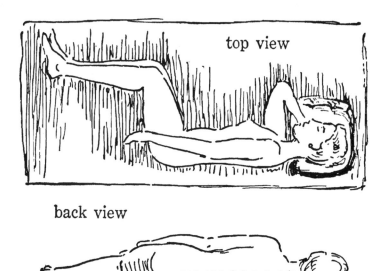

FIG. 84. Position on side for hip and rib balance, in sleep.

will take less time to reestablish it than if it had never been registered.

Sleep often only partially restores the balances of the working systems of the body, though sleep is better than no sleep because, as has been wisely said: "Sleep being a negative phase cannot be compelled. Consciousness, being a positive phase, can be compelled even unto death." The ordinary background of fatigue coincides with the daily round of living. When clocks were invented and men began to do for pay what they did not really want to do, human inertia began, and with it the rigidity of fatigue. The cumulative effect of these fixities is exhaustion. Cumulative fatigue develops patterns of restlessness, muscle states of over-mobilized energy—more power than can be used hisses on the threshold.

Dr. George Crile's physical interpretation of fatigue begins with studies of exhaustion in animals, for instance the salmon which becomes exhausted after a thousand-mile swim to the spawning grounds.

Studies carried out in the Mellon Institute, include data on the stimulating effects of early fatigue:

Fatigue toxins behave like other narcotic agents; in small concentrations they actually improve performance, in large concentrations they impair it. This shows in the factory worker's increased speed in the latter part of the day; but more obviously in the intellectual worker; his persistence of attention increases while his field of attention diminishes. With fatigue, he becomes less able to admit factors of change, he becomes fanatical about a single issue. . . . This improvement in performance may be in itself a sign of bodily impairment. It is merely the narrowing of all energy to a particular task, not increase in energy for general expenditure.

If a particular worry were the focus, this too would absorb more energy after the fatigue point had been reached and fanaticism might center upon this single issue. Thus the vicious circle continues. How can it be broken? Better still, how prevented?

The duration of the process is of the first importance. The process should be interrupted soon enough and often enough to permit recovery from movement by rest. Man alone of all animals disobeys in his living plan this law of rhythm of motion and rest.

Next to duration of movement in the cause of fatigue is frustration of movement. As we have previously stated:

There is a dynamic or active pressure for a movement which does not take place. The agents of movement have been stimulated without being directed to act. In other words, movement has been frustrated; the natural sequence which should follow that type of stimulation has been repressed or restrained. The result is that the arrested pattern of movement tends to become prolonged—to persist rather than to break up and resolve, as it would had movement taken place.*

NEURON STRAINS

The nervous system is made up of a series of single nerve cells called neurons. Each neuron has a cell body and branching

* Our Strains and Tensions, by Mabel Elsworth Todd.

dendrites, the receiving members, and a single axis cylinder, the axon, passing on the messages from dendrite to dendrite. The dendrites, a little remote from the nerve cells, become the

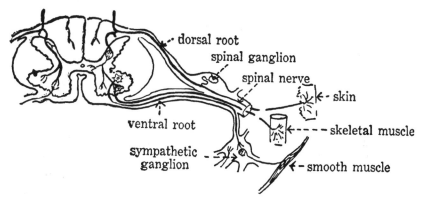

FIG. 85. Diagram of transverse section of spinal cord and neuron chains. (Redrawn after Morris.)

nerve fibers. These fibers supply all portions of the body. The neuron is the source of nervous energy. This energy arises from chemical changes in the cell, just as the energy of a muscle is dependent upon its own chemical changes. It is understood that both the nerve cell and the muscle cell suffer fatigue, although the nerve fiber shows little evidence of fatigue.

When neurons are ready to act and the opportunity is present, to act is agreeable. When not ready to act, and forced to act, to act is very disagreeable, the unpleasantness varying with the degree of the "set" against acting. Also when neurons are ready to act, not to act is unpleasant.

Sherrington,* in trying to solve some of these problems, including functions of mind, asked himself, "Are suites of acts the whole of an animal's behavior?" He could find no answer other than that "the relation of mind to brain is not only unsolved, but devoid of a basis for beginning. . . . The two, for all I can see, seem to remain disparate and disconnected." Ac-

* Integrated Action of the Nervous System, by Sir C. S. Sherrington.

cording to his findings, there are only "mental experience and brain happenings," coincident in "time and space."

Behavior in man and animal alike results from an integrated mechanism adjusting to the environment. This is done through responses made by individual parts and systems in movements adequate to the "total situation." Behind this unit lie the vast exchanges, affording information through the neurons, to insure mechanical and chemical means of meeting the needs.

To establish poise, in which thoughts are supported by emotional readiness, is the principal reason for the forming of new habits, for the opening up of new pathways of discharge. As this proceeds, old blockades will dull and fade in proportion to new interest. Habit has been called the fly-wheel of society. The fly-wheel in a machine controls its definite time and speed. "The intelligence of an individual may be measured by the speed with which he orients himself to new situations."

Man is a storehouse of chemical energy. The reserve must be replenished by food and oxygen or no more energy can be liberated; therefore, rest must be taken to adjust inner balances before more energy can be liberated.

OUR NERVOUS MECHANISMS

We hear much scolding about nerves. But what a lifeless, helpless and ineffectual mass would be the human being without the two nervous systems: the autonomic system which controls our unconscious, our vegetative activities, and the cerebrospinal system, which controls the bodily framework, informing us about our world and supplying a means of motivation.

For a long time, the brain was supposed to have some peculiar function of its own, relating the "mind" closely to "spirit" and directing its precious currents over the body through the nerve fibers. Our present knowledge of the brain and the nervous system has developed since the improvement of the microscope. We now know that the nervous mechanism of the living being includes the brain, and that the two parts of this mechanism, the autonomic and the cerebrospinal systems, interlock, relaying through the brain important information which determines our responses. We no longer speak of mind as independent of these systems. Through the complicated interdependence of the brain, the cerebrospinal and the auto-

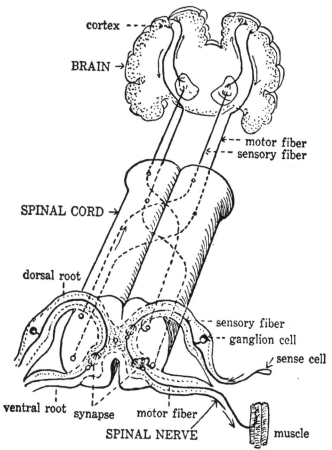

FIG. 86. Spinal nerve. (Redrawn after Woodruff.)

nomic nervous systems, we receive stimuli from our environment, correlate them, and act in relation to them. Most of that action is long habituated and unconscious.

Thus through the cerebrospinal system we become acquainted with our world and make our responses to it. Through the autonomic, our various systems are kept in orderly rhythms, individually and collectively, and are enabled to make such adjustments as may be needed, with sufficient energy to survive.

The autonomic mechanism includes the sympathetic, or thoracico-lumbar system, and the parasympathetic or cranio-sacral system, two opposing systems of nerve ganglia within the great system. These two systems of the autonomic mechanism oppose and augment each other successively in action. The sympathetic and the parasympathetic, however, interact and cannot be considered separately. The sympathetic is a chain of ganglia on the lateral sides of the vertebrae, having one ganglion to each spinal nerve root, except at the cervical where there are but two; and in the upper three or four thoracic ganglia, where they form a single ganglion. Also at the lower end of the spine there is only one coccygeal ganglion. In the abdomen, the solar ganglion, known as the solar plexus, and the superior and inferior mesenteric ganglia function in connection with the viscera.

In general, the sympathetic stimulates the functions of bodily mechanisms needed by the animal for speed and power when meeting emergencies, and simultaneously slows up viscera not needed to function in these responses. Dr. Walter Cannon* demonstrated that, without the sympathetic, the animal's capacity for work is greatly reduced. Also, that without reserves of the sympathetic, the liberation of adrenalin, heart acceleration, dilation of structures of vascular and respiratory systems, redistribution of blood to the working muscles, recovery of body temperature, and bodily responses, all would be inadequate to meet environmental emergencies. Dr. Cannon emphasizes the immediate stoppage of the digestive secretions and of peristalsis, due to arousing fear, anxiety or anger. The terrified cat at the top of the elm, his muscular strength greatly enhanced by his adrenalin secretion, stops digesting because of his more pressing needs. Rescue him, and he curls up in his corner and is soon fast asleep, recovering his equilibrium. Man, however, being the only animal that can be afraid all the time, prolongs his conflicts even after the danger is past. Proust died of introspection long before he died of pneumonia, burned out by the chemistry of seven volumes of "Remembrance of Things Past."

* The Wisdom of the Body, by Walter B. Cannon.

EMOTIONAL FACTORS AND CONTROLS

Life is either an harmonious adjustment between emotions, or a struggle between emotions. We cannot argue ourselves out of emotional imbalances. One persistent emotion can be changed only by another emotion of greater intensity. We may observe daily in ourselves and in others, muscular hypertension, posture strains and irregularities in breathing rhythms, coming from emotional changes, and affecting both physical and mental activities of the day.

In civilization, situations of emotional pressure must be met often. The human animal cannot run away or fight whenever he is disturbed by fear or anger as his jungle brother would have done in the same situation.

If the civilized human being could work off, through bodily expression, all emotional drives, as the uninhibited animal does, hypertension would not result. But social amenities fortunately are with us to stay and man must grapple with his tensions to the best of his ability—the more intelligently the better. Hypertension is the static contraction of muscles gripping the bones; it is the muscles crying to break loose when they have been shackled.

Either hypertension will turn in and destroy one with a final explosion, or it will eventually break its bounds and bend its fury upon someone else. Capping Vesuvius will benefit no one. Therefore, unless the human being's psychological technique is a very sound one in established conditioned reflexes, his various systems suffer the extremes of these unbalances. All the inhibitions of his heretofore comfortable, organic functioning, create changes in pressure within his vascular, nervous and muscular systems, and prohibit the freedom of the rhythms of his entire body. He will try to hold his bones very still, so that his discomfiture will not be discovered.

Every human being has his pet areas where he "grabs himself"—the back of the neck, the jaw, the knee, the abdominal muscles, the coccyx; no matter where the grasp takes hold, the muscles are held as tightly as possible, to keep the bones "fixed," to give a sense of security in space.

This introduces new mechanical strains into the structural problem of balance. The muscles are unable to use the energy generated by the mechanisms responding to fear and anger. With the drive of adrenalin in the blood incident to the emotions of fear and anger, these muscles continue to prepare for fight or flight. Expansive movement being inhibited, muscles stimulated for work become tense and "set" on the bones. Few there are who have not experienced this. We hear on all sides, "I can't let go"; "I am all keyed up"; "I can't get a deep breath." These are all expressions of muscles gripping the bony structure, interfering with nervous, muscular and vascular balances and the mechanical reactions of the bodily framework.

Interpret "expression," in all of its forms, as pressure of forces to get out; and a new sympathy will come to you for muscles having emotional pressure to express, without being allowed to express. The only type of expression that a muscle has, in response to pressure from within, is to contract, and in contracting it moves bones. Failing this outlet for expression, it is blocked.

There are but two avenues of escape for the inhibited human being: a knowledge of the universal forces involved in bodily expression—organized movement; and a knowledge of "old associations"—primary patterns of movement responding to the emotional emergencies met in the hazards of living. Man must learn to give his skeletal muscles something to do when there is a central drive of emotion put upon them beyond their endurance.

Efforts to cope with the prevailing confusions, and to restore something approaching order within the narrow limits of individual life, is the ambition of everyone. The problem can be attacked from the mechanical level, reaching the deeper and more subjective levels by first meeting the more objective and tangible unbalances which can be brought under personal control. We can overcome the emotional pressure in our muscles by putting them to work. We can obtain balance of bone by shifting individual parts while working, so that all energy transferred may be used for the work in hand, instead of being wasted in holding out of balance parts which should be moving in rhythms of mechanical reaction. Holding individual parts of the body in some fixed way restricts the free action of the whole, and produces conflicts between materials and forces, conscious and unconscious.

Even if we are conscious of what it is that is making us angry or afraid, such as being angry at a particular person or afraid of a family situation, we may find it impossible to deal with the emotion philosophically. Since the chain of events producing it is impossible to retrace, we can deal only with the physical effects as we find them.

The physical effects are usually a high center of gravity, with accompanying high breathing, and a drive for action in the executive appendages of the body, especially in the arms, jaw and head. We will find that hypertension exists in all of these members. We are fighting within, and the aggressive fighting apparatus responds. But we have no objective enemy to grapple with because we are civilized and "control ourselves." Hence the stance muscles are stretched upward since the need for their use to increase ballast offsetting the fighting apparatus has been denied them. Therefore the stance and lower accessory breathing muscles do not pull the weights or the breathing down to coordinate with the locomotor apparatus. They have all of the drive without the need to use it. But the inner fight still goes on. Digestion is interfered with, and adrenalin is poured into the blood, and, not being used, disturbs chemical balances. The conflict continues until the weakest part gives way and a breakdown occurs. The fatigue limit has been reached.

But it is possible to eliminate pressure from unused stimuli, and regain mental and physical balance by diverting the energy to other muscular uses. To eliminate these pressures, use the tense muscles that have pulled upward to move the bones encased in this upper fighting and breathing apparatus. *Think movement* in the direction of their vertical axes, as though the bones were separated and insulated from their muscle mass, and could move freely within it. As Gerald Manley Hopkins expressed it, consider your bones "sleeved in flesh."

Imagine pricking your ribs into the spine narrowing the back; imagine pricking your upper arm bone through the flesh at the elbow. Use the front of the shoulder blade at the acromion as a hammer head and tap it forward. Hang a weight on the ends of your shoulder blades, stretching them down out of the neck mass. Hang the arms at the sides and let the bones stretch into a heavy pendulum. The heaviest part of the jaw is the broad vertical bone just in front of the ears. Let the bone drag down from the temples in this line. Drop the head forward and let it drag heavily as a fifteen pound weight on the back of the neck, keeping the spine erect at the same time. These are tangible uses of the blocked-up energy of the upper fighting apparatus.

The ability to put this apparatus into some kind of action will effect relaxation far more quickly than trying to deal with the floating anxieties that are so closely linked with the strains. They are not tangible. One finds no point of attack until the fatigue sensations have ceased pouring into the centers from a body unbalanced by hypertensions. These floating anxieties are produced through social relations, therefore the use of such unsocialized positions will help to release strains, develop a kinesthetic sense and recondition us to an awareness of the natural balance of physical forces.

CEREBROSPINAL BALANCE

Sherrington found that: "Much of the reflex action expressed by the skeletal musculature is postural." Bony levers of the body are maintained in certain postural attitudes, in regard to the horizon, to the *vertical* and to one another. "Reflex tonus is the expression of a neural discharge concerned with the maintenance of attitude. The tonus of skeletal muscles is an obscure problem. The proprioceptive and the labyrinthine receptors seem to have in common this, that they both originate and maintain tonic reflexes in the skeletal muscles, and they, at least in some instances, reinforce one another in this action."*

Man is physiologically equipped so that most complicated patterns of movement are possible. Innervation and coordination are constant in the execution of a movement and for the maintenance of a posture. The execution of movement is made through the influence of many unseen forces in the bodily economy, rather than by simple direct control of individual parts.

I move my arm forward, but the process is merely the establishment of conditions that produce the desired result. Through the reflex arc, stimuli and inhibitions are set up in opposing muscles to move about twenty-five bones in a given direction. Mechanically there are numerous power levers acting upon these several weight levers, and all parts in succession opposing each other, to create an axis of movement. The axis takes the line of direction.

As you read these lines, tap the table with your right forefinger. Note that you did not have to ponder long to decide which was your right forefinger, and also note that the tapping process started instantaneously with practically no intellectual measurements necessary. Analyzed, connections are made between definite location at the surface of your body with a controlling center in the brain before movement can take place. This is the first condition established in your mechanism to produce the movement you have demanded. There must be accuracy in *location* of the bodily part to be moved to determine the right connection.

The second condition that nature must establish to carry out your desire is *direction* of movement; the more clearly defined and specific, the straighter the aim. All of this will not be smoothly accomplished, if not motivated by *your desire* to *move*. The quality of your movement is determined by all these factors including the emotional drive behind the movement.

If you are impatient, there will be more speed in action but less accuracy in direction. With a sore finger there is retarded

* Integrated Action of the Nervous System, by Sir C. S. Sherrington.

speed. If you have many inner conflicts and inhibitions producing an unconscious stubbornness in bodily responses, you will have jerky, uneven rhythms in this simple act.

NATURAL VERSUS UNNATURAL RESTRAINT OF MOVEMENT

As it is true that the nervous breakdowns so prevalent today are due in large degree to maladjustments to social environment, so is it also true that these maladjustments produce strained behavior, which, in final analysis, is found to include hypertension in muscles and fatigue in neurons.

Civilization is the outcome of biological evolution. The problem of the individual adaptation to society, both intimate and remote, is a dynamic one, never a passive. Man meets his environment actively, not with flaccidity.

The neuromuscular units with relaying centers through cord and brain, receive stimuli, correlate them and respond to them. Intelligence should point the way as to how the appropriate response should be made, either softly or drastically, according to the needs of the situation.

Observe the surgeon, operating with such precision on the cataract; or the baseball pitcher having equal precision but with more expansive movement. The same accuracy is needed in both although the difference in radius is extreme. However, the energy expenditure must be precisely adjusted in each case. There must be no hypertension to restrict free movement here—no flaccidity of muscle.

With every turn of the surgeon's knife, there must be a steady controlling center, that no line of force from unbalanced body weights may project to make it slip. It is a similar restriction in radius of movement required for balancing of parts that makes standing and sitting difficult. Mechanical balance of parts must be more perfect when radius of movement is restricted, because muscles fatigue more easily under continuous repetition of contractions. This is one of the facts which makes the essentials of mechanical bodily balance important to the study of relaxation and rest.

Surplus energy may be captured and used, or it may be wasted

recklessly and ineffectually in hypertension. When it is mis·
applied, mentally, emotionally or mechanically, it reacts on the
entire being through the disturbance of balance between bodily
systems. Alternate activity and rest are essential in the time-
space-movement of all parts of the organism. It is necessary to
keep parts moving even within a narrow radius so that the rest-
activity rhythms may be maintained. Fixity interferes with these
natural rhythms.

We frequently hear advocated the merits of "just being
natural" or of doing something in a "natural way." How can
we know what is a natural way? It may be merely a way that
has become habitual to us. Individually or as a race we may
have formed unintelligent habits. The habitual way may not be
the natural way. We cannot say that any mechanism is "natural"
in its functioning unless we understand the laws that govern it.
Factual thinking is necessary. The imagination must contain
factual thinking, not notional thinking.

Through the imagination power is liberated. In learning consciously to employ the *motivating picture* to create the conditions for appropriate movement responses, one must have
cognizance of three things: exact location, direction and desire
to move. When conditions are right, movement takes place. "It
moves," exactly as "it snows," "it rains," "it hails." Muscles
respond instantly to thought, and appropriate action takes place.
The accuracy and skill are determined by the vividness of the
imagined response or the importance of it to life. In other
words, the emotional drive, or the feeling for the idea, is one
of the important conditions for a specified type of movement,
just as condensation is one of the important conditions in rain
or snow. Other factors could also be tabulated in both products,
but they are each experienced as a unit of expression: moving,
raining, snowing.

Only the adult blocks free expression by separating the parts
from the whole. The child says "I run," "I jump," "I sing."
He does not say "I am toeing out," "my shoulders are back,"
"I walk on the balls of my feet," until the adult has split his
attention, making details the focus. To recondition, an image

must be formed and movement encouraged in the direction of the desired vision. *This is effected through the imagination.* When sufficient information has accumulated and a desire is released, expression follows, "it moves," or "it snows," or "it rains." In the thinking the follow-through stroke in golf is accomplished. Practicing on details alone would never have brought the necessary coordination.

HABIT BUILDING

It is not only that postural unbalance results in the waste of energy in general—we have a great deal more energy, by and large, than we ordinarily need in daily life—but it results in the deflection of energy and the use of it by some parts to the detriment of other parts.

Balance holds a profound meaning for all living tissue. Less human energy is consumed by working with than against natural forces; learning to breathe, to walk, to sit, to stand in such ways as to center the breathing and the bones is one of the first disciplines for human economy. Youth is alert, forward looking— as if faith were a part of elasticity and a component of balance. Old age is not measured chronologically. One becomes old when fixities of habits are established—set permanently—when the formation of new habits is no longer welcome. The sensitivity is dulled by lack of alertness toward environmental changes. Acceptance of routine and running into a rut of dull repetitions tend to slow the responses and to allow inertia to gather weight.

We should fall into balance, and seek rest through balance frequently, but to do this the old words and old positions must be analyzed in the light of new knowledge and new feelings for their more dynamic concepts.

In the words of Dr. James Harvey Robinson: "Any most familiar object will suddenly turn strange when we look it straight in the face. As we repeat some common word or regard keenly the features of an intimate friend, they are no longer what we took them to be. Were it not for our almost unlimited capacity for taking things for granted, we should realize that we are encompassed with countless mysteries, which might oppress our hearts beyond endurance, did not custom and incuriosity veil the depths of our careless ignorance."*

Old words, old fixities, traditions of a past age must give way to new realizations of facts or truths, as they relate to modern living. The old military posture, with its implications of stiff discipline, has given way to a more alert erectness, dynamic instead of static, favoring a better acquaintance with natural functionings of the living structure.

ACQUAINTANCE WITH THE DIAPHRAGM

To acquaint oneself with the action of the diaphragm: lie upon the floor, with knees bent and arms crossed (as described earlier in this book), and hiss through the teeth, until it becomes impossible to exhale further. Rest, without taking a full breath, if you can prevent it. Repeat several times. If your breathing rhythms have become seriously disturbed by nerve and muscle tensions, you will be unable to rest between hisses without gasping for breath. Repeat until you can take several long narrow breaths between hisses instead of wide gasping breaths. It is important to hiss through the teeth and without explosive pressure of breath. Exhaling through the nose or through the lips produces the different muscular results already described. A little practice in this will give you the feeling of the action of your own diaphragm when freed from the upper accessory muscles. Note the changes in the body-wall in breathing, while in the supine position.

Pressure of the floor upon the bones will prevent any extreme mechanical reactions throughout the spinal axis which may have become habituated in high breathing and high carrying of weights in the upright position. Bad upright postures may have produced pulls on the axial skeleton by subscapular muscles, rhomboids, scalenus and pectoral groups. As the hissing continues, the lateral diameter of the thorax will narrow, the

* The Humanizing of Knowledge, by James Harvey Robinson.

upper external muscles will release their hold, and the latissimus dorsi and the trunk extensors will begin to pull down, as is their normal function. The chest cage will begin to decrease its dimensions in three directions, under which conditions the diaphragm may make its deepest excursion.

Experiment with breathing rhythms, by inhibiting the upper accessory muscles and favoring the lower in this way. Eventually this will free them all for natural breathing. We breathe all over.

Exhaling is vastly more important for our consideration than inhaling. If through the use of expiration, freedom of the upper accessory muscles and a deeper excursion of the diaphragm have been established, we have increased internal breathing by more frequent and complete changes of internal pressures, augmenting the front body-wall for integration of tensile members for body support.

At the same time and by the same means we have freed the spinal extensors from their static gripping upon thoracic vertebrae and sacrum, allowing them free play. The spinal extensors will then pull down, the lengthwise dimension is thus added to the crosswise in enlarging the chest cavity, and the low accessory group of muscles are again functioning. They are taking part in the breathing rhythm and at the same time acting with spinal muscles and front body-wall to balance compression and tensile forces for integration of the body in action.

In forced expiration, we can expel about three pints of air besides the tidal air. The lungs, it will be remembered, have a residual three quarts of air. The lung area offers the blood about fifty times the amount of the surface of the entire body through which to effect a change of gases. We always have plenty of oxygen in the lungs for our needs.

The descent of the diaphragm raises the pressure in the abdominal cavity, and as it ascends, the abdominal muscles are toned. We should find in the action of expiration, the renewal of vigor and a stimulus for deep inspiration, as it is in this phase that the exchange of gases is made in the deep, body tissues.

TESTING KINESTHESIA WHILE SITTING

To test your kinesthesia in different ways of sitting: Slouch in a chair, in a very lazy and devitalized manner; shift and see if you can emulate a pouter pigeon successfully. The very effort will make you want to sit straight, as the pressure against the abdominal wall will make the lower back ache. Next, sit very upright, as many "back seat drivers" do, with weight all drawn up into your neck, and thence pushing down and forward into the knees, not by any chance being delivered into the seat of the chair, by way of the pelvis through the ischia, as balanced weights should go when one is sitting. Instead, weight is drawn crossways, from front to back, throughout the entire body, from neck to protruding lower sternum and abdomen, to tipped pelvis, to knees. After observing in yourself the tense pattern you have often observed in your friends, try balanced sitting. Give as much weight to the back legs of the chair as to the front legs. Allow your bones to work for you, and release the responsibility of your muscles from holding you up while in the sitting position.

To sit: determine first what bones are in vertical upright alignment when sitting, to support the keystone of the pelvic arch. The joints of the pelvis must have a definite relationship to each other and to the center of gravity, in whatever position the body may assume. In a symmetrical, moving system such as the human body, there can be but one design for the relationship of parts to the center of its dynamic system, that is, to its center of gravity.

The ischia are nearer to the front of the pelvis than ordinarily imagined, in fact their tuberosities, upon which we should try to poise when *sitting*, are directly under the center of the acetabula, where the pelvis rests on the top of the leg bones in *standing*. When sitting, these thigh joints bend at the front of the body.

The design of bone arrangement here is an inverted triangle of bones formed by the ischia tuberosities and the rami (upper forward extensions of the ischia) and the rami of the pubis. When the body-weight in sitting is directed to the ischia, the relation of the vertical axes of supporting structures to the center of gravity of the body would be, in effect, the same as the axes passing through the center of the thigh-joints, the acetabula, in standing. The ischia thus take the place of the legs in upright support of the mass. The legs should rest loosely at the knees, and not pull forward on the pelvis, thus disturbing these axes. The support of the upright spine through the pelvic keystone and arch must be such as to deliver weight to the chair legs and not to your legs.

If the body-weight is balanced upon the tuberosities of the ischia and there is no pull forward by leg muscles, the planes of force acting upon the keystone of the pelvic arch will be identical to those in the balanced standing position. In other words, within a given system, we cannot have a working design for two centers of gravity. When all parts are in balance, there can be but one center of gravity. With this in mind, it is easy to see that the bones that you sit on must be in the same vertical axes as those you stand upon, or the weight in the pelvic arch cannot be supported, nor the spine maintain the balance of its curves in sitting.

As there are many ways of standing badly, so there are many ways of sitting badly. The center of gravity may change in relation to the mass in movement, but the parts making up the mass must be able to adjust quickly to these changes made in movement, and to the spine which controls the movement. The spine is the focal point of all movement, a powerful muscular "python," carrying the bodily weight about, bending and twisting in response to our needs.

BALANCED SITTING

To determine where weights should be: sit on the tuberosities of the ischia, shrink softly inside yourself, as if you were trying not to touch a scratchy sweater. When aggressive in daily doings, you are constantly pulling yourself up and off balance.

The pulling upward is in direct proportion to the emotional drive in thinking. This "feel" for activity is so persistent that the "drive" is still toward shoulders, neck, knees and feet when

FIG. 87. A good central axis.

sitting. You are ready to spring up and step off. So, even in sitting you can feel most of your own weight is still carried by the legs. And, as the upper back and shoulders are tired, "slumping" seems the only recourse. Change the thinking. Visualize where the weights really sit, on the ischia. Feel them sharp. Imagine them pointing through the chair seat to the floor, making another pair of legs to the chair. Let the weight of your legs slide back into the pelvic basin. Note that this loosens the tense feeling of the knees and of the neck. The legs and feet should feel light and the thighs should be able to lift alternately and easily off the seat of the chair, if all weight has been directed successfully into the ischia.

The end of the spine is not designed to carry weight and the body should not be allowed to slide forward on the chair seat so that weight rests upon it. The ischia must receive all the weight. They extend lower in the body than the end of the spine; learn to sit upon them.

Think of your trunk or spine as a handle of a knife, and the legs as blades that close up and fit into it. Think an acute angle formed by legs at ischia; let the head hang but keep the spine erect; do not touch the back of the chair. Hiss and draw legs back into the spine—the blades of the knife, folding back into the handle.

Stand again and get ready to sit; imagine the thighs as two stilts, pushing the pelvis up in front at the sockets; get ready to sit, without bending the knees, but with a squatting motion in the lower body, thus equalizing the compression forces at the back, which act downward. The abdominal muscles will cease to drag and the abdominal wall will shorten in preparation for sitting.

EMOTIONAL VERSUS MECHANICAL STRAINS

Since man cannot change the response of his various systems to primary emotions, any procedure that would help to counter strains produced by them must be found in the mechanical or the psychological fields of investigation. Confusions which result from the struggle with unbalanced conditions are the sum total of so many impressions that they are often difficult to isolate and to name in any satisfactory way, for philosophic judgment. The first step in dealing with "floating anxieties," for instance, is to recognize them for what they are—bugbears, holding over from many physical tensions, from unutilized energy.

These tensions are muscular and are seen as postural mannerisms or "emotional sets" to which man has become habituated and therefore unconscious. These are less noticeable when he is most comfortable but increase in proportion to his emotional stress, automatically tightening some parts of his bony structure and releasing others. This changes length of leverage and interferes with his normal rhythms of motion. The extreme of this finally brings into consciousness unnatural, unsatisfactory moving and breathing. His locomotive and breathing

FIG. 88. Jack-knife sitting.

apparatus have ceased to act together. He is "all up in the air." What devices can he use to get himself down again? Is there a remedy? Education is the remedy.

And some mechanical devices may be used to lower the center of gravity and of breathing. One way is to lie upon a hard surface (floor) to change gravity pull through the vertebrae. While in this position hang the legs on a chair and fold arms across the chest, thus bringing the locomotive apparatus to a passive state as well as changing the axes of gravity in these regions. In this position hiss the breath out between the teeth several times, being careful not to take gasping breaths between hisses. The spine will lengthen, the body become more narrow and the pressure of the vertebrae more even upon the floor. After ten or fifteen minutes changes will be noticed in comfort and in breathing, and with a little practice relaxation will be attained.

FIG. 89. Relieving spine from strain of leg weights and favoring a return of blood to heart.

THE EFFECTS OF HISSING

Before hissing, speak the letter *H* several times, and make the hissing sound in the same place, starting it rather far back in the throat. Then speak *th* and note the changes in placement when hissing. *H* is more nearly like the low, guttural growl, and *th* more like the hiss of the alarmed animal. Try hissing with both placements and note results.

In expiring through partly closed teeth, in the hiss, the inner thoracic muscles, deep lumbar and pelvic, spinal, trunk extensors and the iliocostalis effect the changes, in depressing the thoracic cavity. From above downward, the muscles effecting this type of expiration are the internal intercostals, which act alternately with the diaphragm, the triangular sternal muscle or the transversus thoracis, found in the interior of the thorax on the anterior wall (its fibers run from the sternum, upward and outward, and insert on the ribs from the third to the sixth) and the subcostalis muscles, on the inner side of the posterior wall (their fibers running like those of the intercostals, except that they jump over one or two ribs). In addition, the iliocostalis pulls upon the ribs diagonally backward and downward, also aiding in the depression of the rib-cage. In fact, most of the trunk extensor group may serve to depress the rib-cage. The posterior serratus inferior, the psoas and the quadratus lumborum, also aid in the depression of the thorax in expiration while hissing.

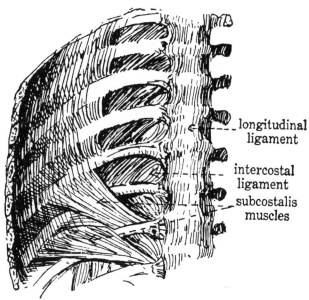

FIG. 90. Right posterior wall of thorax, from front. (Redrawn after Spalteholz.)

Except in hissing, these muscles do not ordinarily function in balanced action to depress the ribs. Try blowing the breath from the nostrils, until no more can be exhaled. The inward pull of the diaphragm on the lower rim of the ribs is noticeable and constriction of the transversalis accompanies this, until the inward pull of the diaphragm is felt quite severely at the lower end of the sternum, tending to bend the body forward.

Blowing the breath out through pursed lips affects the inward pull of the diaphragm on the ribs, as in the foregoing example, but to a less degree. The contraction of the transversalis and the quadratus lumborum and abdominal obliques is increased, but the pull is more even, that is, it does not pull right into the stomach. At the extreme of the exhalation, less bending takes place. In neither of these types of expiration do the iliocostalis and the spinal extensors work to depress the ribs and lengthen the spine at the back, as they do, effectively, in the hiss.

Expiration, with certain pharynx and larynx relationships and

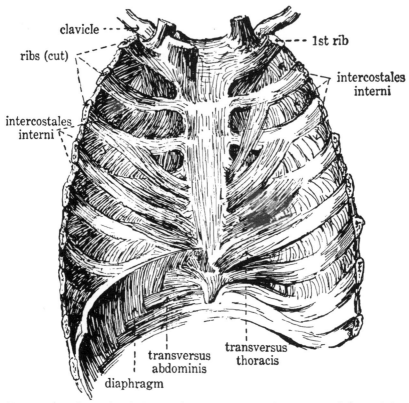

FIG. 91. Anterior wall of thorax, diaphragm having been removed from right side. (Redrawn after Spalteholz.)

with certain lumbar-pelvic adjustments, introduces into the expiratory rhythm the primary animal pattern for augmenting and integrating the fighting apparatus.

The use of hissing as a device for relieving strains and to deepen breathing through imagery and muscular reflexes leads us back to the initial and most important concept that the body is a mechanical structure, subject to mechanical laws and that it is also a living organism and must maintain chemical balance. For its activities to be supported, it must hold its stance and obtain oxygen for the use of its living fires. In the balance of its parts and in deep breathing this is done with least effort. Relaxation through balance is the great conservator of energy.

Relaxation is the equilibrium of the rest and activity phases in the rhythms of living, rest being the passive phase between the active phases of these rhythms, as for example in the rhythms of the heart, diaphragm and reciprocal muscle action.

Relaxation is potential balance, experienced in the ideal state of well-being.

Relaxation is not negation, it is not passivity. The moment it is considered as such, flaccidity is encouraged, both mental and physical. Take hold of your bones *softly*, but do not let go of them. Systems, parts, and parts of parts hang in balance, ready to respond in any direction possible to them when new stimuli are applied.

To find means of attaining relaxation involves the understanding of the natural functions of the mechanisms which have developed in living. Hypertension is the bodily expression of strains superimposed by man's conflicts, maladjustments and ignorance. How to attain release from strain is an important issue for health and for happiness. But this is far from a simple problem. We must study natural as well as strained behavior to find its solution.

Every tired person is advised to "relax," but there is much misunderstanding as to what relaxation, in the sense of bodily rest, really is. Nature provides for this in bodily tissues, as we have seen, in the "rest and activity rhythm." As one part or system works, it automatically throws its working mate into the rest phase of the rhythm. Appreciation and application of Nature's principle enable us to rest as we go. If we understand what relaxation is, we shall have due regard for the two phases of all bodily rhythms. The fact that the vital functions: beating of the heart, rhythms of the diaphragm, peristalsis, are carried on simultaneously and will be continuous without interference under usual conditions, shows the integrity of the vegetative system.

Work balances rest in the rhythms of living cells and systems. The *frequency* of rest periods is stressed in all living tissues, for every movement in one direction there is a movement in the opposite, all controlled automatically by chemical and nerve mechanisms. This principle of work pairing rest observed in the bodily economy under normal conditions can be successfully incorporated into the rhythms of daily activities. As a part of your working scheme, give a proportional time to a resting phase. The frequency of applying it is more important than the length of time allowed for the rest.

While doing very close eye work, for instance, sit near a window if possible, where you can see the sky. Stretch the eyes out to the distant horizon as frequently as you can. Wink often and occasionally close the eyelids and roll the eyes up, down and from side to side while closed. If sitting, stand often. If standing, sit often or move about. Standing is the most fatiguing of daily occupations. We should make various efforts to relax in accord with our needs. Frequent changes of focus, physical, mental or emotional, during active occupation, will favor it. Education and a little care will promote its habit. Rest must be followed by work, and work by rest. Recuperation in bodily tissue depends upon these alternations. In the words of Dr. Richard Cabot: "Rest means the removal of abnormal loads and the promotion of normal activity." In daily living, rest paired with work appears as relaxation, in sleep, play, change—land after sea, sea after land.

Structural unbalance reflects nervous unbalance. It is through the physical manifestations of difficulties that the harm is wrought to our bodies. Confused thinking results. Because of the unity of the physical being, unbalance, even of the most obvious mechanical kind, may have repercussions upon our whole mental and moral status. Whatever the explanation of how emotional and bodily changes are linked, it is as profoundly true that we are as much affected in our thinking by our bodily attitudes as our bodily attitudes are affected in the reflection of our mental and bodily states.

We should not know what lies in the imagination if expression did not reflect it. Often the body speaks clearly that which the tongue refuses to utter. Only as we understand how the materials of the body act in response to the forces of life, can we know how to make a better adjustment to those forces in our thinking. Changing the attitudes of the body is one way to change the mental attitudes; conversely, changing the mental attitudes certainly changes the bodily. And in this movement toward growth we may discover greater freedom for action and greater conservation in living.

Imagination itself, or the inner image, is a form of physical expression, and the motor response is the reflection of it. Memory records the reaction, as noted by Proust when, recovering himself from stumbling over uneven flagstones in a courtyard, he received a sudden release from gloom and discouragement, and upon analysis related it to a happier time, when the same thing occurred to him before the baptistry of St. Mark's in Venice. He notes, "from caverns darker than that from which flashes the comet which we can predict—thanks to the unimaginable defensive force of inveterate habit, thanks to the hidden reserves which by a sudden impulse habit hurls at the last minute into the fray—my activity was aroused at length."

Living, the whole body carries its meaning, and tells its own story—standing, sitting, walking, awake or asleep, pulling all the life up into the face of the philosopher or sending it all down into the feet of the dancer. Each must understand the problems underlying dynamic man, intelligently to lower the center of gravity, to deepen the respiratory rhythms.

Knowledge is the way to conservation and a more efficient use of human energy.

The thinking body stands, moves and performs its skills through knowledge of the natural forces in its dynamic balances.

BIBLIOGRAPHY

BEHAN, R. J. Pain. N. Y., 1914.

BINGER, W. B. What Engineers Do. N. Y., 1928.

BOWEN, W. P. Applied Anatomy and Kinesiology; the Mechanism of Muscular Movement. Phila., 1923.

BRAUS, H. Anatomie des Menschen. Berlin, 1921.

BURNHAM, W. H. Efficient Brain Activity. Essay, American Posture League, July 5, 1917.

BYRD, H. Pathological impulses or currents. Repr. from *Med. J. & Rec.*, 121:141, (Feb. 4) 1925.

CANNON, W. B. Bodily Changes in Pain, Hunger, Fear and Rage. N. Y., 1915.

Wisdom of the Body. N. Y., 1932.

CAPPS, J. A., and COLEMAN, G. H. Experimental observations on the localization of the pain sense. *Arch. Int. Med.*, 30: 778-789, (Dec.) 1922.

COBB, S., and FORBES, A. Electromyographic studies of muscular fatigue in man. *Am. J. Physiol.*, vol. 65, (July) 1923.

FREEMAN, R. G. Fatigue in school children as tested by the ergograph. Repr. from *Am. J. M. Sc.*, 136:686, (Nov.) 1908.

GREGORY, W. K. Man's Place among the Anthropoids. Oxford, 1934.

Bridges that walk. *Am. Museum Nat. Hist. Mag.*, (Jan.) 1937.

and ROIGNEAU, M. Introduction to Human Anatomy. Am. Mus. Nat. Hist., N. Y., 1934.

GRINKER, R. R. Neurology. Balt., 1934.

HILL, A. V. Muscular Movement in Man; Factors Governing Speed and Recovery from Fatigue. N. Y., 1927.

HOWELL, W. H. A Text-book of Physiology. Phila., 1920.

HUXLEY, T. H. Lesson in Elementary Physiology. N. Y., 1926.

JAMES, W. Psychology. N. Y., Ed. 1, 1892; Ed. 2, 1900.

The Principles of Psychology. N. Y., 1905.

JENSEN, M. On Bone Formation; Its Relation to Tension and Pressure. London, 1920.

KEITH, SIR A. Engines of the Human Body. London, Ed. 1, 1919; Ed. 2, 1925.

KEMPF, E. J. Psychopathology. N. Y., 1921.

LAMBERT, G. O. Cardiovascular Pain as a Biochemical Problem. London, 1933.

MACKENZIE, W. C. The Action of Muscles, Including Muscle Rest and Muscle Re-education. N. Y., 1927.

MACLEOD, J. J. R. Physiology in Modern Medicine. St. Louis, 1935.

MARTIN, W. Some types of neuritic reflex pains not generally recognized. Repr. from *Med. J. & Rec.*, 124:782, (Dec. 15) 1926.

PAVLOV, I. P. Conditioned Reflexes. London, 1927.

PIERSOL, G. A. Human Anatomy. N. Y., Ed. 1, 1907; Ed. 2, 1936.

ROBINSON, J. H. The Mind in the Making. N. Y., 1921.

The Humanizing of Knowledge. Ed. 2, N. Y., 1926.

ROMER, A. S. Man and the Vertebrates. Chicago, 1933.

SCHWARTZ, L. *Public Health Rep.*, 192, 42: 1242-1248.

SHERRINGTON, SIR C. S. Integrative Action of Nervous System. London, 1926.

SPALTERHOLZ, W. Hand Atlas and Human Anatomy. Phila., 1923.

STARLING, E. H. Principles of Human Physiology. London, Ed. 1, 1912; Ed. 2, 1936.

STRONG, O. S., and ELWYN, A. Bailey's Textbook of Histology. N. Y., 1927.

STRUNSKY, M. Referred pain in flatfoot. *J.A.M.A.*, vol. 65, (July 3) 1915.

TODD, M. E. Principles of posture. *Boston M. & S. J.*, 182:645, 1920.

Principles of posture, with special reference to the hip joint. *Boston M. & S. J.*, 184:667, 1921.

The Balancing of Forces in the Human Body. N. Y., 1929.

Our strains and tensions. *Progressive Educ. Mag.*, (Mar.) 1931.

TROLAND, L. T. Fundamentals of Human Motivation. N. Y., 1928.

WILLIAMS, J. F. Textbook of Anatomy and Physiology. N. Y., 1926.

Atlas of Human Anatomy. N. Y., 1936.

WILSON, E. B. The Cell in Development and Heredity. N. Y., 1925.

INDEX

Index

A

Abdomen, 18
Abdominal obliques, stretched, 225, 291
Abductors and adductors, 82
Absorption, 21
  shock, 132, 147, 189, 206, 209, 247
Acceleration, 249
Accessory groups, 231, 233, 241, 251
Acetabulum (acetabula), 114, 116, 123, 133, 138, 162, 176, 181
  distance between, 178
Acoustic sense, 27
Acrobat hanging by teeth, 171
Acromial clavicular articulation, 147
Acromion, 144, 149, 156
Action and reaction, 5, 22, 47, 50, 74, 187, 210
Activity and rest, 219
  alternate, 281
Actors and acrobats learn to fall, 202
Actors and antagonizers, 38, 39, 82, 115, 116, 154, 199
Adaptation, 9, 45, 50, 52, 76
  breathing, 9
  functional, 45
  foot, 140
  protective rib cage, 147
Adrenalin, 274, 276, 277
Afferent nerve, 54, 250, 252
Alice through Looking Glass, 172
Alimentary canal, 29
Alveoli, lung sacs, 250
Amphibians, 9, 142
Ankle, 140, 141, 178, 183, 210
  pronated, 183, 209
  rocking motion, 184
Antagonistic action, 117
Antagonizers, 39, 201, 248. See also Actors.
Antero-posterior diameter, chest, 166, 180, 192
Aorta, 223
  main trunk of, 231

Apparatus, breathing, 289
  locomotion, 289
Appendicular skeleton, 10, 80, 113, 142
Arch, femora-ilio-sacral, 114
  foot, 206
  ischio-ilio-sacral, 114
  reinforcement, 116
  sacral keystone, 115, 116
  spread, 117
  support at keystone, 117
Arcuate ligament, 120, 223, 229, 231
Arms, circling, 177
  relation to legs, 154
  "sit" in sockets, 176
Artificial structure, 23
Arytenoid cartilages, 260
Aspirates, elements of speech, 257, 258
Atlas, condyles, 102
  first vertebra, 102
  relationships, 112
  seat for head, 99
Attention, split, 281
  strains, 44, 173
Automatic action of muscles, 77
Autonomic nervous system, 272
    and parasympathetic, 274
  sympathetic, 274
  system, protection, 226
Awareness, 26, 27, 268
Axial load, 93
  skeleton, 80, 113, 149, 154
  stress, 48, 59
Axis (es), 48, 56
  central, 64, 97
  condyles, 100
  crura, 234
  gravity, 59, 190, 289
  legs, 117
  line of direction, 279
  movement, 91, 279
  second cervical vertebra, 102
  spatial relation, 207

Axis—(*Continued*)
  spinal, 21, 64, 94, 95, 108, 154, 166, 211
  three positions, 204, 205
  trunk, leg, spine, 190
Axon, 271

B

Balance, 37, 38, 41, 42, 56, 101, 188, 286, 293
  body, 3
  bone, skeletal, 59, 202, 221, 276
  breathing, relation to, 108
  cerebrospinal, 278
  chest, 153
  compression and tension, 161, 215
  in emergencies, 253
  emotional, 43, 221, 264
  falling, 202
  foot, 140
  head, condyles, 103, 104, 193
  living tissue, 282
  locomotion, 220
  lost in fatigue, 263, 267
  modifiable, 262
  momentum, 202
  muscles, 122, 150
  pelvic, 116, 122, 124
  reduction of curves, 173
  serratus, rhomboids, 153
  sitting, 285, 286, 287
  standing, 189
  strength of spine, 99
  thigh joint, 123
  upward forces, 116
  walking, rebound, 134
Balancing forces, 7
    living, 44
    mechanical, 44
    walking, 194
Base, narrow, 45
  rocking, 62
Beam, 55, 182
Behavior, 1, 30, 272, 280
  artificial, 23
  unconscious, 247
Behan, Richard J., 53
Bending stress, 48, 164, 226
Bicycle, riding pattern, 213, 214
  wheel, 131, 156
Bilateral symmetry, 64, 82
Biochemistry, 266

Biological heritage, 1, 238, 247, 256, 257, 280
  gills and lungs, 218
  influences, 210
Biped compensations, 70
  handicaps, 70
  pattern, 45
  position, 73, 75
Bodily attitudes, 1, 295
  economy, 294
  expression, 295
  rhythms, 293
Body cavity, 188
  compactness, 76
  cylinder, 237
  dynamics, 2
  mechanics, 41, 199
  pattern, vertebrate, 78
  pelvic joints, 205
  as whole, 1
  weight, 42, 206
Body wall, 108, 109, 175, 211, 237, 240, 253
  arm relationship, 192
  breathing muscles, 110
    accessory, 233
  cylindrical, 234
  muscular relationships, 149
  protective, 172
Bone(s), 4, 225, 248
  "add the ground," 207
  balance, 2, 23, 77, 202, 276, 286
  decalcified, 60
  four functions, 7
  as levers, 6
  living fiber, 6, 60
  marrow, 81
  opposing bone, 186
  physical characteristics, 60, 81
  versus steel, 5, 59, 61, 81
Brachial plexus, 252
Brain development, 14
Breast bone, 161
Breathing, 10, 18, 43, 44, 167, 218, 241, 252. *See also* Expiration, Inspiration.
  accelerated, 233
  accessory of, 231, 240, 241, 251
  affected by emotions, 251
  apparatus, 6, 180
  automatic, 232
  bone support, 234
  centers, 249

Breathing—(*Continued*)
  chemical balance, 240
  depth, 18, 247, 292
  expiration, 250
  external, 219
  gills to lungs, 218
  gravity, 247
  hissing, 245, 292. *See also* Hissing.
  innervation, 250
  inspiration, 180, 250
  internal, 219
    increased, 284
  locomotion, 108, 217, 243
  mechanisms in emergencies, 253
  medulla oblongata, 232
  muscles, 107, 231
  primary, secondary, 21, 219
  pulse, 250
  relation in balance, 108
  rhythms, 6, 21, 249, 252, 283
  sensory nerve connections, 251
  spherical, 232
  system, 274
  tidal air in, 233, 240
  tubular, 180, 192, 231
  two phases, 9
  vertical, 241
  voluntary, 222
Bridge, 62
Buoyancy, 203
Burnham, William H., 36, 37
Buttresses, 55
  pelvic arch, 116, 182
  ribs, 70

C

Calcaneus, weight transfer, 141
Canals, dorsal and ventral, 237
Cannon, Walter, 38, 274
Cantilever, 73, 182, 199, 207
Capillaries, 218
Carbon-dioxide, 241
Cardiovascular system, 10
Carotid sinus, 250
Cells, 7, 22, 24, 52, 219, 231, 241, 250
Centering muscles, lower spine, 93, 122
Central nervous system, 78, 220
Centrum tendineum, 221, 229, 231
Cerebellar reflexes, 100

Cerebellum, 29, 30
Cerebral-spinal balance, 272, 278
Cerebrum, 29, 252
Cervical spine, axis, 193
  vertebrae, curve, 95, 239
Chemical balance, 292, 294
Chest, cavity enlarged, 284
  desirable high, 166
  load balance, 97, 153, 167
  muscles, 170
  reduced diameter, 212
  rigidity, 166
  symmetry, 166
  undesirable high, 163, 237
  upper, 226
Circulation, 18, 43, 158, 164, 231
Clavicle, 13, 80, 144, 145, 170, 231
  yard-arm, 147
Clavicular-sternal articulation, 147
Clinical findings in fatigue, 267
Coccyx, 86, 95
Coherence, 46, 47, 49, 65
Collar bone, 161
Communicating system, 248
Composite joint, 115, 123, 199
  crouch, spring, 64, 134, 186
Compression, 54, 59, 77, 107, 211, 288
  forces, 74, 153, 288
  members, balancing, torsion, 175, 182, 190, 215, 255
  operating through spine, 161
  stress, 48, 55
Concavity and convexity, 155
  pelvic, 91
  redirection of curve, 92
  spine, 91, 107
Conditioned reflexes in breathing, 37, 258, 268
Condyles, atlas, 102
  two axes of balance, 99
Conflicts, materials and forces, 277
Confusion strains, 265
Confusions, 288
Conscious control, 6, 41
Consciousness, substrata, threshold, 22
Convalescence, 52
Convexity, spine, 91, 92, 107
Coordination, 17, 33
Correlation, 41, 280
Cortex cerebri, 249, 252
Costal angle, 109
Cranial nerves, 252

Crico-arytenoid, posterior, 260
Crico-thyroid muscles, 260
Crile, George, 269
Cross-pulls, 192
Crura, axes, 234
  diaphragm, 180, 229
  relationships, 234
Crural arch, 234, 242, 251
Cuboids and cuneiforms, 141
Cylinder of body, 68
  hypothetical, 7, 237
  of long bone, 81
  pelvis, 239

D

Daily activities, 294
Darley, F. O. C., drawings, 195, 196, 197
Deformation, 50
Dendrites, 271
Density, 55
Dexterity, 249
Diaphragm, 18, 21, 107, 180, 191, 217, 221, 229, 230, 242, 252
  acquaintance with, 283
  action, 222, 225, 232, 250
  affecting rhythms, 222
  aids lower accessory, 240, 256
  anatomy, 110, 290, 226, 229
  arcuate ligaments, 155
  crura and arch, 128, 155, 233
  cylinder, 237
  excursion, 240, 284
  pelvic, 233
  piston stroke, 242
  rib, 233
  rhythms, rest and work, 222, 244, 293
  tubular breathing, 245
  visceral relations, 221
Diarrhea, 221
Diastole, 38
Digestion, 18, 277
Dinosaur's tail, 174, 210
Distortion in art, 244
Dorsal angles, cavities, 144, 156, 166
"Down the back, up the front," 173
Dynamic balance, 91, 295
Dynamics, 50, 56
  spatial planes, 205, 206

E

Economy, 18, 22, 23, 33, 42, 45, 51, 76, 188, 203, 204, 207, 218, 294
  devices, 258
  minimum effort, 157
Efferent and afferent, 252
Elasticity, 54, 59, 81
Embryo, 17
Emergency, 220, 232, 255
  speed, balanced forces, 243, 253
Emotion and breathing, 232
  expectation, 158
  fighting or escaping, 221
Emotional controls, imbalances, 275
  drive, movement, 281
    thinking, 287
  factors, 219, 275
  readiness, 272
  "set," 288
End-organs, 25, 26, 27, 30
Energy, conservation, 7, 63, 188, 211, 258, 277, 280, 282, 293, 295
  deflection, 282
  kinetic, 225
  ligamentous device for saving, 90
  per cent available, 3
  potential, 225
  replenishment, 272
  storehouse, 249
  used or wasted, 59, 163, 250, 265, 280
Engineering, 46, 74, 200
Equilibrium, 2, 50, 220
  physical and mental, 221
Erect position, advantages, disadvantages, 8
  posture, 46, 70
  stability, 74, 158
Erector spinae muscles, 172
Esophagus, 223, 230
Evolution, 7
Excentering muscles, lower spine, 2, 93, 204
Excursion, diaphragm, 240, 284
Expiration, 167, 218, 250, 256, 258. See also Breathing.
  active phase, 251
  forced, 251, 284
  hissing, 245, 283, 290
  larynx and pharynx, 292
  lower accessory group muscles, 251
  lowering gravity, 258

Expiration—(*Continued*)
  nose, lips, teeth, 245
  muscles engaging, 255
  time element, 222
Expiratory augmenting muscles, abdomen, 259
  muscular release, 261
  reconditioning, 259
  renewal of vigor, 261
  rhythm, 252, 291, 292
Expression, pressure of forces, 276
Extensors of back, strain, 225
  erector spinae, 172
  and flexors, 226
  of spine, 161
External respiration, 219
Exteroceptive, 27
Eye(s), adaptation, 103
  image, work, roll, 32, 294
  rôle in walking, 215

F

Facet, fifth lumbar, sacrum, 176
  posterior, 161
  sacrum, 162
  spinal, 67, 69
Facial nerves, 253
Falling, control of momentum, 202
Fascia, 30, 65, 81, 233, 251
  intermuscular septa, 128
  lata, 128, 138
  pelvis, 127
Fasciculae, 62
Fatigue, 29, 38, 43, 158, 216, 256
  awareness of, 268
  chronic, 265, 267
  clinical findings, 267
  Crile, George, 269
  emotional and mental, 263
  frustration, 270
  habit, 264
  inertia of acceptance, 264
  limit, 277
  Mellon Institute report, 270
  in metal, 268
  from normal activity, 264
  psycho-physical, 264, 265, 266
  toxins, 270
  unbalances, causes, 263, 267
  work impairment, 263
Fear, 267, 274
Feel for second wind, 256

Feeling, 202, 204, 243
  for head balance, 193
"Feelings" for truths involved, 175
Femoral joint, 176
Femoro-ilio-sacral arch, 114
Femur (femora), 70, 96, 162, 174, 181
  alignment with tibia, 138
  balanced tension, 131
  catch weight, 174
  description, 137
  weight re-direction, 134
Fibula, articulating with tibia, 138
  leg flexibility, 140
Fifth lumbar vertebra, 132, 180
  cumulative weight, 208
  slipping load, 172
  spinous processes, 132
  three point support, 133
Fighting apparatus, 292
Flava ligament, 89, 90
Flexibility in foot, 189
  in knees, 189
Flexible upright, curved, 187
Flexors and extensors, 82
Focus, change often, 294
  eyes and hands, 173
Foot, arch construction, 140, 141, 206
  balance, 142, 189
  condition, 203
  planter aspect, 200
  stirrup-like design, 184
  weight transfer, 183, 206, 209
Force, 22, 47, 207
  lines of, 90, 199
  mechanical, 41
  neuromuscular, 41
  planes of, 204
  time-space, 205
  upward thrust, foot, 206
Form follows function, 8, 42
Frustration, fatigue, 270
Function preceded form, 3, 8, 42

G

Ganglia, 53
Gases, 47
Glands, 24, 220
  visceral protection, 218, 220
Glenoid, cavity, 144
  socket, 147
Glottis, widened inspiration, 253

Gravity, 8, 9, 22, 23, 27, 30, 37, 38, 54, 55, 59, 62, 75, 101, 186, 243, 251, 255
  advantage, 256
  affecting function, 8
  bone relations, 244, 286
  center, high, 277
    lowered, 204, 232, 289
    moving, helix, 200
    raised, 164
    shift, 205
  centering of weights, 101
  changed axis, 289
  lower through expiration, 258
  movement, ballast, 255
  relation, lumbar curve, 187
  working design, 286
Gregory, William K., 14
Gutter of spine, 109, 145

H

Habit, 4, 40, 41, 117, 256, 294, 295
  building, 282
  easy standing, 193
  fatigue, 264
  fixities, 282
  fly-wheel, 272
  recognize strains, 179
  weights held off center, 159
Hand manipulation, 13
Haunches, 238
Head, 103, 112, 237, 240
  axial load, 97, 99
  balance, 102, 104
  centered, 187
  dictates movements, 238
  elevated, 212
  "follow through," 159
  freedom, 13
  stabilization, 170, 192
  top load, 94, 193
  weight, 101, 211, 247
Heart, 18, 222, 229, 230, 231, 274
  acceleration, 274
Helix, 200
Hemoglobin, 219
Hiatus aorticus, 231
Hip joints, distance between, 162
  initiate movement, 159
Hissing, 167, 216, 246
  cat and snake, 255
  deepens breathing, 258, 292

Hissing—(Continued)
  effects, 290, 292
  expiration, 245, 246, 290
  lying down, 289
  muscle action, 291
  narrowing thorax, 283
  relieving strains, 292
  sitting, 288
  spine lengthening, 292
  through teeth, 283
Holmes, Oliver Wendell: "Physiology of Walking," 194
Hooke's law, 56
Hoop-skirt pattern, 171
Hormone, respiration, 250, 257
Howell, William H., 252, 261
Humerus, 145, 154
Huxley, Thomas H., 24
Hyoid, 170, 213, 239
Hypertension, 26, 219, 265, 267, 280
  and hypotension, 266
  man's conflicts, 277, 293
  muscle grip, 275
Hypothetical cylinder, 79

I

Iliac fascia, 120, 129
Iliacus muscle, 118
Iliocostalis, 290
Iliopsoas muscles, 160, 181
  balancing obturators, 182
  crura, 234
  ligaments and gluteals, 199
  spine and pelvis, 240
  tone and stretch, 225
Ilium (ilia), 96, 133
  anterior superior spine, 178
  crest, 150, 161
Imagery, 211, 213, 278, 288
Imagination, 189, 211, 212, 213, 250
  importance, 281
  physical expression, 295
  recondition, 282
Impulses, activate muscles, 32
Inertia, 23, 25, 30, 37, 55, 282
  of acceptance, 264
Inhibited movement, 276
Inhibitions, 275
Inner ear, 28
Innervation, respiratory, 250
Innominate bone, 80, 114

Inspiration, 180, 218, 250. *See also* Breathing.
abdominal muscles relax, 259
glottis widened, 253
interrelated structures, 232
oxygen, quantity, 243
voluntary, 251
Intercostals, 232, 240, 251, 252, 290
Internal respiration, 219, 222
importance, 259
increased, 284
lower accessory muscles, 238
Interosseous membrane, 138, 140, 184
Interrelationship, structural, 17
Intervertebral disks, 70, 87, 88
Ischia (sit-bones), 114, 161
alignment, 116
near front, 285
receive weight, 287
Ischio-ilio-sacral arch, 114

J

James, William, 4, 36
Japanese parasol, 213
Jaw bone, 161
Joints, balance standing, 188
centered, 203
rocking motion, 189
Judgments, visual, skin and canals, 247

K

Keith, Sir Arthur, 102
Kinesthesia, 27, 32, 33, 38, 159, 175, 176, 193, 244
testing, 285
Kinesthetic sense, 7, 28, 35, 162, 188, 238, 278
Knees, flexibility, 189
formation, 208
mechanical disadvantages, 208
momentum, 208
rocking, 184
weight control, 183

L

Labyrinthine sensations, 27, 30, 32, 99, 102
Lactic acid, 65
Laryngeal cartilages, 237, 253

Larynx, description, 260
expiration, 292
innervation, vagus, 253
vocal cords, 260
Lateral pulls, reduction, 175, 205
Latissimus dorsi, 148, 150, 155, 156, 281
Lavoisier, 9, 219
Legs, 17, 67, 70, 115, 159, 137, 142, 178
alternate action, 199, 208
arms, relation, 154
axis, 117
over chair, 289
excentering, recentering, 179
and foot, 139
Holmes, Oliver Wendell, description, 194
joints centered, 199, 203, 204
muscle balance, 184
recoil from spine, 187
shorten in action, 199, 208
sitting, 286, 287
spokes of wheel, 207
tripod, 205
Leverage, 4, 6, 205
between three planes, 190
changes, 288
Levers, 33, 62, 63, 80, 176, 190, 210
power and weight, 248, 279
Life-saving situation, 249
Ligaments, 30, 36, 59, 76, 81, 101
anterior common, 88
capsular, 125
flava, 89, 90
longitudinal, 88, 89
pelvic, 115, 123, 124
posterior common, 88
supra-spinatus, 88
trusses, 88
Linea alba, 68
Lines of force, 90, 199, 204
Loads, abnormal, 294
Locomotion, 10, 14, 78, 220
babyhood, 137
balance, rhythm, 220, 249
and breathing, 108, 217, 243, 289
crouch and spring, 160
mammals, 13
problem, 199
uncoordinated, 277
Lordosis, sagging pelvis, 172, 173, 225

Lower accessory muscles, 231, 240, 252, 256
Lumbar, crura, 234
 curve, 95
 deep control, 188, 201
 fascia, 10, 57
 plexus, 252
 spinal curve, 95, 242
Lumbosacral joint, 69, 96, 133, 176, 201, 205
 pyramidal, 133
 di ision of weight, 133
Lungs, 9, 43, 157, 187, 188, 231
 air content, 245
 cavity at back, 240
 lowering, 233
Lymphatics, 21, 43, 231
Lying-down position, 175
 ankle flexion, 178
 rotation, leg, arms, 177, 179
 think through body, 176

M

Machine, human living, 3, 7
 moving mass, 118
Mackenzie, W. C., 46
Maladjustments, 293
Mandible, 170, 239
Mannerisms, 288
Man's conflicts, 293
Manubrium, 111, 144, 164
Mastoid, 170
Macleod, John J. R., 249
Medulla oblongata, 232, 251, 252
Medullary centers, 249, 250, 252
Mechanical action, lung sacs, 250
 advantages, 8, 59, 61, 180
 balance, spine, 93, 99
 coordination, 210
 design, 41
 direction changes, 134
 factors, 40, 55, 59, 97, 132, 137, 141, 147, 155, 170, 209, 210, 243, 250, 292
 gravity center, moving, 200
 pelvis, composite spring, 134
 reduction of curves, 155
 spokes of wheel, 156
 stresses, 33
 yoke, 156

Mechanism, 21, 29, 220
 dynamic human, 4, 7
 labyrinthine, 103
 material functions, 293
 receiving and moving, 13
 and responding, 25
 rotary joints, 176
 supporting and moving, 13
 suspending apparatus, 170
 working skeleton, 80
Mechanics, application, 21, 22, 25, 113, 164, 219
 bicycle, 214
 cantilever, 74
 screw conveyer, 200
 working skeleton, 157
Mellon Institute report, 270
Memory, 1, 32, 248, 295
Mental attitudes, 295
 experience, 272
 focus, 268
 and moral status, 294
Metabolism, 219
Metal suffers fatigue, 268
Metatarsals, radial control, 142
Military posture, 283
Molecule, 46, 47, 49, 54
Motion, awareness, 26
 pelvic arch, 115
 springboard, 190
Momentum, 27, 55, 203, 209, 243
 breaking foot arches, 183
 control, 201
 reduction, 205
Motivating pictures, 211, 214, 238, 278, 281
Movement, 24, 25, 28, 29, 30, 32, 33, 37, 39, 56, 62, 75, 92
 arms and legs, relation, 154
 balance, 205
 conditions for, 7, 279, 281
 execution, 279
 expansive, 242
 expiration muscles, 290
 finger tapping, 279
 grace and efficiency, 159
 gravity and ballast, 255
 head and arms, 102, 232, 248
 hissing, 290
 importance, emotional drive, 281
 leg control, 142, 199
 levers through spine, 279
 location, direction, desire, 279

Movement—(*Continued*)
  many arcs, 148
  natural vs. unnatural, 280
  organized, 161, 204, 248, 276
  patterns, 279
  pelvis as base, 118, 238
  peripheral, 240
  primary patterns, 219, 243, 246
  radius, 280
  reciprocal, 210
  reorganization, 207
  shifting gravity center, 286
  simple, 248, 249
  springboard, 206
  thorax in hissing, 290
  time-space, 210, 249
  toward growth, 295
  trunk as unit, 226
  unconscious, 29
  voluntary and involuntary, 232
Muscles, 62, 148, 248
  abdominal tone, 248
  accessory to breathing, 231
  cells, 249
  electric stimulation, 65
  energy, 3
  fatigue, 62, 63, 66, 263
  fibers, in relays, 222
  forced expiration, 290
  handicap, 63
  intermuscular septa, 138
  living engine, 243
  opposing muscle, 185
  pelvic and femoral, 118
  reinforced by rest, 222
  response to thinking, 281
  saving devices, 63
  skeletal, 220
  "slack," 64
  strain, unbalance, 65, 225
  stretch before contraction, 250
  tone, 63

N

Natural or unnatural restraint, 280
Natural way of doing, 281
Navicularis, 141
Nerves, 25, 248
  afferent, autonomic, 54, 252
  axon, 271
  centers, 26
  cell body, 270

Nerves—(*Continued*)
  dendrites, 271
  efferent, 252
  fibers, 26, 53
  ganglia, 274
  mechanisms, 249
    autonomic, 272
    automatic, 294
    brain, 272
    cerebral-spinal, 272
    locomotion, 218
    respiration, 218
  reflexes, 29, 218
Nervous reflexes, 29
  system, 26, 270
    breakdown, 280
Neural canal, dorsal, 78
Neuromuscular system, 2, 6, 42, 43, 266
Neurones, 248, 252
  fatigue, 263, 266
  cells, 270

O

Obturators, internus, 120, 121, 181
  and externus, 118
  balance ilio-psoas, 182
Occipital condyles, 99
Old age measurement, 282
  animal mechanisms, 248, 276
Optimism, 7
Organism, modifiable, 262
Otoliths, 27, 28
Oxygen, 9, 18, 43, 218, 220, 241, 293
  balance, 241
  cell supply, 243, 250
  exchange, 259
  rapid supply, 249

P

Pain, in foot, 210
  referred, 52, 53, 183
  reflected, 52, 53
Paralysis, 41
Patterns, divergent, 13
  learned, uneconomical, 103
  of movement, 32
  postural, 21, 33
  structural, 8
Pectineus, 118
Pectoral muscle, 148

Pectoralis minor, 153
Pelvic arch, 114, 182
    buttresses, 116
    diaphragm, 233
    equilibrium, 190
    floor, 122
    integration, 161
    reinforcement, 182
    rim, 169
    girdle, 67, 80, 115, 143, 182
Pelvis, alternating substances, 131
    base, 17, 18, 59, 97, 99, 113, 160, 251
    cantilever, 207
    as carriage, 184, 200, 203
    close to thorax, 172, 191, 199, 213, 238, 242
    composite spring, 134
    crouch and spring, 182, 186
    distribution of weight, 132, 162, 226
    hip joints in front, 162
    increased obliquely, 225
    shock absorber, 131
    spring board, 206
Peristalsis, 43, 222, 274, 293
Pharynx, 257, 292
Philosophy, 157
Phrenic nerve, 252
Physiological approach, 2, 36, 75
    balances, 262, 265
    reactions, 36
"Physiology of Walking," Oliver Wendell Holmes, 194
Piersol, George Arthur, 60, 81, 90, 133
Pitch, 36
Plane of force, 190, 191, 205
Pleura, 232
Poise, 40, 272
Postural patterns, 7, 22, 278
    reflexes, 36
Posture, 37
    alarm, 257
    animal hissing, 255
    animals and birds, 255
    bad, 255
    dramatic tradition, 1
    extreme behavior, 261
    false concept, 237
    incessant, 43
    maladjustments, 44, 288
    military, 283

Posture—(*Continued*)
    patterns, 21
    psycho-physical basis, 7
    reflex, Sherrington, 278
    speech, 257
    upright, 7, 70
Potential balance, 293
Prenatal development, 137
"Prepare for the load," 63, 201, 202
Primary breathing, 219
    patterns, 30, 233, 238, 276, 292
    fighting, 253
    movement, 219
    muscles, 1
    reflexes, 210
Proprioceptive mechanism, 27, 30, 36, 101, 130, 159, 176, 216, 252
    sensations, 63
    system, 220, 247
Protoplasm, 6, 7, 23
    and cytoplasm, 24
    behavior, 25
    chemical nature, 24
    defined by Huxley, 24
Proust, 274, 295
Psoas, 118, 181, 191, 229, 242, 291
    integrating curve, 155
Psychic, 217
    disturbances, 264, 265
Psychology, 75, 266
Psychophysical aspects, 7, 23
    fatigue, 266
Pubic bones, arch, 161
    description, 126
    symphysis, 133
Pubis, 96
Pull vs. push, 64
Pulse, respiration, 250
Pyriformis, 118
    action, 122
    origin and insertion, 181
Python, spine, 286

Q

Quadratus lumborum, 118, 225, 229, 291
Quadruped, 14, 67, 73, 113, 175, 209, 244
    into biped, 66
    body weights, 161
    crouch and spring, 160

R

Radius of movement, 280
Receiving, correlating, responding
  mechanism, 2
Reciprocal action, 225
Recondition through imagination, 281
  in inspiration, 259
Rectus abdominis, 154
Referred pain, 53
Reflexes, 33, 43
  arc, 29
Reflexes, 6, 35
  muscular, 250
  nerve, 29
  postural, 36
  primary, 103, 210
  synchronization, 6
Relaxation, 38, 222, 232, 262, 278,
  294
  activity phase, 293
  attained, 290
  balance, 293
  breathing related, 267
  locomotive rhythms, 267
  not negation, 293
  potential balance, 293
  rest phase, 293
Residual air, 241
Respiration. See Breathing
Rest, activity, 219, 248
  alternating work, 222
  as we go, 293
  through balance, 282
  balances work, 294
  frequency, 270, 282, 294
  paired with work, 267
  passive phase, 293
  sitting, 115
  time element, 65, 265
Rhomboids, minor and major, 153
Rhythm, 199, 204, 248
  bodily material, 268
  breathing, 219, 220, 252
  coordination, 219
  falling and catching, 207
  interdependent, 217, 243
  living cells, 294
  motion and rest, 270
  passive and active, 293
  skeletal musculature, 222
  testing bodily, 244

Rib cage, 17, 98, 107, 111, 144, 145,
  221, 225, 290
  in cylinder, 237
  protects arm action, 155, 156
  size of top, 111
Ribs, 107, 251
  antero-posterior depth, 166
  articulation, 239
  braces, buttresses, 70, 192
  cavities, 156
  comparison, 108
  costal angle, 109
  dorsal angle, gutter, 109, 166
  free spinal joints, 166, 167
  interspaces, 232
  muscle attachments, 150, 156
  pulled up, 164
  sternal end, 111
  strained, bending, 164
  suspension, 109, 239
  surfaces, relationships, 110, 112
  unbalance, 164
Richet, Charles R., 206, 262
Rigidity, 54, 56
  chest, 166, 242
  freedom from, 177
Robinson, James Harvey, 282
Rocking, at ankles, 184
  at base, 61
  at knees and thigh joints, 184
Routine acceptance, 282

S

Sacroiliac, 205
  direction, force, 134
  displacement, 117
  equal weight, 133
  formation, 116
  joints, 70, 96, 114
  thrust, 176
  unbalanced by lordosis, 173
  weight-bearing, 116
Sacrolumbar, weight-bearing, 116
Sacrum, 86, 161
  lines of force, 199
  shape, 96
  weight, 207
Scapula, 14, 80, 144, 156, 231
  muscle attachments, 150
  spine of, 149
  vertebral border, 145, 153
Schwartz, Louis, 45, 75

Second wind, 220, 256
Secondary breathing, 219
Self-awareness, 26
Semicircular canals, 27, 28, 216
Sensations, 25, 26, 27, 28, 29, 35
  organic, 30
  peripheral, 36
  proprioceptive, 36
Sense organs, 25, 26
Sensorium, 53
Sensory motor chain, 35
Serratus, 148, 153, 291
Sesamoids, 183
ShanKar, neck movement, 156
Shearing stress, 48, 201
Sherrington, Sir C. S., 259, 271, 278
Shock, 43, 52, 74, 241
  absorber, composite spring, 134
    interosseous membrane, 309
    pelvis, 131
    rebound in walking, 134
    shoulder girdle, 147
      joint, 144
    summarized, 131
    symphysis, 133
  absorption, 189, 247
    at knee, 209
    small parts of foot, 206
    weight distribution, 132
Shoulder, ends of yoke, 170
  girdle, 14, 67, 80, 143, 147, 232,
    238
    bisymmetry, 170
    description, 142
    freedom, 156, 177
    mechanical balance, 170
    proportions, 145
    protection, rib cage, 155
    relationships, 112
    suspension, 170, 176, 192, 239
    unbalance, 154
  joint, 14, 144
    acromion, 144
    coracoid, 144
    glenoid cavity, 144
    spokes of wheel, 156
  muscles, four groups, 148
  round, 186
Sibilants, elements of speech, 257
  production, 258
Sitting, 214, 294
  balanced, 285
  feel for activity, 287

Sitting—(Continued)
  kinesthesia, 285
  legs, 286
  planes of force, 286
  relation to spine, 287
  testing balance, 286
Skeletal muscles, 82, 217
  abductors and adductors, 82
  actors and antagonizers, 82
  centering and excentering, 82
  flexors and extensors, 82
  framework, 148
  tonus, 278
Skeleton, active, 7
  alive, 5
  appendicular, 78, 142, 242
  axial, 78, 103
  axis, vertical, 154
  in balance, 76
  centering and excentering, 243
  development, 10
  locate joints, 177
  mechanics, 157
  nature's triumph, 7
  protective, 42
  shoulder girdle superimposed, 176
  sitting posture, 76
  support of parts, 67
  think relationships, 177
  working mechanism, 78, 80
Skills, 6, 36
  accuracy, 280
  energy expenditures, 280
  jumping and running, 232
  powerful pitcher, 238
  rotary joints, 176
Skull, 59, 80, 102, 149, 239
  condyles, 99
  growth and development, 14
  and neck, 239
  top load, 94, 170
Sleep, 21, 43, 232, 294
  restorative, 269
"Solvitur ambulando," 199
Speech, anatomy, organs, 259
  elements, 257
  emotional factors, 257
  mechanisms, 257
  and posture, 257
Spherical breathing, 232

Spinal column, 82
  action, 242
  axis and ribs, 108
  balance, symmetry, 95, 96
  curves, composition, 91
  horizontal, 67
  lowering weights, 172
  support of weights, 87, 93
  cord, 249
  curves, adaptability, 95
    balance, symmetry, 95, 96
    composition, 91
    convexity, 91
  curvature, 45
    concavity, 91
    development, 94
    dominance of lumbar, 95
    redirection, 92
    returning to front, 254
    subtended angles, 95
    three dimensions, 96
  girder, 69
  mechanics, 87
  nerves, 252
Spine, 68, 75, 78, 94, 242
  accumulating weight, 113
  axis, 94, 108, 166, 175
  balance of strength, 99
  basis of vertebrates, 18
  bilateral symmetry, 82
  central location, 98
  coordinated unit, 238
  degree of curve, 175, 255
  dorsal angle, 108
  elements of strength, 97
  extensors, 161, 232, 240
  flexibility, 240
  flexors, 226
  free rib joints, 167
  integration of curve, 211
  gutter, 109
  integrity, pelvic ligaments, 124
  lengthening, 289, 292
  mechanical balance, 92
    strength, 97
  pulls under, 212
  pyramidal shape, 82
  python, 286
  recoil from legs, 187
  relation to sitting, 287
  rib relationships, 112
  strain, 164
  supporting mechanism, 91

Spine—(Continued)
  three dimensions, 82
  tripod, 212
  two planes of action, 226
  viscera support, 172
  weight bearer, 93
    transfer, 92, 116
Spinous Processes, dorsal, 188
Stability, 8, 47, 220, 226
  gravity, 190
  and instability, 262
  man's, 262
  pelvic joints, 122, 182
Stable equilibrium defined, 191
Stance, 277, 292
  fighting animal, 249
  sports, 158
Standing, 37, 294
  balanced, 191
  compared to walking, 173
  equilibrium, 199
  hands and knees, 175
  psychological factors, 158
  relation to gravity, 286
  still, hard work, 37
  straight, 163
  toeing in, 184
Starving, 222
Starling, Ernest H., 30, 33, 34, 64, 257, 268
Statics, 50
Sterno-cleido-mastoideus, 150, 233
Sternum, 13, 110, 143, 144, 145, 156, 170
  support, 192, 239, 240
Strains, 43, 44, 170, 217, 231, 234
  chest, 166
  compensatory, 104
  emotional, 288
  extensors of back, 225
  false alignment, 204
  foot, 210
  knees and feet, 203
  mechanical, 49, 288
  neurone, 270
  recognition of, 179
  reduction, 209
  as referred pain, 53
  release of, 278
  by hissing, 292
  respiratory, 242
  sacroiliac ligament, 177

Strains—(*Continued*)
vascular, 242
vs. stress, 56
Stresses, 18, 22, 33, 47, 48, 50, 55
computation, 50
five mechanical, 47, 55
measurable, 96
and strains, 49
Structural hygiene, 41, 42, 97, 157
Structure follows function, 3
and force, 46
Styloid, 170
Subcostalis, 290
Subjective chronic fatigue, 266
Subtended angles, spinal curves, 95
Suffocation, 219
Support, 55, 78
accumulated weight, 87
Survival mechanism, 256
Symmetry, chest cavity, 108
wall, 166
thorax, 226
Sympathetic nervous system, 221
Synchronization, 6
Systole, 38
Swayback, 45, 75

T

Talus, keystone, 141, 183, 184, 206
Tarsus, weight-bearing, 141, 189, 206, 210
Tensile forces, 153
members, 54, 77, 107, 284
posture mechanism, 261
Tension, 59, 74, 182, 211
balance compression, 175, 215, 255
balancing femur, 131
operating in back, 161
Tensor fasciae latae, 129
action, 138
Testing balance and rhythms, 244
Thigh, femur, 137
Thigh joints, 117, 205
accelerated momentum, 201
anterior plane, 191
balanced antagonizers, 199
centered, 159
centering forces, 122
close to center, 200
"hub of universe," 207
leverage, 206
location, 178

Thigh joints—(*Continued*)
near front, 285
spring-board, 206, 209
tendons and ligaments, 199
universal, 131
weight thrust, 162
wheel-like, 200
Thinking, 201, 203, 207, 211, 243
better adjustment, 295
bodily changes, 288, 294
confused, 294
down back, up front, 255
emotional drive, 287
factual, 174, 281
movement, 277
muscle response, 268, 281
through bodily expression, 295
Thompson, J. Knox, 75
Thoracic cage, 180
cavity, deepening, 221
curve, 95
dimensions, 232
duct, 230, 231
spine, protection, 192
vertebrae, redirection of curve, 155
Thorax, 59, 145, 156, 170, 252, 290
balanced support, 241
close to pelvis, 191
deepening, 232
diameters, 180
expiration, muscles, 291
and lumbar curves, 242
movements, expiration, 290
narrowing, 289
proportions, 138, 147
protective function, 107
relation of pelvis, 172, 238
ribs. *See* Ribs; Rib cage
beneath shoulder girdle, 176
as side-load, 104
supporting function, 107
twelfth vertebra, 242
weight, 108
Thyro-arytenoid, 260
Tibia and fibula, 138
vertical position, 139
Tibialis posterior muscle, 183, 184, 209
Time-space-movement, 175, 210, 243, 281
Timing system, 39, 117, 220, 243, 257
"Tired feeling," 264, 265
Tonic reflexes, 278

Tonicity, ligaments and muscles, 116
Tonus, fascial, 130
Top-load into side-load, 238
Torsion, animate and inanimate, 48, 51
Total situation, 272
Toxins, 231
Transportation system, 248
Transversalis abdominis, 120, 180, 234
  "belly band muscle," 234
  constriction, 291
Transversus thoracicus, 290
Trapeze performer, 261
Trapezius (shawl muscle), 148, 242
  diversified action, 150
  and latissimus dorsi, 155
Tripod, spine as third leg, 205, 212
Trochanters, 137, 163
Trunk, axes, 190
  extensors and flexors, 225
    pulling down, 284
    thorax depression, 290
Tuberosities of ischia, 285
Tubular breathing, 180, 192
Twelfth thoracic vertebra, strategic, 242

U

Unconscious, 3, 267
Unlearned patterns, 232, 247
  basis for others, 268
  primary, 221
  reacquired, 258
  re-established rhythms, 256
Unsocialized positions, 278
Unstable equilibrium, 191
Upper structures, quick response, 160
Upright carriage, 149
  position, 177, 188, 243
  pelvis and legs, 113
  three planes of force, 190
  stability, 158

V

Vagus, 250, 252
Vascular system, 29, 274
Vasomotor, 249
Vasosympathetic, 249
Vegetative function, 54, 243
  system, 219, 294

Velasquez, 172
Velocity, body weight, 134
Vena cava, 223, 230, 231
Venous circulation, 231
Vertebrae, 65, 69, 85
  adjustments, 88
  bodies, 188
  cervical, 86, 103, 149
  enlarging toward base, 98
  free action, 232
  lumbar, 86
  movability, 226
  protection from pulls, 192
  sacral, 86
  spines, 99
  thoracic, 149, 150
  variable size, 85, 188
Vertebrate patterns, 8, 78
Vertebrates, 143, 147
  air breathing, 218
Vesalius, 5
Vestibule, 28, 100
Vigor, renewal, 284
Viscera, 29, 217, 237, 274
  placement, 172, 191
  protection, 107, 220
  relation to diaphragm, 221
Visceral muscles, 2
  canal, 78
Visceroptosis, 45, 75, 131, 225
Vocal cords, 253, 260

W

Walking, 17, 37, 193, 194, 214, 219
  activity and rest, 119
  analogous to riding, 214
  balanced forces, 194
  bridge that walks, 14
  buoyancy, 200
  centered posture, 159
  control of weight, 201
  examples, 210
  and falling, 207
  first motor skill, 157
  game, 210
  Holmes, Oliver Wendell, 194
  hissing, 216
  leg leading, 204
  momentum, 202
  muscles, 17
  physiology, 194
  problems, 199

Walking—(*Continued*)
running and springing, 238
rôle of eyes, 215
vs. standing, 173
Water, per cent in body, 10
Weight, accumulating in upright, 113
balance, 28, 33, 69, 85, 97, 117,
167
cease holding, 177
control in walking, 201
hanging and braced, 159, 177, 188
managed, 248
manipulation in skills, 176
moving transfer, 33, 37, 61, 117
muscles pulling up, 256
opposing weight, 186
sit, hang, braced, 188
sitting transfer, 114, 159, 188

Weight—(*Continued*)
support in foot, 141, 189
in pelvis, 122, 160
three ways, 61, 66
thorax, 108
thrust and counter, 40, 62, 141
transfer through spine, 85, 92
unbalanced, 62, 225
Wheel-like distribution; arm muscles,
148
Williams, Jesse Feiring, 2, 25
Wilson, Edmond B., 22
Work, balances rest, 267, 294
blood distribution, 274
eye, 294
paying attention, 268
quality and quantity, 264
Working unit, 2, 244

32004142R00193

Made in the USA
Lexington, KY
03 May 2014